CONFIRMATION
OR
THE LAYING ON OF HANDS

CONFIRMATION, OR THE LAYING ON OF HANDS

Volume I.—Historical and Doctrinal. By various writers. 8¾ × 5¾. 350 pp. Cloth boards. 12s. 6d. net.

LONDON: S.P.C.K.

CONFIRMATION

OR
THE LAYING ON OF HANDS

VOLUME II

PRACTICAL

BY VARIOUS WRITERS

LONDON
SOCIETY FOR PROMOTING
CHRISTIAN KNOWLEDGE
NEW YORK AND TORONTO: THE MACMILLAN CO

First published 1927

Printed in Great Britain

PREFACE

THE former volume confined itself to the history and doctrine of Confirmation. In this second volume attention is given to every aspect of the practical work of dealing with Confirmation candidates. The first of its twelve papers provides a comprehensive survey of the whole subject by one whose office includes the pastoral care both of parishioners and of boys and girls at school; the subsequent essays deal with particular parts of the work n greater detail, and, in the case of six of them, are representative of the various distinctive attitudes adopted by the clergy of the Anglican Church. The purpose of the book is to provide, for all who share in the responsible and many-sided task of training candidates for Confirmation, material which shall enable them to learn from Anglican, Evangelical, and Anglo-Catholic alike, all that is best and most profitable.

CONTENTS

CONFIRMATION
OR
THE LAYING ON OF HANDS

CHAPTER I

A GENERAL SURVEY

By O. Hardman

From the inquiry into the history and doctrine of Confirmation, which occupied the whole of the first volume of this work, we now proceed to the consideration of Church of England practice in the matter. In this introductory essay a general survey of the subject will be made, under the headings :

I. Age.	III. The Confirmation Day.
II. The Preparation.	IV. After-care.

The material is drawn partly from the results of a questionnaire which was distributed among a considerable number of Anglican clergy of varied experience ; and the writer's sincere thanks are here offered to the many who answered it with courteous readiness and a most helpful frankness and fullness.

I. Age

The missionary Church is prepared to administer Holy Baptism and Confirmation to approved adult candidates without regard to age. And in lands where it has established itself it finds it necessary not only to continue its proper missionary work of seeking and admitting such converts from without its borders, but also to add to them, for the purpose of Confirmation, adults of varying age who are in the anomalous position of standing outside the sacramental life of the Church, though they have been baptized in infancy. It is usual, for example, to find that the age of the candidates at any of our parochial Confirmation services in the Church of England ranges from thirteen, or a little under, to fifty or more years, sometimes many more ; and there is this much justification for those who say that it is idle to attempt to fix a proper age for Confirmation. We must be prepared to receive persons of riper years when they choose to come, whatever their age. With this in mind some parish priests have replied to a question as to the " best " age by saying, " Confirm people when they are ready ; there is no best age." But at least it is necessary to consider the question of a minimum age ; and, further, we may not unreasonably expect to find a plan of growth in the spiritual life which admits of description as normal, upon which a regular, though not too rigid, system may be usefully built up by the Church without in any degree departing from the truth that people are to be confirmed when they are ready.

By far the greater number of candidates for Confirmation in the Church of England are, after all, from thirteen to eighteen years of age ; and it is therefore true to say that, in practice at least, we have come to a general understanding that the adolescent period is the best age. But this period, brief though it is, is characterized by great and rapid changes, so that it is necessary to distinguish between its early, middle, and later stages ; and we have not yet decided among ourselves which of these stages is to be regarded as the most satisfactory for Confirmation.

While much support is found for the psychological argument against the middle years of this well-studied period of growth, there are not a few of the clergy who remain fixed in the opinion that fifteen or sixteen is the happiest age for Confirmation. They claim that in their experience they have proved the familiar descriptions of disturbance and unsettlement associated with this age to be largely fanciful, and that, on the contrary, young people are then for the first time in their lives really " up against things," eager to know, keenly desirous of being found loyal, and very ready for the right sort of help. It is argued, in particular, that instruction on sex matters is usually dangerous before this age, because it is then given

in anticipation of the emergence of real trouble in connexion with the new bodily powers that are being acquired,
whereas the sixteenth and seventeenth years are the very
time when these difficulties become acute, so that the
need of counsel is realized and help is welcomed. We shall
be well advised to correct any overdrawn pictures of the
storm and stress of the middle period by fairly weighing
a body of opinion based on an intimate knowledge of
many young people. Confirmation in the sixteenth or
seventeenth year is not always mistaken, in spite of much
psychological theory to the contrary. Yet it must also
be remembered that the psychological arguments are by
no means purely theoretical, though they may sometimes
be overpressed in unduly picturesque terms. They rest
upon much observation ; and, further, they are supported
by a very large volume of clerical testimony based on wide
and discerning pastoral experience.

Indeed, the majority of the clergy seem to be in favour
either of the approach to and the beginning of the adolescent
period or of its later years. They would avoid the middle
years, judging it best either to make wise preparation
for them or to make use of their more settled and responsible
sequel ; and it is between these alternatives that the
necessity really arises for careful judgment. The middle
years need not be rejected as invariably unsuitable—they
cannot be so regarded in the light of much experience ;
yet they anticipate by a very short time a stage of much
greater maturity and stability, and, on the other hand,
they are removed, by a period which admits of a considerable
acquaintance with sin, from the opportunities that belong
to the ripeness of childhood. Is it better, for the most
part, to wait until the seventeenth or eighteenth year, or
ought we to make ready, as a rule, before the age of
thirteen ? There is a strong tendency at present in the
Church of England towards the latter position ; and it is
important to consider whether this tendency is to be
approved and encouraged.

In the minds of those who advocate the deferring of
Confirmation until the later years of the adolescent period
there are two dominant ideas, held singly or in association,

with varying degrees of emphasis. They all count it essential that candidates shall have arrived at a sufficient stage of intellectual and moral enlightenment adequately to apprehend the nature of the step they are taking; and many of them consider it to be of chief importance that there shall be such spiritual ardour existent at the time as to make it possible for each one to dedicate himself whole-heartedly to Christ. There must be understanding and there must be conversion, in the sense of surrender to God. Inquiry must turn on these two ideas.

First as to understanding. What kind of understanding and how much of it is meant? There are a few in our Church who are impatient of any mention of under-standing as a qualification for Confirmation. These would gladly adopt the Eastern practice of infant Confirmation; and in defence of their position they ask the question, " If an infant is capable of receiving the Holy Ghost in Baptism, why not in Confirmation?" Or again, more generally, " Is it possible that God's action in conferring grace is limited by the understanding of those upon whom He bestows His favour?" It would appear that the answer to these questions lies in the recognition of the idea of growth as the reconciling factor between the divergences of Eastern and Western practice. If Confirmation be regarded not so much as something completed in a few moments of time but as the initiation of a continuing process of life, justification may be found for the administra-tion of the rite in infancy or in childhood, in adolescence or in later years. That this is the Anglican way of regarding it is made clear by recalling some of the words which the Prayer Book places in the Bishop's mouth. " Daily increase in them Thy manifold gifts of grace," he is to pray over all who are presented for Confirmation; and on behalf of each candidate he is to ask again, as he lays his hand upon him, that he may " daily increase in Thy Holy Spirit more and more, until he come unto Thy everlasting kingdom." Confirmation is the bestowal of an abiding and increasing gift; and so long as the Western Church practises infant Baptism, the Eastern Church can justify its use of infant Confirmation. Yet the Roman Church defers Confirmation until the age of seven, declaring that " the sacrament of Confirmation can be administered to all after Baptism, but yet it is less expedient that this should be done before children have the use of reason." [1] And the Anglican Church requires that candidates for Confirmation shall have attained to " years of discretion " or " a competent age." What is the wisdom of this delay ?

It lies in the fact that God's increasing communication of Himself to man keeps pace inevitably with man's capacity and conscious desire to receive Him—that is to say, that grace cannot be added faster than man can appropriate and assimilate it ; and, again, that the life of fellowship, while it grows stronger day by day, is yet subject to crises of development which are of the utmost importance. To administer Confirmation in infancy is consistent with the recognition of the former fact, but it takes no account of the latter. It commits everything to the steady, uninterrupted growth of the child and the corresponding development of operation of the indwelling Holy Spirit ; but it fails to make provision for that upward leap of the spirit which may be effected by the Church's careful teaching, inducement of expectation, and solemn conferring of the added power of the Spirit of God at an appointed time. Not until the disciples understood sufficiently was it possible for God to pour out upon them the gift of the Holy Ghost ; but when He acted they were swiftly borne to a new spiritual level. There was a close psychological congruity between the earthly side and the heavenly side of that remarkable crisis of endowment. The Holy Spirit could not be given in fullest measure until Christ had overcome sin and death and ascended into the heavens. But, again, He could not really be given until the disciples were ready to receive Him ; and the culmination of their preparation consisted in the sorrow and darkness of Holy Week and the joy and light of Easter and the Great Forty Days. So also there must be a sufficient measure of understanding in our Confirmation candidates if God is to be enabled to give them such a gift as to effect a crisis of development in their spiritual lives and at the same

---

[1] *Catechism of the Council of Trent,* pars ii, cap. iii, q. 18.

time to remain with them as an abiding pledge of continued progress.

All this goes, at first, to strengthen the position of those who would defer Confirmation until the final stage of adolescence. There is no comparison between the fitness of the child of seven and that of the lad of seventeen or eighteen for the apprehension of such a movement of the Spirit as is promised in Confirmation. At the later age the mind is capable of receiving the great truths of Christian doctrine ; moral resolution is possible on the basis of a realization of the nature and authority of conscience and of the range and power of sin ; and, further, there is a good prospect of the permanent attachment of the soul to Christ with those strong emotional powers which emerge only during adolescence and are not found in the child, for all the sweetness of its affection and love. This brings us to conversion, the second of the dominant ideas mentioned above. If in every soul we are to look for a definite turning from comparative apathy to enthusiastic disciple- ship, there is much evidence to suggest that the time of its occurrence is more likely to be found in the second half of the adolescent period than elsewhere in the course of the life ; and of its value in connexion with Confirmation there can be no question. Where there is little warmth in the soul there is a serious impediment to the further work of the Spirit. And it is a most inadequate conception of Confirmation, though fairly common in some quarters, to regard it mainly as a " moral tonic." A conclusion, then, in favour of late Confirmation seems inevitable. Is there anything to be said against this ?

The first thing is, of course, that we should be setting a very wide gap between Baptism and Confirmation, which are properly to be regarded as but two steps in a single rite of initiation. In the case of the convert from without, baptized and confirmed at one time or with but a very small interval of time between the two parts of the Sacra- ment, the association is clearly seen. But if we are habitu- ally to baptize our children in infancy and to delay their Confirmation until they are seventeen or eighteen years of age, it will be difficult to persuade people, from our normal practice, of the reality of the connexion, and Confirmation will be increasingly regarded as an independent rite, and will stand in danger of being warped further and further from its true significance.

Again, it is not permitted to the baptized but unconfirmed to receive the Holy Communion, since their admission to full Church membership is not yet completed. We should therefore be found depriving young people of the joy and strength of that Sacrament through some of the most critical years of their lives. This is seen to be so serious a deprivation that a suggestion has recently been advanced by one who favours later Confirmation that admission to Communion shall be made independent of Confirmation, and allowed to precede it by some six or seven years. Such a large extension of the practice, found in the Roman Church, of anticipating Confirmation by First Communion can hardly be expected to commend itself very widely. It would be a complete departure from the use of the whole Church through all its history ; it would isolate Baptism from Confirmation so effectually as to constitute it in itself the complete rite of initiation ; it would deprive Confirmation of every appearance of advancing candidates to full Christian status by the sealing of the Holy Spirit, and would necessarily transform it into a mere occasion for the public profession of the baptismal vows. The advantages claimed for the postponement of Confirmation to a later age might be multiplied tenfold, for the sake of argument ; and yet it would be impossible to consider such a presumptuous redistribution of the Church's sacramental system in order to secure them. The alternative, however, is to allow young Christians to grow up to the age of eighteen without ever receiving the sacrament of the Lord's Body and Blood. This presents a dilemma of so serious a nature as to suggest that arguments resting upon a conviction of the religious opportunities of the seventeenth and eighteenth years had better be diverted from the subject of Confirmation to some other form of dedication and empowering. Let us return to that presently.

If, then, in order to give young adolescents the benefit

of partaking of the Holy Communion, we are to provide for the administration of Confirmation during the years of immaturity, how far back are we to go, having an eye to the desirability of plainly declaring the essential relationship between Confirmation and Baptism, and remembering the practice of the Eastern and Roman Churches respectively ? To those who would have us learn from what they hold to be the wisdom of the Roman Church and administer Confirmation at the age of seven, it may be pointed out that the degree of moral and spiritual understanding and the power of self-dedication associated with that age are very slight, though these things are not entirely lacking. There still remain some five or six years of child-life before the moral difficulties of adolescence begin to declare themselves ; and there seems to be no sufficient reason for refusing to make use of the more developed powers that belong to the eleventh, twelfth, and thirteenth years. It is a matter of weighing over against each other that special opportunity of building up the devotional life of the soul by a regular approach to the altar in early days, which is the strongest argument for Confirmation at the age of seven, and the greater prospect of securing an intelligent and responsible surrender to Christ and an earnest expectation of the enabling grace of God which belong to the year or so immediately preceding the beginning of puberty. And while we balance them we must remember that a good deal of the plasticity of childhood remains at the age of twelve, so that it is not yet difficult to form new devotional habits ; and, moreover, the near approach of adolescence makes the opportunity of teaching and the actual addition of spiritual strength singularly valuable. On the whole, in view of our existing practice and of the English tendency, strong in parents, to lay stress upon the necessity of understanding, it will almost certainly be found that we shall not be willing as a Church to go lower than the age of ten ; but that there will be an increasing sense of the rightness of bringing children from ten to twelve years of age to Confirmation.

Our action in every case will require to be governed, not

only by the stress we are prone to lay upon the sacramental
life on the one hand or upon the need of personal religion
and conversion, as though that were an entirely different
thing, on the other hand ; but also, and mainly, upon the
standard of the child's development and the conditions of
its life at home, at school, or in the world.   Children of
twelve are sometimes exceedingly childish and undeveloped,
and it is necessary in their case to postpone Confirmation
until they have reached " a competent age " in growth,
whatever their years may be.   Children of ten and eleven,
again, are not infrequently found to be sufficiently " grown
up " and understanding to justify their Confirmation
without delay.   But it will always be hazardous to present
young children for Confirmation unless there is a guarantee
of strong support in their home or school.   When they are
themselves ripe and in the hands of adults who are faithful
Church people and regular communicants, there is full
justification for early Confirmation.   If the home or
school atmosphere in respect of spiritual things is not
satisfactory, it is better to wait until the child has acquired
a greater power of standing alone.   Godparents may do
something to supply the lack in the home, but it is not
wise to put too much upon them.

In places, then, where the Church's system is working
well and the children, having been brought to Baptism in
infancy, are carefully trained at home, in the school, and
in church, it ought to be found that candidates are presented for Confirmation from ten years of age upwards,
and that the majority of them are children of ten, eleven,
or twelve.   These will have been prepared by the whole
of their spiritual training from early infancy, but especially
by the intensive teaching given immediately before the
Confirmation.   And they will have been tested by their
understanding and by their keenness of desire, declared in
attendance at public worship and at classes, in ability to
profit by instruction in the way of prayer, and in increase
of happiness, helpfulness to others, and moral self-regimen.
Criteria of fitness are not to be hammered out into a rule
of thumb for the use of the undiscerning ; but the things
that are mentioned are all deserving of consideration when

the time comes to accept responsibility for the offering of souls to the Holy Spirit ; and it is by them that the true age of a candidate is to be estimated rather than by the number of years he has lived.

It will be seen that this conclusion constitutes in effect a plea that the Bishops will agree to recognise the wisdom of allowing their clergy to present to them for Confirmation children of from ten to twelve years of age, in cases where the conditions are wholly favourable.[1] There remains a further suggestion in the interests of these child candidates, in recognition of the strength of the arguments advanced by those who favour later Confirmation, and in view of the situation established in the Church of England by the Enabling Act of 1919. At the age of eighteen members of the Church of England now become eligible for the inclusion of their names on the parochial electoral rolls. This implies their recognition by the Church as lay members enjoying full ecclesiastical privilege. It is an important step in the churchmanship of the individual, though it is not yet very generally recognized as such ; and it is of obvious advantage to the Church that all who are qualified to take it should do so. If it were provided that young people who are nearing the age of eighteen should be admitted to a course of instruction and spiritual training in preparation for their enrolment, it would enable the Church to seize upon just that opportunity that is so rightly pressed by advocates of later Confirmation, without depriving them of the help of Holy Communion through the years of adolescence, without divorcing Baptism unduly from Confirmation, and without disturbing the Church's established order of initiation followed by Communion. Then there should be a solemn service for the admission and reception of the instructed adolescent communicants

---

[1] It may be noted that the fixing of a minimum age for Confirmation would relieve the clergy of some uncertainty as to the proper form to be used in the Baptism of children. If ten is fixed as the earliest age for Confirmation, then the form for the Ministration of Publick Baptism of Infants would necessarily be used until that age was reached ; but for children of ten and over the form for the Ministration of Baptism to such as are of Riper Years would normally take its place.

to adult status and privilege, the chief feature of which should be a public renewal of the baptismal vows, supplemented perhaps by a pledge of loyal service to the Church. This would enable the Church to require of candidates for Confirmation only a simply expressed intention of striving to follow Christ and to do the right, such as would be well suited to children of ten or twelve years of age. By such an arrangement the Church's sacramental system would be rightly used and its true significance plainly taught, and the whole path of individual progress to full citizenship in the life of the Church would be satisfactorily covered.[1]

II. The Preparation

Under this heading it will be necessary to consider the persons to whom the work of preparation should be entrusted; the preliminary work that must precede the work of the actual classes; the length of the preparation and the general methods of training to be adopted; and, lastly, the subject-matter of the instruction.

1. *To whom entrusted*

Responsibility for the preparation of all parochial candidates rests with the parish priest to whom is committed the cure of souls. In the larger parishes he is accustomed to share the work with assistant priests, deaconesses, and other workers; and even in the smallest parish he will be wise to enlist the aid of some good woman to help him in the preparation of women and girl candidates. But he will count it his duty faithfully to oversee whatever may be done by others according to his direction, and to establish some measure of direct contact with all candidates alike. The art of combining a real delegation of responsibility to fellow-workers with the retention of effectual control is a gift which is invaluable here, as in so much else that belongs to the work of an incumbent; and it is particularly necessary for some men to remember that the trained woman-worker, especially the deaconess, is capable of bearing a larger share of the work than is involved in the giving of

[1] See also p. 14.

instruction on the seventh commandment and the care of a few backward candidates.

Some of the clergy are doubtful about the wisdom of preparing their own children and servants. They consider that it is more helpful to entrust them, at least in part, to clerical friends who will arouse fresh interest, supply the deficiencies of their own general training and influence, and give new points of view. Others, again, resent the idea of surrendering in any degree what appears to them to be a peculiar privilege and responsibility. They regard its abandonment as a confession of serious inconsistency between profession and practice in the presence of those to whom their private lives are well known. This is most certainly an injurious misrepresentation of the case ; and, while it is natural and right that a father who is a priest should desire to take part in the preparation of his own children, and of his servants, for what is to be regarded as a very important crisis in their spiritual history, there can be little doubt that it is due to the children, and in a less degree to the servants, to give them the benefit of the counsel and instruction of one who can deal with them solely on the plane of the spiritual pastor, where this assistance may readily be had.

A more difficult problem arises in the case of some of those who, though resident within the parish, are receiving their education at schools and institutions of various kinds where it is the custom to attach importance to Confirmation and to provide preparation for it. If these institutions are equipped with chapels and priests are licensed to them with cure of souls, so that after Confirmation all the candidates continue to make their Communions there together until they leave the place, there is no room for any parish priest to feel aggrieved. A parish within a parish for the sake of a special community with particular needs presents an obvious example of practical wisdom in ecclesiastical administration. But if the school or institution in question possesses no chapel or chaplain, or if, again, though it possesses both of these, its members are not all able to make regular use of the chapel but are thrown back on their parish churches for Sunday worship, a different and a somewhat difficult situation is encountered. It is a great advantage to boys and girls at school that Confirmation should be intimately connected with the life of the school rather than that, in so important a matter, religion should be made to appear a thing remote from the daily round. The ideals of life, the early friendships that mean so much, the many temptations to wrong-doing, are all part of the texture of the corporate life of the school. Confirmation should be a part of that life also. And if the school authorities, with their intimate knowledge of the scholars, are ready to add to their manifold activities the work of preparation, nothing can be more impressive and helpful to the candidates. It is, of course, to be understood that preparation by laymen and laywomen can never be accounted sufficient. If no priest is available on the school staff, then the parish priest's aid must be sought ; and he will be wise to enter into hearty co-operation with the school authorities and to refrain from giving the impression that, in his opinion, his own part of the preparation is all that really counts. But if there is a chaplain or other priest available, so that the whole of the preparation can be carried on apart from parochial classes, it is not uncommon to find the parish priest somewhat aggrieved against the school, even though he be duly informed, as he should be, of those of his parishioners who have become eligible to communicate at the parish altar. Sometimes he is suspicious of the adequacy of the preparation, especially when laymen have a share in it ; but more often, and with far greater reason, he is moved by the reflexion that those who have not passed through his hands will never be associated with him and with the life of the parish in quite the same affectionate and intimate way as the others, even after they have left their school. He is apt to forget that, if it were not for the school, many of these boys and girls would never have been confirmed. Those who are already in close touch with the life of the parish frequently elect to be prepared by their parish priest ; and even when they prefer to be prepared with their schoolfellows there need be no real weakening of the parish's hold upon them, if the parish priest wishes to have it so. But the great majority of those who are prepared at school come from homes into which the parish priest rarely or never enters, and it is probable that few of them would ever be presented for Confirmation if they were left to his seeking and persuasion. There would seem to be room for some appreciation of a co-operating agency which can supplement the work of a parish by making an effective appeal to some of those who are scarcely touched by the Church's parochial system.

Further, it must be pointed out that, if the scheme indicated above [1] were adopted, by which young people of eighteen would be admitted to adult membership in their parish churches and duly enrolled as electors after a course of instruction, there would be a recognized means of attaching to parochial life those whose religion had been hitherto mainly associated with school life, and it would then be possible for the parochial clergy to establish that close personal contact which they rightly desire.

2. *Preliminaries*

The work of collecting candidates for Confirmation begins, normally, with the administration of Holy Baptism to infants. If the connexion between Baptism and Confirmation is to be truly taught, the parish priest must be careful to see that godparents thoroughly understand the nature of their office at the time of the Baptism, and, as the child grows up, he must allow neither them nor the parents to forget the necessity of completing the rite of initiation. In his work in Sunday school, Catechism, and Children's Service, and in his regular visits to the home, he will all the time be engaged in collecting and preparing candidates ; and in order to leave the matter in no doubt whatever in the minds of those who share his responsibility, he may think fit to copy the valuable example of one who for ten years after Baptism sends out to every godparent an annual reminder in the form of a printed card bearing a suitable legend. The final card runs thus :

[1] P. 10 f.

> On .... you stood Godparent at the Baptism of
> ....
> This is the last card of reminder. The time for Confirmation will
> soon be here, for the softer the wax the deeper the impression of
> the seal. I hope that these cards have not seemed to you intrusive.
> As we admitted the child to the Church under your suretyship, we
> felt bound to remind you of your obligation ; and we are grateful
> for your co-operation with us in bringing this child to God.
>
> ....
> Vicar.

The expense and time and energy consumed in sending out these cards are undoubtedly well used. But in large parishes with inadequate staffs it may be found impossible to achieve such thoroughness, even though lay help be enlisted, and it is then most desirable to supply every godparent at the time of Baptism with such a card as the following [1] :

> *Suffer the Little Children to come unto Me*
>
> I ....
> have solemnly undertaken to act as
>
> ## GOD-PARENT
>
> on behalf of ....
> Baptized at ....
> on .... 19 ......
> Therefore I must :
> 1. Pray for him.
> 2. Set him a good example by my own way of living.
> 3. See that he is brought up to follow the footsteps of our Lord and Saviour Jesus Christ.
> 4. See that he is taught the Faith, especially the Creed, Lord's Prayer, and Ten Commandments.
> 5. Take care that he is brought to the Bishop to be confirmed.
> 6. Encourage him to become a regular communicant.
>
> *Prayer.*—Grant, O Lord, that this child may not be ashamed to confess the faith of Christ crucified, and manfully to fight under His Banner, and to continue Christ's faithful soldier and servant unto his life's end. Amen.
> S.P.C.K., No. 2972.

[1] An alternative is S.P.C.K., No. 3076.

In addition to the young children who are thus collected year by year, there will be some unconfirmed adolescent and adult parishioners whose names have been noted at various times. To these a direct invitation will be addressed by word or by letter, or by both. The following copy of such a letter will serve to show the kind of appeal that is to be made in these cases :

THE VICARAGE,

. . . .

. . . .

DEAR FRIEND,

The Bishop proposes to hold a Confirmation Service at . . . . Parish Church on Thursday, June 6th, at 8 p.m. I hope that a large number of our people will offer themselves for Confirmation, and that you will consider the possibility of offering yourself as a Candidate.

In the Church of England we make much of Confirmation, but in doing so we are in complete accord with the New Testament, in which the rite is called the Laying on of Hands. And experience tells me that many in . . . . have been helped by their Confirmation and their preparation for it.

In these days of difficulty one cannot afford to pass by any of the helps which God gives for leading a Christian life, and on this ground, as well as with the desire of following the Lord fully and becoming a full member of the Church, I trust that you will come forward.

Previous to the Confirmation, classes will be held, one of which each Candidate is expected to attend every week. Even if you have not yet decided to become a Candidate, you will be welcome at the classes. At these classes subjects relating to Confirmation will be dealt with. After the Confirmation the classes will be continued for three weeks to consider the subject of the Holy Communion. I hope that all who are confirmed will become regular communicants.

You will find in this letter a list of the classes. If possible, will you attend the opening address at the Parish Church on Sunday next, at 8 p.m., and will you attend in the first week the class which seems most convenient to yourself ?

Yours sincerely,

. . . .

VICAR.

Most of the candidates will be secured by these means ; but the net must be cast wider still, by direct teaching on the subject in the pulpit, by announcements in church and in the parish magazine, and by the issue of general printed notices, including forms to be filled in by intending candidates. These things should all be done at least four or five weeks before the date of the first class, for people are sometimes slow to make up their minds. It is perhaps advisable to refrain from presenting possible candidates with much instruction [1] or a formidable list of questions ; but there is some difference of opinion on this point, as will be seen from the following specimens of notices actually in use.

A

CONFIRMATION

The sacred rite of LAYING ON OF HANDS, otherwise called CONFIRMATION, will (D.V.) be administered...

Names of intending candidates should be given in *at once*.

The LAYING ON OF HANDS was practised by Christ's Apostles—is often mentioned in the New Testament (see Acts viii. 14–17 ; Acts xix. 5–6 ; Heb. vi. 1–2)—conveys a real spiritual blessing, and gives you the right to receive the Holy Communion.

It is intended for all—grown-up people as well as young persons. The Clergy will gladly arrange separate instruction for Adults.

Name.. *Age*..........

Address ....
....

This slip, when filled up, should be sent direct to the clergy.

S.P.C.K., No. 3050.

B

CONFIRMATION

Please fill this up and bring it with you to the first Class.

Full Christian and Surname..

Address ....

Date of Birth ....

........*Day* ....*Month* ....*Year.*

Where Baptized..

Exact date of Baptism (if known)......................................

Your first class will be ....

On.......................... *at*..............................

in ....

Please say at once if this time is not suitable.

S.P.C.K., No. 3051.

[1] Suitable literature should, of course, be provided in the tract-case in church for all who seek information without wishing to commit themselves in any way.

C

CONFIRMATION, 19..

CANDIDATE'S APPLICATION FORM

To..

Please accept me as a member of the Confirmation Preparation Classes which are now being formed.

I hereby promise to attend the classes regularly and punctually.

Surname ....

Christian names in full..

Address ....

....

Born on the..........*day of*.....................*in the year*..........

Baptized on the..........*day of*.....................*in the year*........

Baptized at..

....

State if not baptized..

Please fill up and return this form without delay to your parish priest.

TEAR OFF THIS SLIP, AND KEEP FOR REFERENCE

CONFIRMATION, 19..

The first meeting of all Candidates will be held at....................
at........ p.m., when classes will be arranged at times most convenient to the candidates.

The Confirmation Day is..

The Church is..
S.P.C.K., No. 3081.

D

CONFIRMATION, 19..

CANDIDATE'S APPLICATION FORM

To..

Please accept me as a member of the Confirmation Preparation Classes which are now being formed.

I hereby promise to attend the classes regularly and punctually.

Surname ....

Christian names in full................................

Address ....

....

Born on the..........*day of*....................*in the year*..........

Baptized on the..........*day of*.................*in the year*..........

Baptized at...

....

State if not *baptized*.................................

Please fill up and return this form without delay to your parish priest.

TEAR OFF THIS SLIP, AND KEEP FOR REFERENCE

CONFIRMATION, 19..

The weekly classes are as follows :

	Time.	Place.
Adults	....day........p.m.	....
Boys	....day ......p.m.	....
Girls	....day ......p.m.	....

The Confirmation Day is...............................

The Church is..

S.P.C.K., No. 3081A.

E

HOLY TRINITY AND ST. MARY, ...

CONFIRMATION, 19 . .

The annual Confirmation will be held in Holy Trinity Church on
.... at 7.30 o'clock. Candidates are requested to
fill in one of these papers and return it to one of the Clergy, or place it in
the box at the Vestry door in Holy Trinity Church.

There will be a service at St. Mary's Church on ....,
at 3.15 p.m., which all the Candidates are expected to attend.

The Classes will begin in the following week. Special arrangements will
be made for the preparation of any Candidate for whom none of the Classes
is convenient.

There will also be an *Instruction on the Holy Communion*, which all the
Candidates are expected to attend, in St. Mary's Church, on the six Sundays
in Lent, at 3.15 p.m., beginning on Sunday, February 21st, 19 . .

I wish to offer myself as a Candidate for Confirmation.

Name in full..

Age...................

Address ....

....

F

WHY SHOULD YOU BE CONFIRMED ?

(A word to those who have not been confirmed.)

BECAUSE

1.—*God needs you.* He wants your help in the world—in building up a new world. In Confirmation we pledge ourselves to take our stand on His side.

2.—*You need God.* In Confirmation God comes to help us in a special way, by giving us His Holy Spirit to strengthen us to fight life's battles.

3.—*Confirmation is found in the Bible* (Acts viii. 14–17, etc.), and that is a good enough reason for most of us.

4.—*It naturally follows on Baptism,* as soon as we have reached an age when we can choose between right and wrong, and are therefore able to make *as our own* the promises made in our name at our Baptism.

5.—*It leads on to Holy Communion.* At Confirmation we become full members of the Church, and entitled to all the rights and privileges which such membership brings ; greatest of all is the privilege of coming to the Holy Communion.

6.—*It is intended for all* who want to serve God more faithfully, not simply for the " extra good." No one is too old, no one is too young, provided they are able to know their own minds and desire to follow Christ.

If *any* of the above reasons appeal to you, and if you want, as a true Churchman, to take your share in helping forward the Kingdom of God, please fill in the subjoined form. By so doing you will, of course, in no way be pledging yourself to be confirmed unless you really wish it. It simply means that you would like to think more about it. In any case it is worth thinking about.

Please tear off here.

ST. MATTHEW'S, ...

I should like to hear more about Confirmation.

Name in full (Mr., Mrs., Miss)..

Age ....

Address ....

....

This form, when filled in, should be sent to the Vicar, *or* placed in the Box in the Church labelled " Communications for the Clergy."

G

A CONFIRMATION SERVICE

Will be held in....................Church on....................
All who were baptized in our parish church as babies were baptized on the
understanding that *as soon as possible* they would be brought to the BISHOP
TO BE CONFIRMED.

All regular communicants, particularly PARENTS AND GODPARENTS, cannot
fail to be deeply concerned about the offer made to those they love, by a
CONFIRMATION in our own church on ...., a great
day in the history of the parish.

No one is too old to be confirmed, but it is well for the young to be
confirmed, if possible, before they leave school and go out into the world.

If in doubt about the importance of Confirmation, read Acts viii. and xix.,
Heb. vi., and the Book of Common Prayer. Note in the Prayer Book the
TWO names :

" CONFIRMATION, OR THE LAYING ON OF HANDS ON THOSE WHO HAVE BEEN
BAPTIZED "

It would be a great help if, as soon as possible, those who are wishing to
be confirmed would kindly fill up the form below, or in some other way
communicate their desire to the Rector.

To the Rector of ....

I wish to give in my name as a Candidate for the Confirmation on
.... I will do my best to attend the instructions.

I was baptized at..

Signed.................... ....

Address ....

....

Date........................

H

HOLY CROSS CHURCH, ...

On ...., the Bishop of .... will hold a CONFIRMATION IN .... CHURCH. I hope to present to him for Confirmation a good number of people. But, as I wrote to the Bishop on .... last : " I intend to make no effort to secure mere numbers, but shall try to present no one who does not give promise of continuing an earnest communicant."

Everyone who wishes to be confirmed must be ready to :

1. Attend the 9 a.m. Service EVERY SUNDAY, before Confirmation as well as after ; and, if absent, to tell me the reason AT ONCE AND IN WRITING.

2. Keep PUNCTUALLY every appointment made with me.

3. Remember, Confirmation means WORK FOR AND WITH CHRIST for life.

SOME OBJECTIONS AND THEIR ANSWERS

1. " *Too old.*" Never : CHRIST needs your help, and you need HIS.

2. " *Too young.*" Not if old enough to choose CHRIST and resolve to serve HIM truly : twelve is quite old enough for one not weak in the head.

3. " *Not good enough.*" Quite right. If you thought you *were*, you would be useless to CHRIST. You need HIS help, HE NEEDS YOURS.

4. " *I shall never keep it up.*" With most people this means, " I *don't want* to keep it up." If you want to serve CHRIST and keep close to HIM, you can leave it to HIM. If you don't want that, don't be confirmed.

5. " *I don't see the need of it.*" With most people this means, " I don't want to see the need of it." CHRIST NEEDS YOU IN HIS ARMY.

.............., Rector.

FORM TO BE FILLED IN BY EACH CANDIDATE

(Fill in in PENCIL, tear off, and return to the Rector.)

Name in full..

Day and year of birth...

Address ....

....

School (past or present)..

Occupation (with name of employer).................................

Date and place of baptism..

Do you agree to be faithful in attending the HOLY COMMUNION EVERY SUNDAY *wherever you are (unless really prevented) ?*..........................

Signature of Candidate...

Date.....................

Signature of parent or guardian....................................

I

ST. SAVIOUR WITH ST. PETER, ...

CONFIRMATION

If you want to attend the Confirmation Classes, please fill up this form and give it to one of the Clergy.

Christian Name in full...

Surname ....

Address in full....................... ....

....

Have you been baptized?...

If so, at what Church?...

What is the date and year of your birth?.............................

What Church do you attend on Sundays?..............................

What time do you attend Church on Sundays?.........................

Have you ever been present at Holy Communion?.....................

Why do you wish to be confirmed?...................................

....

Has anyone asked you to be confirmed?...............................

Think about the following statement and sign it if it is true of you.

I REALLY WISH TO BE A SERVANT AND DISCIPLE OF JESUS CHRIST.

Signed..

N.B.—It should be clearly understood that attendance at classes by no means necessarily involves Confirmation.

Kindly state if you will be able to attend a class on Saturday?...............

If not, what nights in the week can you come?...........................

J

ST. JOHN THE DIVINE, ...

CONFIRMATION

I desire to offer myself as a Candidate for Confirmation.

Name in full...

Address ....

....

Date and year of birth...

Place where baptized..

Date of Baptism, if known...

To be returned to one of the Clergy.

As the papers filled in by intending candidates are received, the particulars they furnish should be entered in a small register which will be used subsequently to record attendance at classes. It is of the utmost importance that full details of Baptism shall be secured, and that verification shall be made in cases where the smallest doubt exists. A few of the clergy insist upon the production of a baptismal certificate as an invariable rule. Failing this, they baptize shortly before the Confirmation Service, conditionally if there is any suggestion that Baptism has already taken place. Most of the clergy, however, are content with a definite statement on the authority of the parents as to date and place, or better still with the production of a baptismal card.[1]

Arrangements must next be made with every candidate for attendance at a particular class in each week ; and, as this is a matter which especially concerns parents and mistresses, the first necessity arises for a visit to the home, a duty on no account to be neglected. One priest tells how he was shamed into an unfailing performance of this duty by a man who said : " My girl is being confirmed this week, and you haven't once been near us all the time of the classes. It wouldn't have been so if we had stopped on at ——." The result of visiting at such a time is not only to establish confidence, to secure co-operation, and considerably to extend one's knowledge of candidates, but not infrequently to win to the Church adults who are themselves unconfirmed and otherwise negligent. In the course of the first visit the prayers of the family should be asked for ; and it is the good custom of some priests to reinforce the appeal then made by sending such a letter as the following after a few days.

MY DEAR FRIENDS,

As your child is a candidate for the coming Confirmation, I am writing to ask your kind help for myself and the children in this solemn time of preparation.

---

[1] It is distinctly helpful in this connexion to provide for each child at Baptism such a card as S.P.C.K. No. 240. This has spaces in which the dates of Baptism, Confirmation, and First Communion are to be entered by the responsible priest, who signs his name against the entry.

(1) You are, of course, remembering to pray daily for your own child. There is no need to ask you to do this. But please do not forget to say a prayer for the others who are to be confirmed at the same time as your own child, and for me as their teacher.

(2) Please encourage and help your child to attend the 11 o'clock service on Sundays and to be regular at the instructions.

(3) If you can manage to come yourself on Sundays at 11 o'clock, it would be a great help to all of us, but especially to your own child.

(4) If there is any matter you care to discuss with me by which I may be able to help you, or by which you may be able to help me in our common concern and responsibility in the preparation of your child, who is so dear to our Lord, please do not hesitate to call on me or ask me to come and see you.

May God make this coming Confirmation a blessing not only to the children concerned, but also to all parents, relatives, and friends.

Your sincere friend and Rector,

. . . .

3. *Time allowed, and General Methods adopted*

The length of time devoted to the work of preparation varies in different parishes from six weeks to six months, one class a week being the almost invariable rule. On the whole, the tendency is distinctly in the direction of regarding anything less than four months' work as inadequate ; and experience is leading many priests to give a full half-year to their candidates. It is especially interesting to notice that insistence upon a prolonged and intensive final preparation is most commonly found among those clergy who also stress the fact that preparation for Confirmation is to be spread over the whole of a child's life up to Confirmation age. The greater the attention and care that are given to the work, the larger the appreciation of its value, and the more the readiness to spend increased time and energy upon it. A few priests report that they have continuous Confirmation classes, six months being devoted to general training in the devotional life, and six months to special preparation for Confirmation and First Communion.

The problem of the odd candidate who appears after the classes have started is a difficult one. There are those who solve it by invariably requiring such people to wait ; and, generally speaking, this is right. It is most important that the whole ground shall be covered in every case, and that it shall not be covered at a forced pace. But it is sometimes necessary either to admit late-comers or to risk losing them altogether, as, for example, in the case of young people who are unexpectedly called upon to leave home in order to take up some work that has been offered to them. In these cases it is usually possible to provide for the continuance of instruction after the Confirmation ; but few will feel justified in presenting such a candidate unless a very considerable proportion of the instruction has already been given.

In addition to the weekly classes throughout the period of preparation, there will be one, two, three, or more personal interviews with every candidate to be arranged for, in order that the priest may come into closer contact with each soul to learn of its state and to move it to a true desire. There can be no question about the necessity and value of such interviews ; but it may well be questioned whether it is a good thing to attempt to prepare candidates solely or mainly by means of private interviews, or even to increase their number beyond three or four in the course of the preparation. Some are nervous under the process, some adopt a defensive attitude, some again find it a sheer delight to be the object of such attention and to expose their inner life to close scrutiny. One short interview at the beginning, one somewhere near the middle of the course, and one rather longer and more searching talk right at the end, is probably the best plan. And even this will require much careful contriving, wise circumspection, and earnest preparation by prayer.

It need hardly be said that public and private prayer should be offered for all Confirmation candidates throughout the period of their preparation. The clergy will pray for their candidates by name. At the Holy Communion they will make the bidding, " Let us pray for all in this place who are preparing to seek the gift of the Holy Spirit through the Laying on of Hands." At Morning and Evening Prayer one of the following prayers should be included.

O God, who through the teaching of Thy Son Jesus Christ didst prepare the disciples for the coming of the Comforter: Make ready, we beseech Thee, the hearts and minds of Thy servants who at this time are seeking the gift of the Holy Spirit through the laying on of hands, that, drawing near with penitent and faithful hearts, they may be filled with the power of His divine indwelling; through the same Jesus Christ our Lord. *Amen.*

O Heavenly Father, send Thy grace upon Thy children who are now preparing to dedicate themselves to Thee and seek Thy Holy Spirit in the laying on of hands. Give them an earnest desire to yield themselves to Thy service, to live as Thy true children, and to take up their cross to follow Christ. Defend them from the distractions and temptations of the world; keep them in safety under the shadow of Thy wings; and so fit and prepare them, O Lord, for this holy ordinance that they may receive the fullness of Thy blessing; through our only Mediator and Advocate, Jesus Christ. *Amen.*

Eternal Father, behold with favour those who are now preparing to be confirmed by Thy Holy Spirit. Mercifully direct the efforts of all who teach them and intercede for them; grant them a true desire and a right understanding; cleanse them from evil, and strengthen them in all good; through Jesus Christ our Lord. *Amen.*

The multiplication of classes is a necessity where there are many candidates; but regard should always be had to the limited capacity of most men for retaining their freshness and impressiveness when required to teach the same lesson many times over in quick succession, and also to the general convenience of the clergy from the point of view of carrying on their other work, as well as to the convenience of the candidates. Sacrifices must be made on both sides, and it is well to make some demand upon candidates rather than to make everything very easy for them. A large number of candidates would require to be broken up into small groups even if they were all of the same age, education, intelligence, and spiritual development. When, as commonly happens, they are of different capacities, they must be divided, not only in order to secure the advantages attaching to small classes, but also because of the necessity of accommodating the teaching to the candidates' powers of reception. The sexes will be separated; school children will be grouped apart from those who have left school; young men and young women will be instructed at other times than their seniors; and married couples will generally be taught two by two.

The one method of grouping which is certainly injurious is that which recognizes false distinctions and suggests privilege, of whatever kind. For this reason it is not good to treat choristers as a separate class; though it may be distinctly useful to provide for them additional instruction specially adapted to their office.

Some of the clergy are accustomed to hold all their classes in church. Others use the vestry or the parish room or the study, according to convenience and the character of the class. A general instruction for all candidates, and for any others who care to attend, in church after Evensong on Sundays, is often found valuable; but the ordinary classes are more profitably held in places other than the church, where, without any loss of reverence and devotion, the candidates are free to ask questions and to share in the lesson in such a way as to prevent it from becoming a mere lecture.

Classes should invariably be opened and closed with prayer, either in the form of a short devotional preparation or conclusion in church, or more briefly in the room where the class is to be held. In practice the latter plan is usually the more convenient, and the following forms are offered as suggestions for use.

I

Before.
> Hymn.
> Lection.
> Litany of the Holy Ghost.
> Lord's Prayer and Collects.

After.
> Thanksgivings.
> Special Intercessions.
> Hymn.
> Blessing.

II

Before.
In the name of the Father, and of the Son, and of the Holy Ghost.

Let us pray.

Lord, have mercy upon us.
Christ, have mercy upon us.
Lord, have mercy upon us.

Our Father, . . . from evil. Amen.

Grant us, O God, the light of Thy Holy Spirit, that in our preparation for Confirmation we may learn to know more perfectly Him who is the Way, the Truth, and the Life, and may gain strength to follow obediently where He calls; through the same Thy Son, Jesus Christ our Lord. *Amen.*

After.

Let us pray.

O God, who hast given us Thine own Son, abiding ever one with Thee in Thy glory, to share our life upon earth: Grant that we may always remember Thy nearness; so that we may both confide in Thy protection, and be restrained by Thy contemplation; through the same Thy Son, Jesus Christ our Lord. *Amen.*

The Grace . . . evermore. *Amen.*

Opinion is divided as to the wisdom of supplying candidates with typewritten or printed notes of the lessons, or requiring them to make their own notes during instruction, or of writing answers to questions set at the end of each lesson. Some are strongly opposed to anything which suggests the remotest resemblance to school-work. These would lay all the stress upon the appeal to the heart and the quickening of right desire and affection. Others, again, set themselves to equip the mind with a store of definite, if limited, knowledge, and consider that any appeal to the heart is likely to prove transitory in its results unless it is fortified with such equipment. The latter are certainly right. It is more helpful to stir the emotions and instruct the mind than merely to stir the emotions. But there is much to be said for the avoidance of any suggestion that preparation for Confirmation is preparation for an examination and that at least a moderate amount of scholarship is necessary for all candidates. Everything depends upon the type of person that is being dealt with. Printed skeletons of lessons and written answers to questions will help some to greater clearness of understanding and deeper impressions, but will confuse and even alarm others. The same is to be said of memorizing. Some candidates will learn without difficulty the Catechism, some of the Prayer-Book collects, and chosen passages of Scripture[1]; and these should be encouraged to the necessary effort, seeing that it will be so well repaid. But there are others

[1] Bickersteth, *Simple Bible Teaching* (S.P.C.K., 2*d.*), will be found useful.

who learn by heart with the utmost difficulty, and it would be harmful to suggest to them that inability to recite even the Catechism debars a candidate from Confirmation. Understanding is by no means limited to those who are found capable of learning rapidly and of writing down their thoughts easily.

Printed notes have some value in cases where classes have been unavoidably missed ; but something more is needed than the mere handing over of summaries of what has been taught. It is important, though sometimes tiresome and difficult, to arrange for the separate instruction of any who have missed a class, so that no part of the teaching and general influence is lost. It is in this connexion especially that it is essential to keep a register of attendance and a record of the work done at each class.

Finally, some insistence is necessary upon three matters which, strangely enough, escape the attention of not a few of those who are earnest and capable in the work of instructing Confirmation candidates, so far as the actual imparting of instruction and arousing of good intentions are concerned. The first is that from the beginning of the preparation the duty of regular attendance at public worship should be stressed ; the second is that each candidate should be provided at once with a suitable form for his own private prayers ; and the third is that, from the outset, he should be guided as to the daily use of the Bible.

It is scarcely necessary to argue the position here that sound Churchmanship involves church attendance, and that nothing else can be offered as a sufficient substitute for it. Preparation for Confirmation plainly implies a readiness on the part of candidates to commit themselves to the Church's way of life ; and it denotes either gross negligence or deplorable misunderstanding if a priest who is preparing candidates fails to urge upon them at the beginning of his instruction the necessity for regular attendance at the Sunday services in church. It is, perhaps, not quite so certain that this should include non-communicating attendance at the Holy Communion, but there is much to be said for it. The preparation is for Communion, not only for Confirmation ; and it is a real help if, in addition to oral instruction about the service, familiarity with it is acquired by attendance at the actual service each Sunday during the course of preparation. Further the intention of the Church is then left in no doubt. The ideal in the matter would seem to be that parents should take their children to the service of Holy Communion occasionally from quite early years in order to teach them the nature of the privilege that awaits them, and so to stimulate desire ; and that weekly non-communicating attendance should begin with their preparation for Confirmation as an integral part of that preparation, leading on to First Communion after Confirmation and regular weekly Communion from that time forward. Such a system would undoubtedly go far to check the disastrous process of producing lapsed communicants.

Definite instruction and help in the way of saying private prayers is an urgent need in the case of the vast majority of Confirmation candidates, and should be offered at the earliest opportunity. Prayers for use night and morning (morning prayers especially need to be insisted on) ; prayers on visiting a church, and before and after service ; and forms for grace at meals : these are essential, and should be provided for every candidate, not that all may use a stereotyped form, but that all may have a model on which to fashion their own prayers or a foundation on which to build by the addition of suitable prayers of their own construction or choice. It is not sufficient that a child should be found ready to give an assurance that he says his prayers ; and no priest should be content to be put off by the suggestion that his communing with God is of so sacred and intimate a character that he could not bring himself to write down what he says or to communicate it in any way. This need not mean hypocrisy ; but it generally means self-delusion and unreality in prayer and a need of quite definite instruction. Since forms of prayer suited to the use of children are not easily found, some suggestions are provided below.

The daily reading of the Bible, preferably one of the Gospels, should be recommended in association with the saying of evening prayers, a scheme of reading being provided so that all the candidates keep pace together. And it is possible, even with very young candidates, to introduce them to the early stages of meditation by the distribution of some very simple guide and a careful explanation of the method to be used.[1] All these matters are clinched in some parishes by collecting the candidates for a week-end Retreat at the close of the preparation.

CHILDREN'S PRAYERS

MORNING

In the Name of the Father, and of the Son, and of the Holy Ghost. Amen.

O God, Heavenly Father, I thank Thee for Thy loving care of me throughout this night and for the gift of sleep. Preserve me this day from every kind of sin and danger ; grant me grace to resist temptation and to please Thee in all I do ; and help me to help other people : for Jesus Christ's sake. Amen.

Bless, in mercy, O Lord, my father and mother, ...
....

Look with tender pity upon all who are sick or in sorrow and anxiety, especially ....

Let Thy light shine upon all who are with Thee in Paradise, especially ...., and grant unto them rest, refreshment, and peace. Amen.

Our Father, . . . for ever and ever. Amen.

O my God, I believe in Thee ; increase my faith.

O my God, I hope in Thee ; strengthen my hope.

O my God, I love Thee ; make me love Thee more and more. Amen.

God the Father, God the Son, and God the Holy Ghost, bless, preserve, and keep me, this day and for evermore. Amen.

EVENING

In the Name of the Father, and of the Son, and of the Holy Ghost. Amen.

O God, who art all Love, I thank Thee for every blessing received this day. Mercifully accept anything in me that has pleased Thee; and of Thy goodness blot out all that has grieved Thee, especially.............
....

For these my sins I am truly sorry. Forgive me, O Lord, and help me to-morrow to serve Thee better, for Jesus Christ's sake. Amen.

Bless in mercy, O Lord, all my relatives and friends ; look with tender pity upon the sick and sorrowful and needy ; help all men and women to be loyal and kind in their work ; guide with wisdom those who lead ;

---

[1] Suitable help will be found in a 2d. series written by the Rev. A. C. Buchanan, and published by S.P.C.K.

make Thy Church in all the world pure and strong and true ; and hasten the coming of Thy Kingdom, for Jesus Christ's sake. Amen.

[*Particular intercessions.*]

Our Father, . . . for ever and ever. Amen.

I will lay me down in peace, and take my rest : for it is Thou, Lord, only that makest me dwell in safety.

Glory be to the Father, and to the Son : and to the Holy Ghost ;

As it was in the beginning, is now, and ever shall be : world without end. Amen.

Prayers in Church

1. *On visiting a church*

Bless, O Lord, those who minister and all who worship in this Thy House of Prayer. Give them love and understanding ; protect them from evil ; and nourish them with all good ; for Jesus Christ's sake. Amen.

2. *Before Service*

O God, Heavenly Father, I come to worship Thee and to learn of Thy loving-kindness. Help me to be reverent ; fill my mind with good thoughts, and my heart with love ; for Jesus Christ's sake. Amen.

3. *After Service*

O my God, I thank Thee for the joy of worship. Forgive whatever has been unworthy ; accept my desire to praise Thee truly ; and be near to me at all times, even as in this Thy House ; through Jesus Christ our Lord. Amen.

Grace

1. *Before Meals*

Bless, O Lord, this food to our use, and us to Thy service ; for Jesus Christ's sake. Amen.

2. *After Meals*

Thanks be to God for these and all His mercies ; through Jesus Christ our Lord. Amen.

4. *Subject-matter of Instruction*

The range of the instruction that is necessary in the preparation of Confirmation candidates is readily determined by a moment's consideration of the end in view. The nature of Confirmation itself and of the Sacrament of Holy Communion must be fully taught ; and since Baptism, the prelude to Confirmation, involves the acceptance of the Faith, the renunciation of evil, and the quest of the good, instruction in the Creed and in the Christian way of life must be added. That is to say, there are four sections in the teaching to be given, and each of them must be adequately dealt with in summary manner, however carefully much of the ground may have been covered previously in the case of some or all of the candidates. If this special instruction is largely revision of what has been done before, so much the better : but none of it may be omitted, either on the score that it has already been taught, or because what remains is thought to be sufficient to produce in candidates a state of emotional expectation. This is the great opportunity for thorough revision, for driving home the essentials of Christian belief and life, for providing an equipment of definite knowledge which shall serve as a protection to the soul against the assaults of error and sin.

Starting with the intention of providing twenty lessons (which, together with some revision lessons, will cover the ideal six months' preparation), we shall find it possible to devote three weeks to the consideration of the call and the response that belong to Confirmation, five weeks to the study of the Faith, eight weeks to the understanding of Christian practice in fulfilment of the law of love, and four weeks to the examination of the Service of Holy Communion. Thus the complete syllabus will stand as follows :

A. THE CHURCH

Lesson 1. The Meaning of Baptism and Confirmation.
„ 2. The Communion of Saints.
„ 3. Vocation.

B. THE CHURCH'S FAITH

Lesson 4. The Bible.
„ 5. The Four Gospels and the Acts.
„ 6. The Creeds. The Blessed Trinity. The Incarnation.
„ 7. The Atonement.
„ 8. The Future Life.

C. THE CHRISTIAN WAY OF LIFE

Lesson 9. Our Duty to God.
„ 10. Our Duty to our Neighbour (1).
„ 11. Our Duty to our Neighbour (2).
„ 12. Prayer, Fasting, and Almsgiving.
„ 13. Prayer : (1) The Lord's Prayer.

The complete course of instruction is set out in the summaries that follow, which are intended to serve merely as a general statement of the content of the teaching to be given.   It will naturally require to be adapted by simplification or expansion, and by varied illustration, according to the understanding of the particular candidates in view.

A. THE CHURCH

1. THE MEANING OF BAPTISM AND CONFIRMATION

When you were baptized the minister ended the service by saying to your Godparents, " Ye are to take care that this child be brought to the Bishop to be confirmed by him, so soon as he can say the Creed, the Lord's Prayer, and the Ten Commandments, in the vulgar tongue, and be further instructed in the Church Catechism set forth for that purpose." The time has now come for you to make ready for Confirmation, and we must begin the preparation by trying to understand exactly what Baptism and Confirmation mean.

I. THE HOLY SPIRIT AND THE CHURCH'S SACRAMENTS

1. Open your Bibles, and turn to the second chapter of the Acts. Here is St. Luke's account of the way in which Jesus Christ sent the Holy Spirit to His Church according to promise (St. John xv. 26 and xvi. 7). God had never left Himself without witness in the hearts of men and women (Acts xiv. 17), and the Holy Spirit had been able long before to give special inspiration to some who are known as prophets (St. Luke i. 70 and Heb. i. 1) ; but not until our Lord had triumphed over sin and death, and been exalted to the right hand of the Father, could the Holy Spirit dwell with men as He desired to do, for their hearts were not ready. Now at length, however, He could come in the fullness of His power.

He is still present with all men everywhere, in some measure ; but the Church is His true home on earth, because the Church is made up of people whose hearts are open to His movements. Read the hymn, " Our blest Redeemer."

2. The Holy Spirit is always active in the hearts of the members of the Church, but especially when we use what are known as the Means of Grace, *i.e.* when we read the Bible, when we pray, or when we receive one of the Church's Sacraments. These Sacraments are pledges which are used by God to give us His grace, or life, or strength. Taught by Christ, the Church takes and solemnly uses simple things such as water and bread and wine, or it solemnly performs some simple act such as blessing by the laying of a hand upon our head, and God the Holy Ghost comes, in answer to the Church's prayers, and graciously bestows His gifts.

II. THE CLEANSING AND STRENGTHENING OF NEW MEMBERS

1. When people who are not yet Christians learn to love Jesus Christ and seek admittance to His Church, they must first be washed clean from all sin and then strengthened with the Holy Spirit so that they may remain pure. They must be baptized, as we say, and then confirmed. This has been the Church's way from the beginning. Turn to Acts viii. 5–17 and xix. 1–7.

The strength which we gain through Confirmation is not, of course, strength of body, but moral strength (*i.e.* power to refuse the wrong and to do the right) and spiritual strength (*i.e.* power to trust in God, whatever may happen). Turn to the collect in the Confirmation Service, where the seven gifts of the Holy Spirit are named, and to Isai. xi. 2.

2. In Christian families the children are received by the Church in Holy Baptism soon after their birth ; but they are not confirmed, or strengthened by the Holy Spirit, until they really need His strength and know their need of it. This is what is meant by coming to " years of discretion." You have now reached this stage.

Open your Prayer Books at the place where the service for the Publick Baptism of Infants is to be found. Read the last paragraph of it. Now skip the other two services of Baptism which follow, and you come first to the Catechism and then to the Order of Confirmation. Turn back and read the heading of the Catechism, and you will understand why the Catechism is put in between Baptism and Confirmation in the book. It sums up the things you must be taught before you come forward for Confirmation.

III. How to prepare for Confirmation

1. You must learn the Catechism, if you can, and try your utmost to understand and to remember all the teaching that is given to you in your preparation. See St. Mark iv. 9, 23. Never miss a class, if you can help it. Be punctual ; and be very attentive.

2. Attend the services of the Church regularly on Sundays. This is very important. And, now that you are preparing to become a communicant, you may attend the service of Holy Communion regularly during your preparation, not of course to receive the Sacrament, but to pray and to take note of the order of the service, following carefully from your Prayer Book.

3. Every morning and every night you must say your prayers with all reverence and care, praying especially for the gift of the Holy Spirit through the Laying on of Hands. At night you will add to your prayers the reading of a passage in the Bible, which you will stay to think over for a short time.

4. In all that you do you will try to please God. It is your bounden duty to be active and helpful, bright and happy, full of thought for others, and always true to the best that you know. Be very earnest.

2. THE COMMUNION OF SAINTS

By Baptism and Confirmation we are admitted to full membership in Christ's Holy Catholic Church, which is, as the Prayer Book puts it, " the blessed company of all faithful people." This is so great a privilege that we must take time to consider its full meaning.

I. The Saints of God

1. Some Christians have shown such wonderful faith and goodness in their lives that they have come to be known as saints, or holy ones ; *e.g.* among men St. John, St. George, and St. Francis of Assisi ; among women St. Mary, St. Margaret, and St. Catharine of Siena ; and among children St. Agnes and St. Faith. Some of these died a martyr's death, like St. Stephen and St. Alban ; others died a natural death ; but all of them, whether they lived a short time or a long time, showed in their lives the wonderful power of the Holy Spirit. In every one of them the grace of God was clearly seen.

2. The Church has always numbered such saints in its fighting ranks, and it has some of them to-day in various parts of the world. Together they form a great company of brave and pure-souled Christian people, many of them now in Paradise in the Church Expectant, some of them still in the Church Militant here in earth, but all of them members of the one Church, that great family to which we belong. They are our big brothers and sisters.

II. " Called to be Saints "

1. These brothers and sisters of ours are a constant reminder of what is expected of us, for all the members of the Church without exception are " called to be saints " (Rom. i. 7 ; 1 Cor. i. 2). The Church is holy, because it is the chief dwelling-place of the Holy Spirit on earth ; and He is striving to win every Christian to perfect holiness, or sainthood. When His work in us is finished, there will be " a great multitude, which no man could number, out of every nation, and of all tribes and peoples and tongues, standing before the throne and before the Lamb, arrayed in white robes, and palms in their hands " (Rev. vii. 9).

2. Our power is drawn from God's Holy Spirit ; the perfect ideal we set before us is found in the life and teaching of our Lord Jesus Christ ; but it is a great source of strength to us to know that so many Christians have achieved such faith and goodness, and that we are joined with them in the warfare against evil. " Therefore let us also, seeing we are compassed about with so great a cloud of witnesses, lay aside every weight, and the sin which doth so easily beset us, and let us run with patience the race that is set before us, looking unto Jesus the author and perfecter of our faith, who for the joy that was set before him endured the cross, despising shame, and hath sat down at the right hand of the throne of God " (Heb. xii. 1, 2).

III. The Prayer-Book Calendar

1. The Calendar in our Prayer Book contains a list of names of chosen saints, each one set down against a certain day. This makes it a family birthday-book, which helps us to remember, and to rejoice in remembering, the greatest and most lovable members of our family. Their birthdays, it should be understood, are not the days on which they were born into this world as babies, but the days on which they died and were born into the peace and happiness of Paradise.

2. These saints, whose birthdays we keep, are known as Red-letter Saints and Black-letter Saints. The Red-letter Saints are the most important of all, and it was to mark their importance that their names were printed in red. All of them are found in the New Testament.

3. The Black-letter Saints are of two kinds. There are, first of all, saints who lived outside these islands, but are remembered and loved by the whole Church. Such are St. Monnica, Matron, mother of the great St. Augustine; St. Benedict, Abbot of Monte Cassino and Doctor, whose wise Rule was followed by most of the monks of the West; and St. Giles of Provence, Abbot and Confessor. Then there are our own national saints who lived in these islands and played a part in our history. Such are St. Hilda, Abbess of Whitby; St. Oswald, King of Northumbria and Martyr; St. Alphege, Archbishop of Canterbury and Martyr; and St. Hugh, Bishop of Lincoln.

4. It will be a great help to us in our efforts towards sainthood if we will read the lives of the Saints, and make special remembrance of them on their birthdays, praying that we may be made strong and faithful, pure and good, as they were. "We therefore pray Thee, help Thy servants : whom Thou hast redeemed with Thy precious blood. Make them to be numbered with Thy Saints : in glory everlasting."

3. VOCATION

When you read the lives of the Saints you will find that they were all quite different people and that they were called by God to do very different things. They did not choose for themselves, but in answer to a call they walked in the way that was appointed for them and set themselves to do the will of their Master.

I. The Call to Suffering

1. There is one call which every saint hears—the call to suffering. Our Lord said to His disciples generally, " If any man would come after me, let him deny himself, and take up his cross, and follow me " (St. Matt. xvi. 24). When He called St. Paul to be His servant, He said, " I will shew him how many things he must suffer for my name's sake " (Acts ix. 16). The Saints do not all suffer alike ; and whatever the degree of their suffering they learn to rejoice in it. " I rejoice in my sufferings for your sake," writes St. Paul to the Colossians (i. 24). But they all suffer ; and no follower of Jesus Christ must expect to escape suffering.

2. The suffering takes so many forms in different lives that there is not much use in trying to find out in advance just what it is likely to mean for us. (Read the list of St. Paul's labours in 2 Cor. xi. 22–30, and vi. 4–10.) But when the call comes to us we must be ready to set our own desires on one side and to endure contradiction and sorrow and pain, if need be, for Christ's sake.

3. Some people to-day are teaching that, if only we are full of faith in God, we shall suffer little or no pain in our bodies and we need never be ill. That is not true. It is quite true that many people suffer bodily distress through sin and through want of faith : but it is also true that great faith and much suffering sometimes go together. It is a mystery why it should be so, but we do not reproach God for it ; rather we try to suffer gladly in fellowship with Christ, believing that our sorrows are somehow helping God to banish evil and to " wipe away all tears."

II. The Call to Work

1. The word " vocation," or " calling," is commonly applied to the work we do. Here we must remember that God does indeed call, and that we are not to count ourselves free to choose selfishly and foolishly. God gives us certain gifts and powers ; He gives us certain friends and opportunities ; and He gives us certain suggestions in our minds from time to time. In choosing our life's work we are to be guided by what He says to us, by what He says to our friends, and by the opportunities He makes for us. Whatever profession or occupation we choose, in answer to His calling, we are to work with all our powers, to please God and to serve our fellow-men.

2. Some Christians are specially called to the direct service of the Church in various ways. " He gave some to be apostles ; and some, prophets ; and some, evangelists ; and some, pastors and teachers ; for the perfecting

of the saints, unto the work of ministering, unto the building up of the body of Christ " (Eph. iv. 11, 12). This calling is a very great privilege, on no account to be refused, even when the difficulties in the way of accepting it are great.

In the Church of God to-day, as at the beginning, men may be appointed to serve as deacons, or as priests, or as bishops ; and women may minister as deaconesses. Or again, both men and women may serve the Church as lay-workers. If the call comes to you now, or later on, see that you pray about it, and talk it over with your parents and friends, and do all that you can to answer it. You must not refuse to lend God the help He asks from you, whether it is to be given at home or in the mission-field abroad. " I heard the voice of the Lord, saying, Whom shall I send, and who will go for us ? Then I said, Here am I ; send me " (Isa. vi. 8).

III. THE CALL TO MARRIAGE OR TO SINGLENESS

1. When men and women marry, it ought to be because God calls them to live together. This He does when He causes them to love one another truly, so that they desire to make a home together and to help one another to love and to serve Him for the rest of their lives. When a man and a woman are thus called to the holy estate of Matrimony and agree to marry, they come to church to ask for God's blessing and to promise before Him to be faithful and loving to each other all their days.

2. But sometimes it happens that men and women are called to work which makes such special demands upon them that they must not think of the responsibilities and the joys of married life. For the sake of the Kingdom of God they must live alone, free to make many friends, but not to have a home and family of their own. There are other reasons which sometimes make it clear that people are not meant to marry ; and always a good Christian will listen to God's calling in the matter and act according to His bidding, though it may be at great cost to himself.

B. THE CHURCH'S FAITH

5. THE FOUR GOSPELS AND THE ACTS

The Gospel, or Good News, of the life and work of Jesus Christ, is set out for us in four different ways in the first four books of the New Testament. This is the very heart of the Bible, and the part to which we should give most attention. Then there follows a book called The Acts of the Apostles, in which we are told of the spread of the newly founded Church from Jerusalem to the great city of Rome. All this is history ; and on this history our creed is based.

I. Our Lord's Early Life

1. As the opening verses of St. John's Gospel make clear, Jesus Christ is the eternal Word of God. " In the beginning was the Word " (St. John i. 1). In the fullness of time He was born as a babe at Bethlehem, of Mary, the Blessed Virgin, and adored by shepherds and by wise men from the East. To escape the wrath of Herod He was carried into Egypt. On His return He was taken to Nazareth, the home of Mary and His foster-father Joseph the carpenter, where He was brought up as their child.

2. For thirty years the life at Nazareth was interrupted only by visits to Jerusalem " to keep the feast." According to Jewish custom our Lord took part in these from the time that He was twelve years old, and St. Luke tells us of His desire to be about His Father's business on the first visit that He made.

II. The First Part of the Ministry

1. When our Lord was thirty years old, St. John Baptist came out from the desert to announce the Kingdom of God. Jesus accepted this signal, left His carpenter's shop, and went forth to fulfil His vocation as Messiah. He was baptized with John's baptism ; and immediately afterwards He spent a time of earnest prayer in the wilderness, overcoming the temptations of Satan to do His work in a wrong spirit and in a wrong way. Then He began His ministry.

2. His purpose was to reveal to people the love of the Father, to wean them from sin and to win them to goodness, and so to establish the Kingdom or Reign of God. He chose twelve disciples to be with Him ; and together they travelled about through all the villages of Galilee, spending much time especially on the shores of the Sea of Galilee. Our Lord constantly taught the people, by means of stories called parables, and He worked many miracles among them. Crowds followed Him wherever He went ; but though they wondered at Him and wished to make Him their king, yet they did not rightly understand Him. The disciples alone grew in understanding, and at length recognized Him as Messiah. He then revealed to them the suffering that would come to Him ; and shortly after this He was transfigured before three of them.

III. The Second Part of the Ministry

1. Our Lord and His disciples now journeyed to Jerusalem, preaching the Kingdom in Samaria, Judæa, and Peræa, on the way. The religious leaders in Jerusalem hated Him for His teaching and for His claims, and, after He had raised Lazarus from the dead, they plotted to destroy Him. He entered Jerusalem as the Messianic King on Palm Sunday, purged the Temple and taught many things during the next four days. On Maundy Thursday He instituted the Memorial of His Passion, gave the disciples the new commandment, and was then betrayed by Judas Iscariot.

2. He was tried by the High Priest on a charge of blasphemy, and by Pontius Pilate on a charge of sedition. Through fear of the mob Pilate gave Him up to be crucified. On Good Friday morning He was put to death on the Cross, and in the evening His body was taken down and laid in a tomb.

3. On Easter Day the mourning disciples were amazed and rejoiced to find Christ with them again, risen from the dead. During forty days He appeared to them from time to time and continued His teaching; and on Ascension Day He went back to be with the Father in heaven.

IV. The Acts of the Apostles

1. After a short time of waiting, the disciples received the Holy Spirit to strengthen them for their work, and at once began to build the Church on the Foundation that had been laid. The Apostles took the lead, their number being made up to twelve again by the election of St. Matthias in the place of Judas Iscariot; and they were helped by St. Stephen, the first martyr, and six others, whom they appointed. Soon it became necessary to appoint presbyters, as well as these deacons, so that the three orders of the ministry came into being.

2. For some time it was thought that only Jews could become Christians. Then the Holy Spirit made it clear that the Church is Catholic, and that Gentiles as well as Jews were to be admitted.

3. The second part of this book tells of the wonderful missionary work of St. Paul, who carried the Gospel through Asia Minor into Europe, daring greatly and suffering greatly. It is a constant call to us to preserve the missionary character of the Church, supporting its work overseas by our prayers, our alms, and our service.

6. THE CREEDS—THE BLESSED TRINITY—THE INCARNATION

The Church's faith is summed up in three Creeds, the Apostles', the Nicene, and the Athanasian. These summaries were wrought out by the Church, in the course of the first few centuries of its life, in the process of teaching candidates for Baptism and correcting teachers who went astray. They can never be abandoned, as though we belonged to a Body which did not care to know and to declare what it believes ; nor can they well be changed, unless the Church is to change its faith.

I. The Creeds

1. The Apostles' Creed gives us the full faith of the Apostles in its simplest form. It is arranged in three paragraphs, the first concerning God the Father, the second concerning God the Son, and the third concerning God the Holy Ghost and His work in the Church. We use this Creed at baptisms and when visiting the sick, at Morning and Evening Prayer, and in the Catechism.

2. The Nicene Creed keeps to the same arrangement, but it is longer. It was necessary to make it longer, because it was found that people did not all mean the same thing by the words that were used about Jesus Christ in the Apostles' Creed. A Council of Bishops met at Nicæa in Asia Minor in the year 325 to consider what was really meant by calling Him the Son of God, and this Creed shows what their answer was : He is " Very God of very God." We use this Creed always at the Holy Communion.

3. The Athanasian Creed differs from the other two in its form. It is a hymn of faith, in which some Christian of the fifth or sixth century set forth the truth concerning the doctrines of the Blessed Trinity and of the Incarnation as these were maintained by the great champion St. Athanasius.

II. The Blessed Trinity

1. God is One, and God is Three in One. This is the Church's teaching about God, on the authority of Jesus Christ. He often spoke of His Father and prayed to Him ; He promised to send the Holy Ghost, the Comforter. When Jesus was baptized the Holy Spirit descended upon Him in the form of a dove, and the Father's voice was heard, approving Him. Hence we baptize people into the Name of the Father, and of the Son, and of the Holy Ghost. We make frequent use of St. Paul's prayer : " The grace of the Lord Jesus Christ, and the love of God, and the communion of the Holy Ghost, be with you all " (2 Cor. xiii. 14).

2. The wonders of God's nature are far beyond our understanding, yet the doctrine of the Blessed Trinity helps us very much when we try to think clearly about God's relationship with what we call Nature and with the human family. He creates, He redeems, and He sanctifies ; and all the time He is in Himself perfect Love.

But the doctrine is revealed to us chiefly in order that we may worship God rightly and pray to Him aright. Everyone who prays has some idea of the Power to Whom he is praying, and the nature of his prayers depends very much upon his idea. True prayer is possible only to one who thinks rightly about God. The prayer of the idol-worshipper is not the same as the prayer of the Jew or of the Moslem ; and the prayer of the Jew or of the Moslem is not the same as the prayer of the Christian.

III. The Incarnation

1. In order to save man from sin and to bring him into perfect fellowship with his Maker, God the Son lived on earth as Man, died upon the Cross of Calvary, rose again from the dead, and ascended into heaven. There He is now, at the right hand of the Father, still in His Manhood that He took upon Him when He was conceived by the Holy Ghost. His Incarnation (that is to say, His adoption of our human nature) began at a moment of time by His own will, but it continues, also by His will, for ever and ever.

2. Just as we are not able to declare fully the mysteries of the Being of God, so the manner of the Incarnation passes our understanding. But we know that He was, and is always, perfect God, so that He can save us, and again perfect Man, so that in Him we can be saved. He is not a mixture of God and man, but in His One Person both Godhead and Manhood are found in their full power and perfection.

3. In His life upon the earth the Son of God was known first as a carpenter's son, then as a carpenter, then as a teacher, then as the Messiah, and at length as the Son of God. He Himself grew into an understanding of His Person. But all the time He was the same unique and perfect Son of God, tempted, yet always without sin.

7. THE ATONEMENT

By our sins we are separated from God, and we have no power of ourselves to get back again into fellowship with Him. But God has provided a way out of the difficulty. He so loved the world that He gave His only-begotten Son, Who by His death upon the Cross, made God and man " at one." This is what we mean by the word at-one-ment, or, as we now say it, atonement.

I. A Ransom

1. " The Son of man came not to be ministered unto, but to minister, and to give his life a ransom for many " (St. Mark x. 45). In these words of our Lord we are taught to think of ourselves, before He comes into our lives, as slaves—slaves to sin, fast bound in the chain of bad habits and sinful ways. Then comes Jesus Christ to ransom or redeem us from our slavery, and on the Cross He pays the price of our emancipation, or deliverance.

2. Sometimes men have thought of Satan, the father of sin, as the one who holds us in bondage ; and then they have naturally gone on to think of the ransom as a payment made to him. They have sung of the Cross as a tree

> On whose dear arms, so widely flung,
> The weight of this world's ransom hung :
> The price of humankind to pay,
> And spoil the spoiler of his prey.

But this is not the best way in which to think of it. When we sin, suffering always follows. A price has to be paid ; but there is no profit in asking to whom it is paid, for it is not really paid to anybody. Our sin not only brings trouble upon ourselves and upon other people, but it hurts God. God's hurt is far worse than ours, and there is so much love in it that it becomes redemptive, it breaks our chains.

II. A Sacrifice

1. " He, when he had offered one sacrifice for sins for ever, sat down on the right hand of God " (Heb. x. 12). This is another important way of thinking about the Atonement. Like most other peoples, the Jews were accustomed to offer actual sacrifices to God ; and it is striking that our Lord was crucified on the very day of the year when the Passover lambs were killed. Christians were taught to think of Him as the " Lamb of God, that taketh away the sins of the world."

2. Now, if it was wrong to think of God paying ransom-money to Satan, is it wrong to think of God's Son offering Himself as a sacrifice to His Father ? Only if we think of the Father as an angry God Whose wrath must be turned away by the offering of a very precious life. God gave His Son in love, not in anger. And the Son gave His life in love, not in fear. As the Head of the human family He offered to His Father the best that the human family had to offer, namely, His own perfect obedience and perfect life.

And the Father gladly accepted it as a pledge of the obedience and righteousness that will appear in time in the lives of all those who are " in Christ." The offering made upon the Cross wins for us acceptance with God in advance. God receives us as sons because of the great sacrifice of His unique Son.

3. In heaven Christ acts as our great High Priest, continually seeking to confer upon us the benefits of His sacrifice. On earth the Church joins with its Head in the work of intercession, especially in the service of Holy Communion, where we plead Christ's death.

> And now, O Father, mindful of the love
> That bought us, once for all, on Calvary's Tree,
> And having with us Him that pleads above,
> We here present, we here spread forth to Thee
> That only Offering perfect in Thine eyes,
> The one true, pure, immortal Sacrifice.

III. An Appeal

There is yet a third way of considering the Atonement. The Cross is like a wooden pulpit; and Christ, Who hangs upon it with outstretched arms, preaches to all men a silent sermon on the love of God. " I, if I be lifted up from the earth, will draw all men unto myself " (St. John xii. 32). When we gaze upon the Cross we see the ugliness of sin and the beauty and glory of love, triumphant in its suffering.

> See from His Head, His hands, His feet,
> Sorrow and love flow mingled down ;
> Did e'er such love and sorrow meet,
> Or thorns compose so rich a crown ?

Being drawn to Christ, one by one, through the power of the Cross, we enter into a close fellowship of mind and spirit with Him, sharing His hatred of sin and His attitude towards suffering, and thus gradually becoming conformed to His likeness and completely " at one " with God.

8. THE FUTURE LIFE

Most men have believed in a life after death, both because such a belief is reasonable and because they have a feeling that man was not made to die. But apart from our Lord's Resurrection there can be no certainty in this matter. Easter Day is the one sure ground of our faith and hope. " If we believe that Jesus died and rose again, even so them also that are fallen asleep in Jesus will God bring with him " (1 Thess. iv. 14). To die is to be " with Christ," and that is " very far better " (Phil. i. 23). Little can be known by us about that life, and we must be content with the few things Christ has taught us, refusing to trust to the teaching of those who believe in Spiritism.

I. Paradise

1. When we die, the soul is separated from the body, and passes to Paradise. This is not the same as Heaven, but is a further stage on the way to Heaven. In it the soul is cleansed and strengthened by the love of Christ, so that sometimes this state is spoken of as Purgatory, or the place of purging. But we must not think chiefly of suffering and pain in the process of cleansing. There is great joy in the soul, because it knows that it is being fitted to dwell with God for ever. The penitent robber was greatly comforted when our Lord said to him, " Verily I say unto thee, To-day shalt thou be with me in Paradise " (St. Luke xxiii. 43).

2. The souls in Paradise form the Church Expectant, which is closely bound up with the Church Militant here in earth. They strive and pray for the perfecting of the Kingdom even as we do, and it is well for us to remember this in our prayers. It cannot be doubted that those who prayed for us while they were living here still pray for us now that they are in Paradise. So, too, we who prayed for them when they were here with us in the flesh will continue to pray for them now that they are nearer to God. We shall ask that God will grant them rest, refreshment, and peace, and that light perpetual may shine upon them.

II. Resurrection and Judgment

1. When this world comes to an end, our dead bodies will be raised up even as our Lord's Body was raised on the third day, and soul and body will be reunited. But the resurrection body will not be a body of flesh and blood. It will be changed so as to serve the soul better than the body which is ours while we are here. " Flesh and blood cannot inherit the kingdom of God. . . . We shall all be changed " (1 Cor. xv. 51 f.).

2. Then will come the last judgment, before the throne of Christ. Each of us will appear in his true character, and will be approved and accepted as fit to dwell with God, or—condemned and cast out. God is all Love, and He is full of mercy and loving-kindness ; yet He is not able to make light of sin, and the judgment will be solemn and searching, and, for all who have set themselves against God, very terrible.

III. Heaven and Hell

1. After the judgment those who are accepted by God as fit to dwell with Him will live for ever in His Presence, enjoying to the full His love and goodness. This is what we mean by Heaven, or the Beatific Vision.

> Father of Jesus, love's reward,
>   What rapture will it be
> Prostrate before Thy throne to lie,
>   And gaze and gaze on Thee.

None of the evil things of this life find any place in it ; there is no pain or sorrow, there are no tears, and death will be no more. As for its joys and blessings, they are pictured in symbols by St. John, in the wonderful book of visions which closes the Bible. These joys are so perfect and intense that all sense of time is lost, and life is eternal.

2. Those who are judged unfit to live with God are cast out of His Presence. They will know what they have lost, and that is what we mean by Hell. Some think that they will suffer for a time and then die eternally ; others think that God's love will win every one of them in time, and that they will then be added to the number of the blessed. But these things are not revealed to us ; and we do better to dwell on the thought of Heaven than to dwell on the thought of Hell. " Strive to enter in."

C. THE CHRISTIAN WAY OF LIFE

9. OUR DUTY TO GOD

If we wish to keep our bodies well, we must observe the laws of health. So also, if we wish to keep our souls pure and holy, we must obey the laws of holiness. God taught these laws to His chosen people many hundreds of years ago in the table of the Ten Commandments. These we still use, but with a deeper and wider meaning than they had at first, because our Lord has taught us their full scope. In the Sermon on the Mount He had much to say concerning the Christian way of life; and at another time He summed up all the commandments in the saying, Love God, and love your neighbour. Four of the ten commandments are included in the first part of this saying, and the remaining six in the second part.

I. The First and Second Commandments

1. In the first commandment we are taught that God claims the first place in our lives. There is no other person, and there is no creature or thing, worthy to be compared with Him. We must be perfectly loyal to Him. If any friendship comes between us and God, it must be abandoned. If we care for riches, or pleasure, or even work, so much that we fail to find a proper place for God in our lives, then we are sinning grievously, and we shall not grow aright nor shall we find any real peace for our souls. It is in our own best interests and for our own true happiness that we should be able to say with the Psalmist, " I have set God always before me."

2. The second commandment forbids the worship of any *thing* in the place of God. It requires us to think rightly about God, so that we are not found worshipping a false god of our own imagination; and it warns us that, if we use pictures and images in our worship, it is to be understood that they are lawful only so long as they help us to get into touch with God, Who is a Spirit.

II. The Third Commandment

1. This is the law of reverence for God and for all His works. It requires us to guard our lips from every form of bad language, but especially that which is profane. The use of oaths betrays either a lack of education or a serious want of self-control, frequently both; it commonly goes with a certain coarseness and vulgarity in the way of life, and it tells of a failure to realise the presence of God. Far worse than common swearing is the use of blasphemous language, which is a grave sin. Always speak of God, and of His Son, and of the Holy Spirit, and of the Church, and of the Bible, and of death, with due seriousness. These are not subjects for jesting or for use in angry moods.

2. Remember also that reverence is due to God in our treatment of little children, animals, birds, flowers, and all the wonderful works of His hands that are put in our power. To mock at a child's innocence and simplicity, to cause any creature unnecessary pain, to destroy without any reason, all this is to break the third commandment.

III. The Fourth Commandment

1. " Six days shalt thou labour." Work is for us one form of the worship of God, and every man is commanded to work for six days in the week. Most of us have to work in order to earn our living ; but we should remember our Lord's words, " My Father worketh even until now, and I work " (St. John v. 17), and we should be glad to labour with God, for Him and for the good of our fellows, doing our very best at all times.

2. The Jews rest on the seventh day of the week, *i.e.* Saturday, believing that God requires them to keep that day free from toil in order that they may make it a holy day. They worship God in their synagogues on this day, which they call " the Sabbath," and they make a special point of refraining from every kind of work.

3. Christians keep Sunday, the first day of the week, as their holy day, because on that day our Lord rose again from the dead ; and it is for us a day of worship and of spiritual refreshment rather than of mere rest. It is our bounden duty to go to church for public worship every Sunday ; and as to the rest of the day, the part not occupied by church-going, we must use it with care so as not to rob the whole day of the true spirit of worship. Games of various kinds are not in themselves sinful on Sunday, but on the whole it is better to refrain from anything that would help to make Sunday just like any other day. It is well in this connection to remember St. Paul's words, " All things are lawful ; but all things are not expedient," and to have a care for our neighbour when we are planning our use of the Lord's Day (which, by the way, should not be called the Sabbath).

10. OUR DUTY TO OUR NEIGHBOUR (1)

The love of God and the love of our brother are closely bound up with each other. As St. John very vigorously says, " If a man say, I love God, and hateth his brother, he is a liar : for he that loveth not his brother whom he hath seen, cannot love God whom he hath not seen " (1 St. John iv. 20). Our duty to our neighbour is, in fact, a part of our duty to God. In serving him and behaving properly towards him, we are really loving and serving God. Read our Lord's words in St. Matt. xxv. 31 to end.

I. The Fifth Commandment

1. Our first duty to others is honour, respect, and courteous consideration. This is to be learnt at home. We owe a great debt to our parents for all the love and care they have bestowed upon us, and for this we ought to yield them not only affection, but also reverent obedience and truest courtesy. Even when we grow up and leave home we should still defer to their wishes as far as we possibly can, and, if necessary, minister to their needs with generosity and gladness.

2. Outside our own families there are all the other people who go to make up the great human family, people of various colours and classes, rich and poor, wise and foolish, friendly and unfriendly. We have a duty towards all of these, as our Lord taught us in the parable of the Good Samaritan : and it is impossible that this duty should ever be rightly discharged until we have learnt to " honour all men." Love your family, then ; love your school ; love your country ; and love the Brotherhood.

3. As to the promise that is attached to the commandment, we need not suppose that we are bound to live a long time on the earth if we pay proper respect to others ; but by so doing we shall certainly be preparing to take our place in the family life of Heaven, where our days will be without number.

II. The Sixth Commandment

1. All life comes from God. In man it reaches its highest level, and we are all responsible to God and to one another for a reverent care of it. Animals may be killed for food, but they should not be put to unnecessary pain. Men may agree to take away a man's life as the punishment for a very serious offence ; but this must be done in defence of God's laws and by proper authority. Men are forbidden to take their own lives ; each man must wait God's time. And they are forbidden to take one another's lives, whether in kindness so as to save them pain, or in anger, jealousy, and revenge, or for any evil purpose whatever.

2. There is more in this commandment, however, than a mere forbidding of actual murder. In the Sermon on the Mount our Lord teaches that we are to control our tempers, and this is its real meaning for all of us. " Keep your temper," as they say in America ; " it's of no use to anyone else." We must not be sulky ; we must not be passionate. We must not allow ourselves

to hate other people, even when they injure us ; but we must try to follow our Lord's command, " Love your enemies."

III. The Seventh Commandment

1. God has provided that children should be born of love. When a man and a woman marry, God commonly crowns their love with the gift of a child. For some time the child lives near to the heart of its mother, and then, when it is fully formed, it is born into the world. For a long time after that it depends upon the care of mother and father, living with them in their home and receiving loving attention at all times, and yet adding to their love and helping to make their home a real home.

2. The sin that is forbidden in this commandment is the sin of yielding to lust, or strong desire, in disloyalty to God and the home, and without the possibility of providing properly for God's gift of new life, if He should grant it. Again, it covers every kind of impure act and thought, whether between married people or those who are not married. It insists upon the sacredness of life, which must never be taken away in anger or impatience, as we have just seen, and must never be renewed except in pure love according to God's provisions.

3. It is not good for us to set our thoughts on these things. We should dwell, rather, upon what is good and pure and holy, and keep our bodies clean and healthy by means of cleanly habits, the use of plain food in moderation, and sufficient outdoor exercise. Above all, " think on " things that are pure, and fear God. Read Phil. iv. 8, 9.

11. OUR DUTY TO OUR NEIGHBOUR (2)

Last time we were considering the sacredness of life. We learned that it is to be reverenced and cared for in all men as the very power of God. Now we have to learn what is our proper attitude towards life's possessions, the things that belong to other men during their stay here on earth, or, in the case of their character, for ever.

I. The Eighth Commandment

1. Honesty is said to be the best policy. But it is more than that ; it is God's law, and we must always respect our neighbour's right to enjoy his possessions in security. Thieving is thieving, whether the thing stolen is money or some other possession, and whether it is valuable or of small worth. Stealing is usually done in secret ; but there is also open stealing, which takes the form of borrowing, with no intention to repay. Stealing from a company or association of people is just as bad as stealing from one person, though most people seem to do it with an easier conscience. The most despicable form of theft is that which is committed against people who have been good to us.

2. Boys are sometimes heard to say, " Finding is keeping." But that is not the law of the land, nor is it God's law. If we find anything that is clearly lost property, we must make every effort to discover the owner.

3. Cheating is to be regarded as a form of stealing. This is seen especially when it is practised in order to win money. And some people consider that we come very near to stealing when we are successful in some lottery, or raffle, or other competition involving neither work nor skill. On the whole it is better to avoid these things, since they offend the consciences of a good many Christian people.

II. The Ninth Commandment

1. Of more value to each man than his property is his character. To bear false witness against anyone is to rob him of this, his most precious possession, in the eyes of other people. It is true that it does not damage him in God's sight ; it damages only the person who speaks what is false. Yet it is a grave wrong and may lead to serious injury. Beware, then, of discussing other people too freely ; do not repeat stories which are not to their credit, even when you know them to be true ; try always to find out the good in others, and, when you speak of them, talk about that. When it is your duty to speak unpleasant truths against anyone, speak without fear but with all care.

2. There is a tendency in most people to exaggerate their statements in order to lend emphasis to what they say. We must be on our guard against the growth of this habit, for it actually weakens the force of what we say, and it leads to untruthfulness in more serious forms. Lies are commonly told through fear, in order to escape punishment, or with the object of impressing people and adding importance to ourselves. In either case

they are an abomination. No man likes to be called a liar, even though he knows himself to be one, because it means that he is judged by his fellows as disloyal, dishonourable, and unreliable, not deserving of a place in the society which he is doing his best to render insecure. A liar is an Ishmael, always on guard, always ready to hurl a dart, never truly at peace.

III. The Tenth Commandment

1. To covet is more than to desire. It is not a sin to want things when we see them. There are many things we should all like to have, and the mere feeling that we should be glad to have them is not a sin. But if we allow the desire to grow in our minds, so that our thoughts are constantly set upon the desired possession, and we become envious of the person who has it and thoroughly dissatisfied with our own condition because we have it not, then we are covetous, and we have broken God's law. The covetous person is never satisfied; he always lacks something, however great his possessions.

2. There is no need to suppose that a Christian is forbidden to desire, and to work for, a larger income. Poverty is limiting in many ways, whereas wealth is a power that may be used to work much good. Yet we must remember that we may all too easily fall victims to that " love of money which is a root of all kinds of evil." Our Lord's teaching is plainly to the effect that the soul is safer in poverty than in riches. But whether we are rich or poor we should learn to be content with our lot, and to make the best of our opportunities to serve others.

12. PRAYER, FASTING, AND ALMSGIVING

The Jews, to whom God delivered the Ten Commandments, found that there were three practices which would help them to keep the Law—Prayer, Fasting, and Almsgiving. The first has reference to God, the second to the self, and the third to our neighbours; the first looks up, the second looks within, and the third looks around. Our Lord and His disciples practised these three duties, and Christians have striven ever since to follow their example, especially during Lent, but also as a general rule of life.

I. PRAYER

1. There is a great deal to learn about prayer, so that it will be necessary to give three whole lessons to it. To-day we must be content to learn the nature of prayer and some of the rules to be observed if we would pray well. Prayer means remembering God, thinking of Him, listening to Him, and talking to Him. Every time we raise our thoughts from the things of earth to which they cling, and fix them upon God in Heaven, we are at prayer.

2. In order that we may learn to pray in this way " without ceasing," we set apart certain times of the day for deliberate prayer in precise forms of words. These prayer exercises are the means by which we train our souls to apprehend God, and they must be performed regularly at the proper times, when we " feel like it " and when we do not.

3. In church we pray in the sight of other people. But a great deal of our praying must be done in secret, in the quiet of our own room. It is a help to have a special prayer-place, where there are helps to the practice of the presence of God, including any books that we may use for this purpose. Usually we shall kneel to say our prayers; but it is also permitted to stand; and we may learn to pray earnestly when seated in a bus or tram or railway-carriage, or when lying on a bed of sickness.

II. FASTING

1. Strictly this means going without food or drink for certain periods; but it is generally understood to mean going without certain kinds of food, or using only a limited quantity, less in amount than is usually taken. Thus on fast-days (the season of Lent, and Fridays, chiefly) many Christians avoid flesh food, though they commonly use it at other times; they give up all dainties, and they eat sparingly. This is good for the body, since most people eat too much normally; but it is practised rather for the good of the soul. It helps us to gain the power of self-control, and it serves to show God that we are in earnest in our sorrow for past sin and in our intention to please Him better in the future.

2. Fasting must, however, be held to include other kinds of bodily discipline by which we refuse to do or to use things which are in themselves lawful. We do well sometimes to stay away from the theatre or the picture-palace or the dance-room as a matter of deliberate sacrifice; to refrain from smoking,

when grown up, as from overmuch eating of sweet things, when younger ; to refuse to waste time in reading books which serve no other purpose. And as we fast from too much pleasure, so we must learn to fast from too much indulgence of the body in the way of rest, and go to bed and rise again at fixed hours.

III. Almsgiving

1. A part of all the money that comes to us must be given up in the form of rates and taxes for the good of our country, a good in which we share ; a part must be spent on ourselves, our families and friends ; a part should be saved ; and a part should be given to God. The old rule was to give God one-tenth, or a tithe, as it is called. When we have little money, it may not be possible to give as much as one-tenth ; when money is more plentiful, we may well be able to give more than one-tenth ; the tithe will serve as a general reminder of the extent of our duty.

2. But how is money to be given to God ? First, for His work ; the work of His Church at home and abroad, to all good causes such as hospitals, the care of homeless children, etc. And then in charity, that is Christian love, to particular people in need who are within reach and known to us. We ought not to give money to beggars, who may be untruthful, and who in any case will not be really helped by what we give them. Almsgiving is not an easy duty to discharge, and we must take pains about it.

13. PRAYER: (1) THE LORD'S PRAYER

The Twelve were so greatly impressed by the way in which our Lord prayed that they felt almost as though they had not yet begun to pray properly and were in need of being taught again from the beginning. " Lord, teach us to pray," they said ; and in answer they were given the prayer we know as the Lord's Prayer. This is to be the model of all our praying, and our hope must be that we shall grow in the power of prayer until at length we shall be able to pray the Lord's Prayer perfectly.

I. Our Father

1. We begin by fixing our thoughts upon God. " Unto Thee, O Lord, do I lift up my soul." He is the great God of Heaven, Creator of all that is ; and yet He is our Father in the sense that He knows and loves each one of His creatures. When we talk to Him as His children, He listens and takes careful account of every desire of our hearts. Draw near, then, with boldness and confidence, yet with reverent awe.

2. " Hallowed be Thy Name, Thy Kingdom come, Thy will be done —in earth as it is in Heaven." We pray for the greater glory of God, so that in Him all things may come to their perfection. May His Holy Name be reverenced by all men throughout the world, even as the angels regard Him worshipfully in Heaven ; may His rule in men's hearts grow ever wider and more complete, until He is everywhere acknowledged as King and Lord ; and may His plans for the Kingdom, and for the life of each member of it, be carried out without opposition on our part, but with free and joyful co-operation, in the knowledge that " in His will is our peace."

II. Give us this Day

1. Now we come to ourselves and our neighbours. We all depend upon God's goodness for everything, and so we ask Him to provide every one of us with all the things that we need this day and every day—food and drink for the body, nourishment for the mind, and grace for the soul. God our Father, Who cares for the birds of the air and the flowers of the field, cares still more for us, and we go to Him in faith, nothing doubting. But as we pray, let us remember that God requires us to help ourselves and one another by work, and also that He expects us to deal righteously with one another. We cannot truly pray this prayer if we are living selfishly and unjustly.

2. " Forgive us our trespasses, as we forgive them that trespass against us." We believe that God is ready to forgive us our sins, if we truly repent and believe in Him, because we are in Jesus Christ. But we must also be sorry for other people's sins, and very willing to help them to do better ; and that means that we must be forgiving, as we hope to be forgiven. When we are wronged we must not avenge ourselves, we must not allow ourselves to be angry and malicious, but rather we must go more than half-way to meet those who have injured us, and so help them to become our friends

again. God has done this for us, and He cannot forgive us until we are ready to forgive others. Read St. Matt. xviii. 21–35.

3. "And lead us not into temptation : but deliver us from evil." God has given us the power of choosing between good and evil, and every opportunity of making such a choice provides a temptation. By overcoming temptation we are made strong. By yielding to it we become weaker. Because we know our own weakness we pray to God, Who orders all the details of our life, not to present us with such hard choices that we shall run serious risk of falling ; but if such choices are presented to us, then may we be delivered from the power of evil and choose aright.

III. For Thine is the Kingdom

1. After the prayer there follows an ascription of glory to God, in which we express our belief in His authority and power. God reigns over all. He made all that is ; He sustains everything by the word of His mouth ; and in the end His plans for creation will be accomplished, and God Himself will be all in all. It is in this faith that we offer all our prayers to Him, through Jesus Christ, His only Son, our Lord.

2. Sometimes we use the Lord's Prayer without this ending, and sometimes with it. In Morning and Evening Prayer, for example, it is used twice, the first time with this concluding doxology, and the second time only as far as the word " evil." The explanation is that with the ending it has a note of thanksgiving, and is suitable for use after we have listened to the pronouncement of the forgiveness of our sins ; without the ending it is purely a prayer, and stands rightly at the head of the Versicles, Collects, and prayers which follow the Creed.

14. PRAYER: (2) THE WORK OF INTERCESSION

Prayer and work are not to be thought of as opposites. Some people who do not understand prayer suppose that anyone who devotes himself to a life of prayer is idle. But there is a vocation to that way of service in some chosen lives, and to pray is most certainly to work, just as it is true that " to work is to pray." Work and prayer are to be blended together in varying proportions in the lives of the rest of us; but, whatever the proportion of prayer, according to our powers and opportunities, we must be quite clear that we shall never be able to serve our neighbours well unless we are praying for them, and that very often the things we actually do will help them less than the intercessions we offer to God on their behalf. " More things are wrought by prayer than this world dreams of."

I. A ROYAL PRIESTHOOD

1. St. Peter says that we Christians are " an elect race, a royal priesthood, a holy nation, a people for God's own possession " (1 St. Pet. ii. 9). He means that we are " members of Christ," and that as such we not only enjoy a wonderful privilege, but we have also a great responsibility. We who are in the Church are kings and priests, entrusted with the duty of praying on behalf of all sorts of people. Many do not feel the need of praying; many feel the need, but do not know how to pray aright; many pray well and earnestly, and these know best the great need they have of other people's prayers in support of their own. For all these we are to pray, exercising our priestly office gladly and faithfully.

2. Our great High Priest is Jesus Christ, Who " ever liveth to make intercession." He it is Who pleads unceasingly on our behalf, inspires us to pray " in His Name," that is, according to His Will, and, gathering up and strengthening all our feeble prayers, presents them before the Father's throne. This is what we mean when we say at the end of a prayer, " Through Jesus Christ our Lord."

II. ACCORDING TO PLAN

1. We get many opportunities of praying for others. Whenever we see people in trouble in the street, or in the bus, or in the train, we shall ask God to bless them. But in addition to such unprepared intercession we must have a regular plan, setting apart a little time each day for the remembrance of the needs of special people and causes. For this it is necessary to keep a small note-book, in which to write down the objects of prayer for each day. One special cause and four special people each day will be as much as you can do at present.

2. Here is a simple example of such a scheme.

Sunday	A.B., B.C., C.D., and D.E.	The Holy Catholic Church.
Monday	E.F., F.G., G.H., and I.J.	All Rulers and People in Authority.
Tuesday	J.K., K.L., L.M., and M.N.	All Scholars, Writers, Artists, Musicians.
Wednesday	N.O., O.P., P.Q., and Q.R.	All Workers in Industry, etc.
Thursday	R.S., S.T., T.U., and U.V.	All Families.
Friday	V.W., W.X., X.Y., and Y.Z.	All Sinners.
Saturday	M.Q., L.P., K.O., and J.N.	The Sick, the Dying, and the Departed.

III. THANKSGIVING

1. Our prayers will be answered in one of three ways. We shall learn that what we are praying for is not possible, because God in His wisdom knows that it would not be good for the Kingdom. Or we shall find that God gives us the power to do something which will help to bring to pass the thing we seek. Or, again, we shall find the prayer answered in the most wonderful way, without our being called upon to do anything more than to observe and to wonder at God's love.

2. Whatever the answer, we shall learn to accept it as right, and to approve. But, when it happens that God brings to pass the very thing we have prayed for, we shall not only rejoice, but we shall also remember to offer thanks to Him Who has blessed us. The story of the healing of the ten lepers reminds us that of all the people who pray to God and receive blessings from Him in answer to their prayers there are not a few who forget to return thanks. But " it is a good thing to sing praises unto our God. Yea, a pleasant and joyful thing it is to be thankful."

15. PRAYER: (3) COMMON PRAYER

' Where two or three are gathered together in my name, there am I in the midst of them." Every company of Christians, large or small, assembled for worship is thus assured of the presence of the Master; and it has always been the practice of those who follow Him to meet together frequently for common (*i.e.* united) prayer, especially on Sundays, the weekly anniversary of the Resurrection. To be cut off from this public and corporate worship of God, whether by sickness or by any other cause, is a sorrow to every true Christian. None would voluntarily forgo the joy and the help that it provides, to say nothing of the satisfaction of service, or duty, loyally performed.

I. The Holy Communion

1. The chief occasion for the assembling of Christian people is the celebration of the Holy Communion. This is sometimes called " The Lord's own Service," because it is the one service which He Himself instituted and commanded us to continue. Sunday by Sunday we meet together early in the morning to commemorate the great sacrifice by which we are set free from sin, and to receive anew the gift of life.

2. It is important that this service should be regarded as one of common prayer. The priest who celebrates the Mysteries speaks and acts on behalf of all who are present. It is for them to follow closely, to say audibly their part of the service, and to make all the prayers their own by repeating the Amens.

3. Special objects of prayer are often announced as biddings before a long prayer for the Church. These should be carefully attended to by all, and earnestly prayed for; though each person present may have also his own special intention of prayer, and may use the periods of silence chiefly for that purpose. It is open to those who do not desire to receive the Communion, either because they have already communicated or for some other reason, to be present at the service and use it altogether for prayer and worship.

II. Morning and Evening Prayer

1. The services of Morning and Evening Prayer both begin with a penitential introduction. Before proceeding to praise God we must be made clean from all sin. First of all, therefore, we confess our sins and are absolved. Then, in the Lord's Prayer, we thank God for His mercy, and we are ready to begin our service of praise.

2. The central part of these services is made up of psalms and canticles, which we generally sing, and the reading of two lessons from Holy Scripture, one from the Old Testament or Apocrypha and one from the New. Follow the lessons from your Bible; it is well to have a lectionary so as to be able to find the lessons before the service begins.

3. Then comes the Apostles' Creed, in which everyone should join; and, after that, prayers—the Lesser Litany, as it is called, the Lord's Prayer,

Versicles and Responses, and three Collects. This closes the set form of service, and there follows an anthem or a hymn.

4. After this comes a number of miscellaneous prayers and thanksgivings. Here is the great opportunity for prayer at these services, and we must all try to take our full part in the Church's intercession by earnestly fixing our thoughts upon the work that is being done.

III. THE LITANY

This form of prayer is specially suited for use in procession, but the priest's part is often read or sung from a litany-desk placed " between the porch and the altar." Our Prayer-Book Litany is lengthy, for the range of intercession is necessarily wide. We must not, however, let our attention wander as the petitions are offered one by one. Let your voice be heard every time a response is made, and support with all the strength of your soul the suffrage that has just been offered.

IV. COMPLINE

This beautiful service closes the day, and, as its name tells us, completes, or fills up, the day's duty. It is the last of the old daily offices, now happily recovered for us in our new Prayer Book. With it we end our common, or family, prayers to God, and go away to say our night prayers alone before we retire to bed.

16. THE FORGIVENESS OF SINS

In our seventh lesson we learnt the meaning of the Atonement. By Christ's death on the Cross we are saved from our sins and " made one " with God. But in order that we may receive the forgiveness that God is waiting to bestow upon us, we must first of all " come to ourselves," like the Prodigal Son, and then go to the Father in our right mind, and tell Him that we have sinned before Heaven, that we are truly sorry, that we humbly desire His forgiveness for Jesus Christ's sake, and that we firmly intend by His help to do better in the future. Then God immediately puts forth His hand and touches us, to comfort and to heal ; and once more we are friends with Him and are at peace.

I. Conscience, and Self-examination

1. The voice within us which teaches the difference between right and wrong, urges us to the right, and reproaches us when we are disobedient, is called the conscience. It comes from God, both directly and through the lives and teaching of other people. At first, in the days of innocence, it is scarcely to be heard. Then as we grow up it speaks more and more strongly, and, if we are in the habit of saying our prayers and trying to please God, more and more truly ; and so we arrive at what we call " years of discretion." We are able to a large extent to judge for ourselves between right and wrong, because we have the spirit of God.

2. Every night when we kneel down to say our prayers, we must examine ourselves by the light of the conscience. Looking back over all that we have thought and said and done during the day, we shall remember some things of which we are ashamed. Some other things there may be which are doubtful ; these we shall carefully consider. It will help us very much also if from time to time we examine longer periods of our life, so as to get a general view of our characters and discover the weaknesses and failings that are most frequent in us. For this purpose many people use " Quiet Days " and " Retreats," which provide opportunities for making this survey thoroughly.

You must understand that it is very important that you should know yourself well before you are confirmed, and that you must therefore practise self-examination regularly.

II. Confession

1. If we are to be forgiven we must make confession of our faults. We must ask pardon of any whom we know we have offended, and of God we must ask forgiveness for all our sins known and unknown. This we can do immediately after our self-examination at night, or at any other time, in the quiet of our own room, or in any other place ; and again in the public services of the Church, when the whole congregation makes a general confession, we shall join in with the others, remembering before God our own particular offences.

2. In early days it was the custom for Christians to confess their sins publicly in the hearing of the whole congregation, because they felt that each man's sins hurt all his brethren, and also because they recognized that it is the Church's duty to impose discipline upon its members and to require sinners to do penance for their faults.   Later, in order to avoid the possibility of scandal caused by people unkindly talking about sins which had been confessed in their hearing, it was arranged that confession should be made in the hearing of a bishop or a priest alone.   This practice is still observed in the Church to-day, for the relief of the consciences of all who feel that their sins are as new wounds in the Body of Christ, and for the help of those who are in doubt about their sins or about the way in which to overcome them.

III. REPARATION

1. Christ's death upon the Cross served as the " full, perfect, and sufficient sacrifice, oblation, and satisfaction for the sins of the whole world."   For-giveness of sins comes through the merits of His death, and for nothing at all that we ourselves have done or can do.   When we are truly sorry, and fully purpose amendment, then we are forgiven.   Yet it is clear that it is our duty to undo our sins, so far as that is possible, by compensating for any injury we have caused.   If we have told a lie, we must own to it ; if we have stolen anything, we must restore or replace it ; if we have been unkind, we must go out of our way to do a kindness.

2. There is still more to be done.   Though we can do nothing, and need do nothing, to earn our forgiveness, we shall be so thankful to God for that which He gives us freely, that we shall desire to offer Him some little token of our sincerity and of our gratitude.   This is what we call our penance. It may take a great many forms ; but, whatever its form, it is to be thought of, not as self-punishment, not as a payment offered to God, but as a " Thank you " uttered by a grateful heart.

3. It must be added that self-punishment has a proper place in the dis-cipline by which we free ourselves from bad habits, but that is not a part of reparation.

D. THE HOLY COMMUNION

17. THE INSTITUTION AND ITS MEANING

After your Confirmation it will be your privilege to receive regularly " the most comfortable Sacrament of the Body and Blood of Christ." The last four of our lessons must deal with this Sacrament in order that you may come to it with right understanding, proper reverence, and earnest expectation. First we shall consider how the Sacrament came to be instituted by our Lord, and what is its meaning.

I. MAUNDY THURSDAY AND GOOD FRIDAY

1. It was the custom of the Jews to keep a yearly feast, called the Passover, in memory of their deliverance from bondage in Egypt. At this festival a lamb was sacrificed for each family or small group. On the day before our Lord's crucifixion all the Jews in Jerusalem and elsewhere were preparing to keep the Passover on the following day, and our Lord Himself with the Twelve met in an upper room in the city to share in a solemn meal.

2. During the course of this meal He insisted upon taking the part of a slave and washing the feet of all the disciples in turn. Then He gave them the new commandment, which explains why we call the day " Commandment " or " Maundy " Thursday. " A new commandment I give unto you, that ye love one another; even as I have loved you, that ye also love one another."

3. Presently He took bread, and, when He had given thanks, He broke it into pieces and gave them to the disciples, saying, as He did so, " Take, eat ; this is my body." Then He took a cup of wine, and, having given thanks once more, He said to the disciples as He gave them the cup to drink, " Drink ye all of it ; for this is my blood of the covenant, which is shed for many unto remission of sins."

4. Shortly after this they went out, and our Lord was arrested in the Garden of Gethsemane. During that night He was tried before various courts, and, being found guilty through the enmity and fear of His judges, He was crucified on the following day, which we call Good Friday.

II. HIS BODY AND BLOOD

1. You will see that what our Lord did on the Thursday night goes closely with what He suffered and did on the following day. He did not then die the death of a martyr, but He offered Himself as a Sacrifice for the sins of the world so that He might really do the thing that men were vainly trying to do by sacrificing lambs on that very day. On the Thursday night He made the offering by surrendering Himself to the will of the Father ; and on Friday the offering thus begun was fully completed.

2. This enables us to understand what our Lord meant when He said, " This is my body," " This is my blood." He spoke of the Life that He was to lay down on the morrow, rendered back to Him, as it was on Easter Day, glorified and imperishable. This triumphant Life He would add to them by means of the Bread and the Wine whenever afterwards they kept

the Memorial of His Passion, according to His command, " This do in remembrance of me."

3. A sacrament, you will remember, has two parts : " an outward and visible sign " and " an inward and spiritual grace." Here the Bread and the Wine are the sign, and through them there comes to us the very Life of our Lord Jesus Christ, to make us like unto Him.

III. Titles

1. The Lord's Supper. This name is often used, but it is not really correct. It denotes the solemn meal during which our Lord instituted the Blessed Sacrament, and so is rightly applied to the Agape or Love-feast which Christians have sometimes shared in connexion with the Sacrament.

2. The Holy Communion. This is the Prayer-Book name, and is the best name for general use. Communion means fellowship ; and this title reminds us that through this Sacrament the bonds of our fellowship with Christ and the Saints and all the faithful departed are strengthened.

3. The Holy Eucharist. This beautiful name comes from the East, where Eucharist means " thanksgiving." The Holy Communion is the greatest of all thanksgiving services, wherein we praise God's Holy Name for every blessing, but above all for His " inestimable love in the redemption of the world by our Lord Jesus Christ ; for the means of grace, and for the hope of glory."

4. The Mass. This is the term commonly used in the Church of Rome. In its origin it means " dismissal," but it is frequently explained to mean " feast " ; and some members of the Church of England use it because it suggests that fellowship and unity which the Sacrament is meant to promote.

18. THE LITURGY (1)

The form of service used when the Sacrament of Holy Communion is administered is properly called "The Liturgy." It is very important that you should be thoroughly familiar with this service in all its parts, and that you should know something about the practical details of its celebration. In order to explain it with some fullness we will divide the service into two parts, taking only the first part to-day, with a word about what are called the ornaments.

I. THE ORNAMENTS OF THE SANCTUARY AND OF THE MINISTER

1. The word "ornaments" means here not decorations, but necessary equipment in the way of furniture and vessels for the church and clothes for those who minister in it. These should all be good and beautiful, for the glory of God; but that is not why they are called ornaments.

2. For the celebration of the Holy Communion there must be an altar or holy table, having upon it a silk covering and a fair linen cloth. This stands at the east end of the church in the part known as the sanctuary. A service-book resting upon a cushion or stand is placed upon the altar; in the middle of the east side of the table an empty cross with decorated ends speaks of the Resurrection; and a candle on the right and on the left remind us that Christ is the Light of the World and that ours is a " yonside " religion. Behind and above the altar there is usually a reredos, and at the sides riddel-curtains enclosing it. Near to the altar there is a smaller table called the credence, bearing cruets for wine and water, a box or plate for bread, a finger-bowl, and an alms-bason. Then there are the sacred vessels, the chalice and the paten, and the silk and linen that go with them, burse, veil, corporal, and purificator.

3. The priest, when celebrating the Holy Communion, wears the ancient Eucharistic vestments, amice, alb, stole, and girdle, with chasuble or cope; or else he wears a surplice with stole, or with scarf and hood as at Morning and Evening Prayer.

II. PREPARATORY DEVOTIONS

The service of Holy Communion is frequently prefaced by another service which is intended as a preparation for it. This introduction may be a shortened form of Morning Prayer, or the Litany, or a special short service of devotion which takes the form of the recitation of the 43rd Psalm, followed by some appropriate versicles and responses. All three preparations remind us of the solemnity and dignity of the Holy Communion, and serve to put us into a proper state of soul before drawing near to the Holy Mysteries.

III. THE INTRODUCTION, THE MINISTRY OF THE WORD, THE OFFERTORY, AND THE INTERCESSION

1. The service is begun by the priest quietly saying the Lord's Prayer as he stands at the altar, the congregation all kneeling. He alone says the

prayer and the Amen. Then in a louder voice he says the Collect for Purity, and the congregation answers " Amen." There follow the Ten Commandments, or our Lord's summary of them, or simply the " Kyrie eleison," and then the salutation and its answer. " Let us pray," says the priest, and he reads the Collect of the Day. Have the place marked in readiness, so that you can turn to this at once, follow the prayer with attention, and say the Amen.

2. The Ministry of the Word includes the reading of the Epistle and the Gospel, and sometimes the preaching of a sermon after the recitation of the Nicene Creed. Sit during the reading of the Epistle ; stand for the Gospel, say " Glory be to thee, O Lord " when it is announced, and " Praise be to thee, O Christ " when it is ended ; remain standing for the Creed, turn to the east if you are not already facing that way, and say the Creed as though you meant it.

3. The Offertory Sentence having been read, the collection will be taken. Give as generously as you are able, remembering that this offering of your money is an important part of the service of Holy Communion, and that it is generally applied to the relief of the sick and poor, whom we are especially bound to help. When you have made your offering, kneel, and proceed with your own devotions.

4. Listen carefully to the biddings to prayer that precede the Intercession, and see that you pray earnestly, for the peace and unity of the Church, for the rulers of the nations, for all the ministers of the Church, for all others who are teaching the truth at home and abroad, for all Christian people, for those who are in trouble of any kind, for the faithful departed, and for yourselves, that you may have grace to follow in the footsteps of the Saints.

19. THE LITURGY (2)

Last time we went through the first half of the service of Holy Communion, which includes the Introduction, the Ministry of the Word, the Offertory, and the Intercession. Now we go on to consider the Preparation, the Consecration, the Communion, and the Thanksgiving, which make up the second half of the service.

I. THE PREPARATION

1. First comes an Exhortation, reminding us that we must take all possible pains to prepare ourselves for the reception of this Sacrament. To come to it lightly and unprepared is grievous sin, and will not only add no benefit to us, but will certainly injure our spiritual life. This exhortation is not read every time the Holy Communion is celebrated, but we must keep it in mind every time we attend the service in order to receive.

2. There follows the Invitation, the General Confession, and the Absolution, all three being provided in a longer form for use on Sundays and in a shorter form for use at other times. Then the priest recites the Comfortable Words to assure us of the forgiveness of our sins through the Blood of Jesus Christ ; and, kneeling down before the altar, he says the Prayer of Humble Access, expressing to God our sense of utter unworthiness. After this he stands and uncovers the paten and chalice in readiness for the consecration of the bread and wine.

II. THE CONSECRATION

1. This is the central and most important part of the whole service, so far as the prayers are concerned. After the salutation and response there comes the appeal, " Lift up your hearts." That means, " Forget earthly things ; think with all your power of Jesus Christ upon the Throne and of the gift He is about to give." Join in with the priest when he comes to the words " Holy, holy, holy," and then follow with the closest attention every stage of the Consecration Prayer.

2. It begins with thanksgiving for that God, of His tender mercy, gave His only Son to suffer death upon the Cross for our redemption. The institution of the Sacrament is next recalled, with the distribution of the Bread and the Wine, just as it took place on Maundy Thursday. And then we declare our intention of setting forth before the Father the memorial which Christ commanded us to make, and the Holy Spirit is invoked for the hallowing both of ourselves and of the bread and wine, " that they may be unto us the Body and Blood " of Jesus Christ.

3. The prayer continues with the Oblation, or solemn offering of ourselves, our souls and bodies, to God, in union with our Lord ; and it ends with the great Amen of all the people, the most important Amen in the whole Prayer Book. Then immediately we all join in the Lord's Prayer.

III. The Communion and the Thanksgiving

1. The celebrant first receives the Communion in both kinds himself, and then administers the same to any others who are present in the sanctuary and desire to receive. After that he calls upon the congregation to draw near and receive the Body of our Lord Jesus Christ and His Blood, and they come up in order to the sanctuary rail. Kneeling there, each one holds out his open right hand, resting it upon the open left hand, when the priest comes to him. Gloves will, of course, have been taken off and left behind. As soon as the Bread is placed in his hand, he carries it to his mouth, takes it up with his lips, being careful to take up crumbs also, if there should be any, and consumes it reverently with thankfulness to God. When the chalice is presented to him, the communicant takes it firmly in both hands, carries it to his lips, sips the Wine, and returns the cup to the priest; or, if the priest should retain his hold on the chalice for safety's sake, the communicant should put one hand upon it so as to tilt it sufficiently to enable him to receive.

2. When you have received, you remain kneeling at the rail for just a brief space while you enjoy the supreme moment of union with Christ and thank God for it with all your heart; then you rise from your knees and return to your place quietly, to remain kneeling in prayer until all have communicated and the priest begins the last part of the service. This he does after covering the sacred vessels with a linen veil.

3. There remains only the Thanksgiving. First a prayer said by the priest alone; then " Glory be to God on high," in which everyone joins; and after that the Blessing. Then the priest consumes what remains of the consecrated Bread and Wine, unless some of it is to be reserved for the use of the sick; he cleanses the paten and chalice, puts in order the silk and linen belonging to them, and, when he has finished his prayers, leaves the church. You remain kneeling during this, and continue to make your thanksgiving after he has gone. Then get up and go away, determined to pass on to others some of the joy that God has given to you. Do not spoil everything by being impatient if your breakfast is not ready.

20. PRACTICAL MATTERS

We have gone carefully through the Liturgy, and have given a little attention to some of the things that are done during the service as well as to the things that are said. But there still remain some important practical matters to consider, and we must devote our last lesson to these.

I. TIME AND FREQUENCY

1. The best time at which to receive the Communion is not settled by the clock but by our fitness and by our need. Our Lord instituted the Sacrament in the evening, and He had special reasons for so doing. It was to be bound up as closely as possible with His death on the following morning; it was to be the last thing that He did with His disciples in their preparation for the ministry that was to follow, the very crown and summary of all that He had taught them. But for the Church it is a morning feast, telling of the Risen and Ascended Life of our Lord, and furnishing us with needful strength for the day's warfare. Fresh from sleep, unsoiled by the day's temptations and trials, we come to meet Him with gladness in our hearts, seeking His blessing before we attend to the world's claims upon us. If real necessity should ever arise, or physical infirmity should ever compel it, then we may certainly receive the Communion at any later hour when it is provided: but not otherwise.

2. There is a further reason in favour of the early morning. It is convenient then for us to come fasting, and so to observe the Church's ancient rule. This is valuable as discipline, for it means a small sacrifice; it is valuable for reverence, since it emphasizes the superiority of the spiritual food we go to receive; and it is valuable for attention, seeing that we are very clear in our thinking and praying before we have taken food in the morning. But if, after trying, you should find that you are not strong enough to walk to church and kneel throughout the service without taking some slight nourishment beforehand, then take what is necessary, but no more. In every case let breakfast wait until afterwards. In most cases you will find that nothing at all need be taken until then.

(N.B. Our instruction in this matter is notoriously divergent. There are those who count it a duty to encourage all candidates to a strict observance of fasting communion; and there are others who practise Evening Communion, and attach no importance to the preparation of fasting. I give here, as in all these lessons, my own view of the truth, and I believe that there is a growing sympathy with the position I have taken.)

3. Some Christians receive the Communion once a quarter, some once a month, some twice a month, some every Sunday and holy-day, some every day of the week. Each one must find out what is most helpful, and make a rule for himself. But the standard towards which all should strive is the weekly Communion, Sunday by Sunday, together with Communion on week-day festivals.

II. Ceremonies

1. It is customary to bow to the altar on entering the church and on leaving it, and also to bow the head at the mention of the sacred name of Jesus, and at the reference to the Incarnation in the Nicene Creed. This bowing is intended to express and to promote reverence, and must not be allowed to become merely formal.

2. Many Christians are accustomed to use the sign of the cross at various points in the service, though there is no agreement as to these points. The practice is an ancient and helpful one, but, again, it must not become formal, and to that end it is better to refrain from excessive use of it. Learn its meaning, and then use it or not, as you find best ; and do not judge other people in their use or non-use of it.

III. Preparation and Thanksgiving

This last word on the Holy Communion is something that must never be forgotten. To forget it is to insult God, to make it hard for Him to nourish our souls, to find the Holy Communion disappointing, and so to be tempted to give up receiving.

The only way in which to avoid this is to prepare thoroughly for every Communion and to give thanks warmly and generously after it. You will be given a little book in which you will find simple forms to use in your preparation and thanksgiving. Use them regularly and well. Never fail to prepare ; never fail to give thanks. And as you go on your way of spiritual progress you will fill out and enrich these forms more and more, fitting yourself by their use to receive more and more grace through the Blessed Sacrament.

III. The Confirmation Day

1. *Godparents*

The Prayer Book says, " It is convenient that every one shall have a godfather or a godmother as a witness of their Confirmation." This means that the duty of the three baptismal godparents ceases when their godchild is confirmed, and that their place is then taken by a single godparent who enters upon his duties by attending the Confirmation service as a witness. While there is nothing here to forbid the choice of one of the baptismal godparents to act in this new capacity, it is in accordance with the old rule that a fourth person should be introduced at this point. At the Confirmation service all four will meet together, to pray for the child and to witness his Confirmation, the three baptismal godparents looking back over their ten or twelve years of spiritual responsibility to the time when the priest instructed them, " See also that he be brought to the Bishop to be confirmed by him ; so that, strengthened with the gift of the Holy Spirit, he may come with due preparation to receive the blessed Sacrament of the Body and Blood of Christ " ; and the new godparent looking forward to the equally great responsibility to be borne by him during the years that will bring his charge to maturity.

Starting off enthusiastically on the communicant life, the newly confirmed boy or girl may progress without difficulty for some little time. But sooner or later difficulties are bound to arise, and there will be need of companionship and of friendly counsel and encouragement. The understanding godparent will not step in too frequently. He will not attempt to nurse the young communicant all the time ; but he will be always watchful for signs of a lowered spiritual vitality, and will then judiciously administer the needed tonic and stand aside again to pray. Such a friend, voluntarily pledged to spiritual fellowship and assistance, may be of inestimable advantage to a young adolescent who is full of good intentions but liable to sudden changes of spiritual temperature. In the opinion of many priests the majority of our lapsed communicants have fallen away for want of just such help as a godparent might be expected to give. They are like the coin dropped from the woman's hand in our Lord's parable.

Why, then, is the Prayer-Book direction about god-parents almost invariably neglected ? The present practice. of the Church of England, with but very few exceptions, is that godparents are not provided for Confirmation, and that baptismal godparents have come to suppose that their responsibility, lightly carried though it be, lasts for life. The explanation of this is, no doubt, the fact that god-parents are not given any part in the Confirmation service. They are not even allowed to kneel by the side of their godchildren, because it is considered convenient that all these should be grouped together. Apart from the rubric, there seems to be no official expectation that they will appear, and therefore they are not found.

There are two ways out of this difficulty. One is to discover those cases, unfortunately not very common, where a baptismal godparent has faithfully discharged his office, and to arrange with him that he shall " witness " the Confirmation and take upon himself the further responsibility involved in that official action. The other is to supply godparents, or wardens, from among the most trusted communicants in the parish—not one for each child, but two or three for each yearly group of Confirma-tion candidates. Those who are appointed in any year to act in this way attend all the classes with the candidates, taking every opportunity of getting to know them ; they are present at the Confirmation service and at the first Communion, and they afterwards watch over the candidates, not officiously, but carefully, quietly, and unobtrusively, in the way already indicated. In the following year a new set of wardens is chosen to care for the next group of candidates, and so provision is made from year to year and each batch of recruits to the main body of communicants is cared for.

2. Before the Service

All the candidates should come together in church on the evening before the Confirmation day, for the double purpose of rehearsing the service so that there may be no unnecessary nervousness and no hitch in the proceedings, and of sharing in a short devotional preparation. The rehearsal should come first, and if the Confirmation is to take place in the church in which the candidates are meeting, it is well to have present the officials who will order the procession of candidates to and from the Bishop, so that they may rehearse their part at the same time. The candidates should be supplied with copies of the service, they should sit in the actual seats to be occupied by them on the following day, and they should be taken through the service step by step.

A brief address should follow, in which the two notes of dedication and expectation should be firmly struck, and the value of quiet for the next twenty-four hours duly emphasized. It may be necessary in some cases to warn foolish parents against planning attendance at some entertainment on the eve of the Confirmation ; but, if the candidates have been brought into a proper frame of mind by their preparation, they will themselves be aware of the inappropriateness and hindrance of such a thing and will oppose it successfully. After the address a few suitable prayers will close a service which, if it is kept brief, will serve to give the right key-note to the candidates' own thoughts and prayers during the coming day.

The baptism of candidates who have not yet been baptized is often deferred until the eve of Confirmation so that the intimate association of the two parts of the Sacrament of initiation may be emphasized by thus bringing them closely together. " Three, or at the least two, to be their Witnesses, who shall be ready to present them at the Font," are required by the rubric. The Confirmation godparent may very well act as one of these. It should be remembered that in the case of adults there is a Prayer-Book rubric directing that notice be sent to the Bishop at least a week before. It was the practice of one Bishop to send a letter of encouragement to every such candidate. This was so much appreciated that his instructions to the clergy are here reproduced in the hope that they may be adopted by others.

ADULT BAPTISMS

I have thought that the rubric directing that "*When any such persons, as are of riper years, are to be baptized, timely notice shall be given to the Bishop,*" a rubric which is now either neglected or else complied with as a formality, might be turned to good account if it were made to give opportunity for a word to the candidate from the Bishop, as his (or her) Father in God.

I propose accordingly, when I receive notice from "*the Minister of the Parish, the parents, or some other discreet persons,*" to send to the candidates (or catechumens) individually a letter containing a few words of encouragement and exhortation.

And as it is obviously impossible to write such a letter in each case, I have printed one, with space in which to enter the name with my own hand.

It will be subject to revision, and I may from time to time change it and write a fresh one.

Having adopted this plan, upon which I desire to ask God's blessing that He may use it for some help to His children, I will beg the clergy to comply with the rubric (as they already often do), and to do so a few days—the rubric says "*a week*"—before the Baptism. The names, ages, and addresses of the candidates should in all cases accompany the notice. I must rely on the clergy, and I can do so with perfect confidence, to do for me the "*examination*" which is to show how far the catechumens have understood and appropriated the instruction "*in the principles of the Christian religion*" which they received during their preparation. I may add that this examination need not be such in any formal sense of the word.

In some parishes there is a celebration of the Holy Communion on the morning of the Confirmation day, intended especially for parents, godparents, friends, and candidates, the candidates not, of course, receiving the Communion. The experiment has been made of holding the Confirmation service early in the morning and following it immediately by a parochial Communion in which the newly-confirmed take their part. The great value of this is obvious ; but in many parishes there are serious practical difficulties in the way of collecting candidates in the morning, and it is scarcely likely that this practice can be generally adopted.

3. *The Confirmation Service*

It conduces to the convenience of Bishop and candidates alike, and to the glory of Almighty God, if all things are done in order and at the right time, without haste and without hesitation. Seating arrangements must be carefully worked out beforehand, male candidates being placed on the south side of the nave, female candidates on the north, and witnesses near at hand, the rest of the church being left open to the general congregation that assembles for the service. Clergy bringing candidates from other parishes should be accommodated with due regard to the dignity of the priest's office, and should all wear surplice, hood, and scarf. Organist and choir must be thoroughly familiar with their part in the service, for it is in their power to help greatly or to hinder sorely. It is well to provide candidates and congregation with forms of the service and with hymn-sheets.

The clergy must remember to bring to the Bishop the required particulars of the candidates they are presenting and to use official forms for the purpose. It is their duty to arrange that all candidates shall be in their places at least ten minutes before the service begins, and to provide for assistance in the veiling of female candidates at some place near at hand. In the matter of veils the best plan is undoubtedly for each parish to equip itself with a supply of veils—squares of fine linen turned back at one corner and fitted with two tapes—and to insist upon their use. White should be worn by the girls, if it is possible for them to provide it ; and they should be discreetly warned against extravagance and unnecessary decoration. These things are not in keeping with the spirit of the services.

The details of the service are dealt with in a later essay. Here it will suffice to give some brief instructions supplied to the writer by one of our bishops.

1. Commence with a hymn, such as " My God, accept my heart this day," or " Soldiers of Christ, arise."

2. The parish priest reads the Preface, which is followed by the singing of a hymn to the Holy Spirit, all kneeling.

3. The Bishop briefly explains the meaning and method of the service, candidates and congregation all seated.

4. A minute of silent prayer, all kneeling.

5. The candidates stand and the Bishop asks the question ; the congregation remains kneeling.

6. Versicles and Responses (by the candidates alone) and prayer to the Holy Spirit.

7. The Laying on of Hands, first the male candidates, then the female. The congregation remains kneeling.

8. The Salutation and Response, the Lord's Prayer and the two following Collects.

9. The Blessing of the candidates.

10. A hymn, such as " Thine for ever," " Praise, my soul, the King of heaven," or " Now thank we all our God." *Not* " O Jesu, I have promised," because it strikes the wrong note, emphasizing what the candidates have done instead of what has been done for them.

11. The Bishop's address, brief and definite.

12. A minute of silence, followed by the final Blessing of the whole congregation.

Where there are a hundred candidates the service should not last for more than one hour.

Arrangements must be made for the quiet and orderly withdrawal of the candidates at the conclusion of the service ; and in order to effect this it is usually necessary to instruct the congregation to remain seated until all the candidates have left the church.

IV. AFTER-CARE

1. *Records*

In addition the records and notes kept by the parish priest for his own use in the after-care of candidates, entries should be made in an official register kept with the parish records. It is sufficient as a rule to enter the names in full, the date of birth, and the address, of each candidate, with a general entry as to the date and place of the Confirmation and the name of the Bishop administering the Sacrament ; but some think it well to note also the date of the First Communion. If, with the Bishop's permission, any candidate takes an additional Christian name at Confirmation this should, of course, be recorded.

2. *First Communion*

There is a considerable variety of opinion and practice in regard to the arrangements to be made for the First Communion of the newly confirmed. In a very few cases the Communion is received on the same day as the Laying on of Hands, as already noticed ; in many more it is received on the Sunday following the Confirmation service ; still more frequently it is received on the second Sunday after the Confirmation ; and in a smaller number of cases there is a still longer interval, all teaching on the subject being deferred until after the Confirmation has taken place. The danger of the last system is that the First Communion may become something of an anti-climax, and there may even be a little difficulty in holding the candidates together once they are confirmed. It is more natural that the Communion and the Confirmation should come closer together, and that the necessary teaching on the Holy Communion should form an integral part of the preparation for Confirmation, so as to make it clear that it is the communicant life that is being prepared for and not only the receiving of grace through the Laying on of Hands. On the whole the commonest arrangement, namely, the receiving of the Holy Communion on the Second Sunday after the Confirmation, is probably the most satisfactory. It keeps the two in sufficiently close proximity, and yet admits of a short time of special preparation for the Communion service in which to create a right disposition distinct from the expectation that belongs to the approach to Confirmation.

Some welcome the opportunity of using one of the great festivals as the occasion of a First Communion, considering that it adds to the impressiveness of the occasion and helps to fix the memory of it indelibly in a child's soul. On the other hand, it means a longer service and a consequently greater strain, physical and spiritual, and it is probably better for most people that the Sunday chosen should be an ordinary one.

It is usual for all the newly confirmed to attend and make their First Communion together, sitting in one group, and receiving the Communion before the rest of the congregation. Some are of opinion that it is better to make the First Communion as much as possible like the others that are to follow ; and they therefore instruct their candidates to come independently, kneeling where they please, if they all come on the same day, or even coming on different days of their own choice. The only advantage attaching to this is that they are able to kneel and to communicate side by side with members of their own family and with their friends. But it is probably a greater advantage to the congregation as a whole to be reminded of their own First Communion and of their duty of praying for those now added to their number, by seeing them present in a body, the girls dressed and veiled as they were for their Confirmation. It is something, too, that the fellowship of the candidates should be crowned by this association in the first receiving of the Blessed Sacrament. In some parishes it is the custom to invite the newly confirmed and the general body of communicants to breakfast immediately after the Communion service, and to give to the young communicants a semi-formal reception into the communicant fellowship. Such a revival of the ancient Agape, or Love-feast, has much to be said for it, where it can be conveniently arranged.

3. *Shepherding*

It has already been pointed out that much help may be given by godparents or wardens in the after-care of the newly confirmed, and that the rubric suggesting the " convenience " of the provision and attendance of these helpers at the Confirmation service should not be neglected. For the rest, there is no brilliant discovery to be expected which will ensure that all those who have been confirmed will remain faithful. In spite of every effort on the part of godparents and parish priests, some will assuredly lapse. But every effort must still be made to prevent this ; and diligent watchfulness combined with the provision of really suitable and attractive aids may do much. Social organisations have their place in holding young Churchpeople together ; but the work of building up the spiritual life of young communicants must be done in guilds, prayer-circles, and study-circles, of the most varied kinds according to the type of parish and the needs and capacities of the people. Monthly preparation services for the Holy Communion, held on a week-night or after Evensong on the last Sunday in the month, are essential. And to all these things must be added the personal friendship of the parish priest, a factor of the greatest value.

Some of the clergy are convinced that the only hope of retaining and edifying our young communicants lies in persuading them to a regular use of the Sacrament of Penance. If the parents consent and if the young people are truly persuaded, without any unwarranted stretching of the term to make it cover authoritative direction, the system will produce nothing but good in the hands of a good and understanding priest. It is well for our Church that the best of the Evangelical clergy are able to make equally good use of their opportunities in dealing directly with individual souls, guarding and cleansing them from sin, though without resort to the more formal and sacramental method.

Strong complaints received from some priests, especially from some Army chaplains, make it necessary to close this section, and this chapter, by reminding all concerned that the commendation of those who move away from the parish where they were confirmed is a vital part of after-care work. It is no excuse for neglecting this work to say that letters of commendation are often ignored. It remains the duty of a parish priest, in spite of this, to send word to his brethren whenever any of his flock move off to another parish or to some special group ministered to by a chaplain. A kindly and informing letter written on behalf of one who is entitled to continue to receive the attentions of the Church will rarely fail altogether of its purpose, even though it be not answered, according to its deserts, by any word of courteous assurance.

CHAPTER II

ADOLESCENCE AND SEX-INSTRUCTION

By Reginald Tribe

Childhood and adult life are two periods of life that are comparatively fixed and stable, the former lasting for ten or twelve years only and the latter for fifty years. The time between these two periods, that of adolescence, lasting for about ten years, is a time full of change and development. What is characteristic of it at one stage is often in abeyance at another; what is a main feature at one age may exist, but only in a profoundly modified form, at another. Thus it is not possible to speak of the physical and psychical conditions of the period as a fixed whole; they must be described in terms of change and growth.

The study of adolescence is one of immense importance for those to whom the preparation for Confirmation is entrusted. But a warning must be given as to the limitations of knowledge obtained in this way. Scientific study can only produce broad generalizations about the analysed elements of child-nature. No textbook can convey the bewildering variety and rich complexity of the developments of mind and body in individual adolescents. Knowledge derived from books can only point the way to the more accurate observation and understanding of each child as it grows up to full adult life.

Adolescence, then, is essentially a time of change. Underneath the surface this change is continuous, but at times this growth is very much more rapid than at others. This is a fact very obvious to the onlooker. Moreover, the continuous growth, even though it may be quite regular, is only perceived by the observer at intervals; so that the total impression of growth by leaps and bounds is accentuated. This is perceived not only by the onlooker but by the adolescent subject himself, especially in the

93

later years of the stage ; and this spasmodic self-knowledge reacts to cause psychical development by stages and crises.

As a rule, the time of great physical growth is a time of quiescence in psychological development, the physical changes generally preceding the mental. So we often get the phenomenon of a youth with the body of a man and the mind of a boy, or a girl with the physical maturity of womanhood and the inexperience of a child.

The Physiology of Adolescence

It is possible to some extent to consider the physical and psychical aspects of adolescence separately, though they are so closely associated ; and it will be more convenient to follow the physical developments first. The young of the human race is the most helpless of any in the animal creation, more helpless both in point of degree and of length of time than the young of any species. Also, the instincts necessary for self-preservation and for well-being are less developed in man than in any other animal ; their place is taken by reason and by education. This is part of the price paid by man for his high mental development. In consequence the young child cannot be left alone to find out what is good for it and what is not. Childhood must be a time of continual supervision and education by the parents. In the matter of sleep, for instance, the animals choose their time and length of sleep by the light of nature ; the child must learn by inculcated habit. The young of the beasts will rarely eat of food that is not suited to them ; but no infant is averse from a diet of biscuits and other non-fatty substances that will give it rickets. The young animal soon acquires the art of cleaning itself perfectly, but the young human has to be taught the proper toilet of the body, especially with regard to things like teeth or feet.

Although these are facts mainly about childhood and not about adolescence, they are of importance in the subject we are studying, because the neglect of physical education in childhood is often the clue to the understanding of certain abnormal conditions in adolescence.

Chronic constipation, for instance, engendered by parental neglect in childhood, is often the cause of moods and tempers in an adolescent.

The consideration of the relative parts played by instinct, reason, and education in the physical sphere is also very helpful to an understanding of the spiritual sphere, for there is close analogy between the two. In the soul of man, as in his body, there are certain instincts ; there is also the power of natural reason to deal with spiritual conceptions. Together these form natural religion. But there is also revealed religion, and this can only be implanted in the soul by education. Christianity is primarily a revealed religion, but a wise teacher will remember that it is also the summation and perfection of natural instinctive religion.

To return to the physical developments of adolescence, which we will take as being between the age of twelve and twenty-one. Growth in childhood is regular, but slows down between eight and twelve years of age. After that it goes on by fits and starts. There is generally an acceleration at the time of puberty, then a period of retardation, with a further bound forward at seventeen or eighteen in boys and a year earlier in girls. Growth in height is more irregular than growth in girth, which must be distinguished from increase in weight.

In so far as the actual tissues are concerned the most striking changes are in the bones and brain. Man commences life at birth with practically all his bones in a cartilaginous condition and the ends of the bones (*epiphyses*) joined on by non-bony tissue to the shafts. During childhood and adolescence the bones gradually ossify and the epiphyses join on to the shafts by bony union. This process is not complete until the age of twenty-one.

The brain during this period shows to the eye a great development in the complexity and depth of its surface convolutions, but to the microscope it exhibits an even more striking and important change in the development of the *striæ*, or threads of communication between the cells in the surface convolutions. A child is thus, physically as well as psychologically, incapable of forming many of the associations upon which mental life depends.

The muscles, so far as bulk is concerned, are the most important tissues of the body, and the degree of muscular development plays a large part in determining the quantitative regulation of most of the chemical processes of the body.   There is little or no change in their minute structure during development after birth, but there is a marked change in their function.   The nervo-muscular system of the child is not adapted to, and almost incapable of, fine movements.   To teach such movements as writing and musical performance at too young an age is to overstrain the nervous and muscular mechanism with unsuitable work. Premature industrialism, with its monotonous performance of minute and exact muscular movements, is a physiological crime against childhood.   Its results are of great importance from the spiritual point of view, for the physical and nervous exhaustion caused by the premature exploitation of a child's muscular system is disastrous to the proper development of spiritual health and balance.

The greatest of all physical changes during adolescence is that in the sexual organs.   The main features of these changes are well known and need no recapitulation.   The changes of puberty are not limited to the direct organs of sex but pervade others.   In boys the break in the voice occurs, and there is alteration in the quality of a girl's voice also at this time.   In boys there is very often a marked change in the face; the features thicken and become fatter, especially about the eyes.   A similar change is sometimes seen in women at the time of their first pregnancy, especially in the early months.   In both sexes the temporary fleshiness of the features passes off after a time, but the face never regains its old sharpness of outline.   In addition to this the blood-vessels of the face are sometimes in a disturbed condition, causing localized patches of flushing ; and a general flush of the face is often seen, giving to youth the appearance of bloom which is one of its distinctive charms.

Another point not generally known is the nervous connexion between the sexual organs and the tissues of the nose, the nipples, and the skin of the thighs.   An analogous condition exists in birds, where the blood-supply of the comb and the wattles is very largely influenced by the sex reflexes.

In boys the secondary physical changes of puberty are more marked than in girls ; but in the latter the psychological changes are the more profound.

The Hygiene of Childhood

Although this article is written mainly for religious teachers and not for parents, a few notes upon the hygiene of childhood are necessary. A spiritual guide has sometimes the duty, as well as the occasion, to suggest regulations for the physical well-being of his spiritual charges ; and, as we have seen before, a faulty physical hygiene may react upon the spiritual state.

This is particularly the case with regard to the hours of sleep necessary for health at different ages. A new-born child ought to sleep for the whole of the twenty-four hours of the day, an adult ought to sleep an average of eight hours per diem ; there is a gradual and steady diminution through childhood and adolescence from the twenty-four hours of the baby to the eight hours of the adult. Boys and girls between the years of twelve and sixteen, for instance, ought to sleep ten hours daily. This amount is frequently lessened by foolish and ignorant parents on the one hand and by the exigencies of the various irregular forms of child-labour on the other. This particular violation of child-hygiene is intimately connected with the housing question, for sleep, in order to be fully efficacious, must be in a room set apart for the purpose and not in the living-room where light and noise both occur.

Play is an important feature of child-life ; it is the natural outlet for surplus energy and nature's way of educating for future work. A disinclination to play is generally caused by the absence of surplus energy owing to ill-health or to its absorption by physical tasks. Play must, therefore, never be forced upon an unwilling child, and the cause for the want of energy should be investigated. The play of children under thirteen is naturally individualistic as well as spontaneous, and harm may be done in forcing social play or by over-regulating its forms. It is after puberty that play naturally becomes social and organized, and it is only then that the teacher should *insist* upon organized games. Play is educative, and the varying kinds of spontaneous play at different ages should be studied sympathetically, for nature is an excellent guide in this respect. Hobbies will often show for what career a particular boy is fitted. A wise spiritual guide will perceive through children's play of what type the child is—the slow, painstaking, the adventurous, the intuitive, the reasoning—for the same characteristics will generally mark the child's spiritual type.

The later years of adolescence after puberty are not marked by any profound physical changes, but only by growth and consolidation of the changes already accomplished. The growth in physical strength is obvious. In boys, and to a lesser extent in girls, the instinct towards athleticism is nature's way of stimulating growth. Games, swimming, cycling, and a great variety of physical enjoyments all exercise their lure. The chief danger is the obvious one of overstrain of the heart and muscles ; and there is an easy criterion for judging whether a boy or girl is overdoing it. If the person in question is losing colour and flesh and becoming pale and thin, then there is almost certainly overstrain. But a bright, healthy complexion does not necessarily imply no overstrain. Falling asleep during the day after great exertion is also a danger-signal. Over-athleticism may come from weakness of will in the incapacity to resist the stimulus of pleasure or from obstinacy of will in persisting in spite of distaste and lassitude. Obstinacy, in spite of current belief, is not weakness of will, but strength of will without a corresponding development of intelligence.

The appetite, especially for sweet things, is usually enormous in these later years of adolescence. This is again a perfectly sound instinct on the part of nature, for a large amount of physical exercise calls for a large amount of sugar in the diet. This sugar appetite should be satisfied by the parent in the household diet and not by the confectioner.

The appetite at the time of puberty may become very

capricious and perverted. In girls this abnormality may take the form of self-starvation, and if so the trouble is physical rather than psychical. It calls for expert advice from a physician. The mere insistence upon taking food by force of will may lead to psychical trouble being added to the physical.

Adolescence is a time when inherited qualities begin to show themselves with increasing force. Many physical and mental inheritances are not in evidence before this age, but are lying latent. Children in most respects look much alike and are much alike, though coming from very varied ancestral stocks. It is not until the later years of adolescence that most inherited qualities or defects begin to come to the surface. Aptitude for games, for intellectual work, and for various practical things like engineering and art begins to differentiate one adolescent from another and to fix the capabilities and disabilities which will characterize the person throughout life. Certain diseases towards which the young person may have inherited tendencies—mental instability, epilepsy, tuberculosis—are likely to manifest themselves for the first time between fifteen and twenty. This point is in contradistinction to the diseases which are definitely hereditary—syphilis, various eye troubles, certain paralyses—in that the latter usually present symptoms from infancy onwards.

The Physical Side of Sex

It is unfortunate, but true, that the attention of the religious teacher is called to the subject of sex by a widespread sin, that of self-abuse in boys and youths. It is doubly unfortunate because it alters the whole of the perspective from which sex should be surveyed. The habit frequently starts before puberty, and often in complete ignorance of its moral wrongness. There seems fairly good reason, from the experience of other priests whom the writer has questioned, to believe that in such cases of innocent acquirement the prospects of a speedy cure are good, for in such boys there is no task of cleansing a polluted mind but only the task of breaking a physical habit.

But when the habit has been learnt in lasciviousness or in an evil way the task is much harder. This fact opens up the question of sex-instruction to children, which will be dealt with later in a special section.

There are certain temperaments and constitutions more prone to acquire the habit than others. Its association with such things as biting the nails, epilepsy, and perverted food-appetite is a proof of this ; and such cases ought to be dealt with by an adviser with special knowledge of the subject. These cases form the minority ; by far the greater number of youths who practise masturbation do so because in them the natural instinct towards sexual self-gratification is stimulated and augmented by unclean talk and pictures, whilst the controlling power of natural modesty, of knowledge, of parental love and religion, is diminished. The habit will only be cured when there is created a motive force towards purity stronger than the motive power towards self-gratification.

The harmful physical effects of self-abuse have been grossly exaggerated, especially in literature and propaganda designed to promote purity. Truth is a weapon quite powerful enough in itself, and in the long run propagandists will find that exaggerations and misrepresentations fail of their purpose. Self-abuse never causes epilepsy or insanity or any definite disease. What it does is to take off the sharp, fine edge of accomplishment both in sport and in study, and to remove the fine bloom of freshness and health that is a feature of normal adolescence.

These are the physical effects. There are also mental and spiritual effects, and most modern opinion on the subject believes that these come from conscious or sub-conscious worry over the subject. This worry is in the form of conscience informing the boy that the practice is morally wrong or of anxiety about the physical harm resulting from the habit. In support of this view one must remember that sexual gratification brings no evil effect in married life, for it is a normal physiological act. On the other hand, it is possible that any form of unnatural sex indulgence may be harmful *per se*, and self-abuse is unnatural. Practical experience points to the fact that the psychical results of masturbation are always worse in boys whose conscience on the subject is not deadened.

So far the writer has only been treating of a moderate degree of self-abuse. Violent and frequent self-abuse, like all other sexual excess, brings about certain definite physical and physiological ills; and the pathological picture of the masturbator is well defined and typical. Physically the boy becomes of a sallow, blotchy complexion, with all his muscles relaxed in tone, this last phenomenon producing a flabby, loose face with the cheek and mouth muscles quivering at every movement of the body. He acquires a distaste for games and exercise, and is generally sleepy. Psychologically he becomes shy and solitary, not responding to conversation, and resenting most attempts at confidence and familiarity. He is continually on his guard, and always has the air of keeping back something. Fits of moroseness and ill-temper are frequent; his will is weakened, and he loses interest in his personal appearance. Very frequently he indulges in a shallow religiosity, shallow because it is the emotional side of religion which is cultivated, whilst the intellectual side and the sense of religion as a duty are feebly developed. Parish priests of experience will recognize at once how frequently boys of this sort drift their way. The one hope of salvation is to get the confidence of such a boy, for if confidence be given with an acknowledgment of the state of affairs then the ground is prepared for reform.

Nothing can equal the value of Confession in this respect. It involves complete acknowledgment, it gives to the man receiving the confidence a character of office apart from his personality, it gives relief of conscience for past sin—a very important thing psychologically—together with the assurance of grace for help in the future. Moreover, all this takes place with the knowledge that the inviolable seal of the confessional makes it impossible for the subject to be referred to in conversation, and there is nothing that a boy dislikes more than reference to a private subject when he is not desiring it.

Physical harm is caused by self-abuse in the young because it is a premature use of the sexual function, and, like the premature use of any physiological function whatsoever, it will cause damage. In the average boy puberty occurs between the ages of fourteen and sixteen, but the sexual function is not fully established until about two years later; therefore any use of the function before eighteen years of age will cause strain in the present and premature exhaustion in the future.

It is as well to point out that the main physical harm caused by masturbation or by sexual over-indulgence is nervous and due to the nerve-strain of the repeated act rather than to the loss of the physiological material from the body. The teaching of this fact will reassure any youth who is troubled about frequent seminal emissions, for they occasion no harm whatsoever.

The cold bath and regular hard exercise in the open air are the two physical measures that give most help in combating the habit of masturbation. To these must be added the necessity for a simple diet; for a diet that is either too rich or too big is very liable to encourage sexuality. Still more important than the cure is the prevention of the habit, and the early sexual enlightenment of the young boy is by far the most important element in such prophylaxis. As it has been remarked already, a large number of boys fall into the habit through complete ignorance; and if the harmfulness and moral wrong of such a habit were pointed out when a boy is made aware of its existence, a large number of boys would be saved from it. Not only is it important that children should be instructed upon the subject of sex, but it is equally important that they should be instructed with accuracy and with reverence. In most cases when a boy picks up the information haphazard, he is taught with many inaccuracies of fact and from a wrong standpoint. It frequently happens also that boys learn of the facts of sex in the form of a sin involving the misuse of sex. Such a method of acquiring knowledge is bound to pervert the whole attitude towards sex, to make the adolescent regard all sexual matters either as obscene or else as a matter of self-gratification. All this could be prevented and a proper appreciation of chastity be induced if teachers and parents would undertake their duty of teaching boys under their care the true facts and the right estimate of the sexual function.

Unhappily self-abuse is not confined to the male sex. It occurs also amongst girls and women, though not so frequently as amongst boys. The physical effects are very much the same as in boys.

With regard to the treatment of such an ill, it is important that girls should obtain as much rest as possible, for the trouble is generally due to an exhausted and irritable state of the nerves. Sometimes the trouble is aggravated by a local condition of inflammation and irritability of the skin in the sexual area, which necessitates advice and treatment by a competent medical man or woman.

THE PSYCHOLOGICAL SIDE OF SEX

The instinct of sex is a very complex one. Not only is the physical attraction of sex made up of many elements, involving the senses of sight, smell, touch, sound; but the psychological aspect is even more complex, involving many secondary sexual emotions like jealousy, the sense of possession, desire for admiration. The subject is exhaustively treated by Dr. Havelock Ellis in his series of books upon the subject of sex, to which the reader may be referred. In both male and female the positive stimulus towards sex manifestation is inhibited and countered by the natural sentiment of modesty. In the right use of this instinct is to be found the practical basis for the development of the grace of chastity.

The direct attraction towards females is found in boys in the natural state from the earliest months of puberty; but in the artificial condition of middle-class life at the present day, when boys and girls are segregated in schools entirely for one sex, there is generally some delay before the sex instinct looks out from the same sex to the other sex. So that the attraction of women is not a powerful factor in a youth's sexual life until he leaves school and mixes in women's and girls' society. This artificial condition of things often leads either to a turning inward of the sex-instinct with the development of self-abuse or to an attraction for the same sex, homosexuality. The advantage resulting from co-education methods may, however, be outweighed by other losses resulting from the mixed education of boys and girls.

Apart from its intrinsic wrongness, sin between boy and boy or between boy and man is specially harmful in the age of pubescence. At that age the sexual passion is being developed ; and, following the general rule of the perversion of instincts, if the instinct is allowed at this plastic age to find wrong expression there is very great danger that a permanent perversion of sexual desire may be brought about.

In females the sexual complex is more active on the psychological side than the physical. Troubles due to disorder or want of control in the sexual function therefore tend to assume a psychological form. Of these the commonest are unbalanced emotional states characterized by violent affections or antipathies, wild imagination, weeping, and uncontrolled laughter. There is no golden rule for the management of such states ; each must be dealt with according to its special nature, but generally in the direction of developing the exercise of the will either by work and occupation or by the emphasizing of religion as a duty rather than as an emotional expression.

Hysteria is a morbid condition causing much difficulty in the religious training of girls. The term covers very many varieties of nervous disorder. Fits of uncontrolled emotion in which laughter and weeping alternate, moral disorders like lying and stealing, self-infliction of injuries, the unconscious stimulation of organic disease are the most prominent of the multiform conditions grouped together under the term "hysteria." It is probable that future developments of psychiatry may be able to divide up these various ills into different pathological groups, but at present they are believed to be manifestations of one disorder. There has always been a disposition to regard hysteria as a disease connected with the sexual function ; the very name is derived from the Greek noun ὑστέρα (womb). The medical science of the last century learnt to dissociate the disease from the physical organs of sex and dwelt upon its psychological origin, even when the symptoms were physical.   The newest theory of hysteria traces the psychical conditions back to the psychical concomitants of the sex-complex.   According to Freud, who first elaborated the theory, hysteria is due to the blocking-out in consciousness of certain psychical elements and their associations.   Blocked out from consciousness, these elements still remain in the subconscious, with their intensity increased owing to their suppression from the conscious. They escape into expression in dreams.   Unaware of the act of violence which it has done to itself, the conscious mind suffers from it ; so too does the subconscious mind. The derangement of the subconscious thus produced leads to the functional disorder of hysteria, which is essentially a disease of the subconscious self.

The elements thus blocked out are generally rejected from consciousness because of their unpleasant character or associations, *e.g.* a fright in childhood, a painful incident, or antipathy instilled by education.   In most cases the element thus repressed is of a sexual nature ; and it is treated with this antagonism owing to innate shame and natural modesty or to the prudishness of current social teaching.

This is the newest theory of hysteria preached by Freud and elaborated by many disciples, often to the point of the ridiculous.   In order to make it tenable Freud insists upon treating as primarily sexual many features of psychical life which at first sight seem to be only remotely sexual, if sexual at all.

This is not the place for a discussion of the theory or of the curative means which are based upon it.

Actual cases of hysteria should be dealt with by a competent psychologist, for the hysterical subject is ground where angels might fear to tread.   Moreover, the whole matter is still in the region of hypothesis and experiment.

Seeing how much of the subject-matter of sex is matter violently rejected by the conscious mind of the adolescent owing to fear or ignorant shame, Freud's hypothesis of the nature and origin of hysteria is a very strong argument for the teaching of the facts of sex to girls at an early age ; and it must be noted that nineteen out of every twenty sufferers from hysteria are females.

Owing to the physical occurrence of menstruation, many parents are already awake to the necessity of preparing girls for the onset of puberty ; but unfortunately there are large numbers of mothers who will let their girls grow up, and even marry, without the knowledge of the facts of sexual life. Such neglect is a crime.

We have thus arrived by several convergent roads at the fact that the one important thing in the proper management of adolescence, both for boys and girls, is instruction upon sex matters early in life. The age at which this can and should be given is much earlier than is generally thought. The age of nine or ten in both sexes is none too early. The essential point is to forestall teaching on the subject from other sources, because such teaching is likely to be inaccurate and wrongly orientated. Nature is a very good guide in matters of education. When a child begins to realize its ignorance of the way in which babies are born and to ask questions upon the subject, it is a signal that the child is in need of such teaching and is capable of receiving it. It is a matter of experience for those who have tried it, that young children do receive instruction of this kind with intelligence, and that a right point of view results. Those parents and teachers who have done their duty in this respect towards their children always find themselves repaid a hundredfold by the happy results of their courage in facing a difficult task.

Both for the purpose of teaching the young and of preaching from the pulpit it is necessary to have a clear and right idea of the Christian view upon sex. It happens very frequently that teachers take up an entirely negative view of the subject, and their teaching is prone to take the form of a series of prohibitions : " Do not commit self-abuse, do not fornicate, do not entertain thoughts of lust." But Christian morality is essentially positive. The positive teaching of the Church upon sex is to be found in the ideal of Christian Marriage. This is the consummation of the union between two lovers, in body, soul, and spirit, and the subsequent care of the children born to that union. Christian chastity before marriage consists in the sanctified guardianship of the faculty of sex for that purpose. Chastity does not consist in banishing every thought of sex and every expression of sexual attraction by the sheer force of repression. The teaching of such an ideal is neither right nor efficacious. Sex with all its desires and attractions is there, ignore it though we will. The right attitude consists in recognizing it and consecrating it to its right purpose, making use of the universal civilized " instinct " of modesty. It is wrong to frown upon the sex attractions of developing boys and girls as if they were essentially wrong. They are the instinctive impulses by which the human creature is led to select its mate ; and to deny natural instincts savours of the Manichæan. There may be much that is annoying in the clownish love-making of boys, and much that is stupid in the attractions that an adolescent girl unconsciously puts forth ; there may even be things that are both unwise and sinful in boy and girl flirtations with their jealousy and vanity, quite apart from all definite sins of immodest talk and impure fondlings ; but to feel and to express the sexual emotions, *i.e.* the love of man for woman, and of woman for man, is part of the normal healthy soul.

The cultivation of the sense of chivalry which exists in every youth is a powerful aid to the preservation of chastity.

So, teaching that sex is a holy thing in which physical union takes place only after the solemn exchange of vows and the blessing of the Church, we can lay down a positive Christian ideal in which the fact of sex is recognized and consecrated.

The Instincts of Adolescence

Adolescence, as we saw at the beginning of this article, is the time of development between two fixed states—childhood and adult life ; but we can regard it in another way as the time of preparation for adult life. In this age there appear, one after another, the instincts which are the natural means of such education ; nearly all the interesting psychological features of adolescence can be grouped and studied in this way.

Life is both physical and mental.

Most of the instincts necessary for the preservation of physical life appear in childhood and infancy ; we meet very few of them appearing for the first time in adolescence. We have already dealt with the sex instinct, the instinct necessary not for the preservation of the individual but of the species. There remain one or two more belonging to physical well-being, which are of importance to the teachers and guardians of youth.

The instinct towards sport is one obviously leading to activities that will develop the physical faculties needful for life. Some instincts formerly necessary when man lived in the uncivilized state and had to provide his food by trapping and hunting still remain as vestigial survivals. Chief among these are the tracking games of youth, and sport in the form of hunting, shooting, and fishing. Their attraction can be only partly explained upon the basis of the needs of physical life, and other explanations treat them mainly as survivals of utilitarian needs when life was primitive in its form.

Pugnacity, which becomes very strongly marked soon after puberty in males, is the instinct towards self-defence necessary to the young human being when it comes to the age at which the protective care of parents ceases. It is also associated with sex, for in animals at the season of mating the male displays unusual ferocity, often accompanied by growth in the organs of aggression—antlers, claws, etc. This foreshadows the protecting function of the male towards his mate in the breeding season.

But it is in mental life that the adolescent shows the greatest richness of instinctive development.

There is first of all the thirst for information, the insatiable curiosity which is typified in the immortal question, " What makes the wheels go round, father ? " This demand for knowledge begins early in childhood, and continues sometimes even throughout life, but always into adult life. At various ages it takes different forms. In

childhood it demands facts ; from puberty onwards it is
more insistent in its demand for the explanation of facts
by general laws owing to the instinct towards unification
which is the key-note of all the psychology of adolescence.
In later adolescence this intellectual demand becomes
more philosophical and metaphysical. " Why is God
God ? " is a problem that engaged one girl, and " Why are
people born, if they have to die ? " is another. This specula-
tion about ultimate things is the basis for a fact, of which
Dom Bede Jarrett writes as follows : " It is a startling fact
that in modern society the contemplative most frequently
to be met is a boy."

This energy for philosophical inquiry concerns itself
with ethical as well as with metaphysical matters, and if
not disciplined, sometimes results in the holding of pronounced and exaggerated views or the cultivation of
unconventional habits. The conscientious objector, the
hatless youth, the revolutionary anarchist, are each of them
the product of adolescent speculativeness.

Belonging to an earlier stage of adolescence or even to
childhood is the passion to collect and to arrange. Stamps,
crests, post-marks, engine numbers, are only a few out of
the many hobbies whose attraction is due to the instinct
for arranging and codifying. The facility for arranging
data is a very important part of mental life, and is a prelude
to the discovery of the general laws controlling phenomena.

It must be noticed that the collecting habit is due not
only to the codifying instinct but also to the instinct of
acquisitiveness. This again is one of the fundamental
instincts of mankind, the pleasure of possession. The child
who strews its toys all over the house and the developing
adolescent hoarding things in cupboards stand in extreme
contrast. The important part acquisitiveness plays in
our psychological make-up can only be appreciated by
imagining what would be the effect of its absence.

A person who had no desire to possess things could
scarcely remain alive by his own efforts for a week either
in a civilized community or in primitive life. Many of
the failures of life are the men and women in whom this
instinct is ill-developed, both wastrels and spendthrifts.

Acquisitiveness, although not strongly developed until adult life, begins in adolescence. When the instinct is uncontrolled by moral habit it gives rise to stealing, a common moral disorder in young girls. Kleptomania, especially in the form of a monomania for stealing articles of one class only, is the collecting instinct out of control. This explanation must not be invoked to cover the commonest form of thieving in young people, the pilfering of food, for that, as a rule, is due merely to physical hunger.

Another very different feature of adolescence is hero-worship. Equally marked in boys and girls, it is to be explained by the idealistic element which develops in adolescent mentality. In life we have to play a social part as well as an individual, for man is above all things a socialized animal. Just as there are instincts stimulating the development of capabilities to meet the needs of the individual, so there are instincts tending to foster the faculties and activities necessary for the existence of the social whole. The idealizing instinct performs this function. A boy or girl entering upon life with no aspirations or a grown-up who has lost his illusions is an anti-social element. Without the rashness of youth there would be no enterprise, and enterprise is necessary to civilization. Without the visions of youth there would be none of the heroic adventures of mature life. The pioneer, the reformer, the missionary, the founder of a movement, all have the beginnings of their careers laid in the visionary period of their youth; the growth of judgment and will, coming in adult life, completes the mental equipment of the hero.

Even the humdrum maintenance of civilization in its present form is dependent upon the regular entry into social life of fresh generations of the young with their boundless hopes of success and unspoilt faith in humanity. The young mind is concrete in its thinking and generally embodies its devotion to the ideal in the form of some hero of history or a lesser figure of note in the circle of friends.

Ambition is the same spirit of idealism, not embodying itself in an altruistic setting as in pure hero-worship, but identifying itself with the ego. The mere contemplation and worship of a hero is not productive of any achievement unless it becomes identified with the self in order to produce the personal desire to excel as the hero excels. It is a particular case of emotion passing into will.

"Every boy," said a well-known schoolmaster, "is a mixture of a poet, a pirate, and a pig." Of the pirate and the pig we have already treated; the poet suggests that the appreciation of beauty is another of the features of adolescent psychology. Although children have a sense of prettiness, especially in regard to bright colours, and of rhythm in music, it is not until they reach the threshold of adult life that the powers of æsthetic perception and appreciation begin to develop and exercise influence upon action. The sense of colour is generally the first to develop, whilst music, form, and language are later in their appeal. It is in the age between sixteen and twenty-one that the artist is born, though manual dexterity shows itself earlier; and later adolescence is, therefore, the time to be watched for the education of the æsthetic faculties. These tastes account very largely for the pleasure-seeking activities of youth, dancing, the theatre, travelling; but we must add the social-sexual and the purely social instincts to the complex cause of the adolescent love of pleasure.

The phenomenon of a girl or a youth being stage-struck is a very striking one. It is a curious compound of ambition, vanity, and æsthetic taste; but for all its complexity it is a common occurrence, and one needing much sympathy and understanding in dealing with it.

Those responsible for the presentation of religion to young people will do well to remember the strong æsthetic developments of this period of life. It is well to point out that it is those churches which clothe their worship with the music and colour of the time-honoured ritual of the Church that manage to retain their adolescents through this difficult period of their life. Worship accompanied by an austere ugliness will be repellent to the æsthetic instincts of youth, and a gaunt moralism which neglects the dogmatic richness of men's knowledge of God will be equally repellent to the metaphysical cravings of the heart of youth in its search for God.

There is one very important fact to be noted concerning the instincts. Each has a definite time for appearing, it works up to a period of maximum intensity, and then tends to disappear or diminish. If that instinct is not seized and developed by expression and education it is very likely to atrophy, with the result that the faculty dependent upon it will be missing from adult life. Herbert Spencer, for instance, recognized this fact in himself, for the instinct for beauty was never exercised owing to his absorption in study, and it was lost for ever out of his life. The same will be the case with any of those instincts, the moral, the intellectual, the adventurous, the development of which is necessary to the fulness and richness of life.

The key to the understanding of the adolescent thus lies in the study of his instincts as they appear.

The task of education, in particular of religious education, is to develop the successive activities brought into play by each successive instinct; and furthermore to keep each faculty active as later instincts appear and tend to relegate it to the background. But it must not be forgotten that there are certain qualities necessary for life which have little or no instinctive basis, the sense of duty for instance. In such matters education has to create habit, which is another feature of psychological life that is of equal importance with instinct.

This account of the physical and psychical basis of life in adolescence has been written round the instincts, but the reader must bear in mind the limitations of the method and remember that in the complexity of human nature there are other elements, not so powerful perhaps in adolescence, but more powerful in adult life. Reason, habit, and group suggestion are a few of such elements.

THE AGE FOR CONFIRMATION

The study of adolescence from the physical and psychical points of view throws a little light upon the vexed question of what is the best age for Confirmation.

According to English custom the rite of Confirmation

carries with it several things which must be clearly distinguished from one another.

(*a*) A course of theological instruction.

(*b*) An intensive course of spiritual and devotional training.

(*c*) Admission to Communion ;
and we must recognize further in the rite itself,

(*d*) The gift of the Holy Spirit.

(*e*) The solemn renewal of baptismal vows.

Each of these things comes best at a different age. But there is one thing common to them all, namely, that they should never come during the time of puberty.

In the six or twelve months during which bodily changes are taking place the organism is so taken up with the physical changes that the mind cannot be receptive to any big psychological influences. For a year after puberty the psychical system is so unstable that it is wise not to attempt to throw into it any new elements, but to let it carry on with the old. It is an exceedingly bad time for any exceptional religious effort. The two years, therefore, from the first beginnings of puberty are a very unfavourable time for any of the events usually connected with Confirmation.

We may now consider what is the most suitable age for each of these separate events.

(*a*) The intellectual mind of a child is capable of receiving concrete facts only ; the power of dealing with abstractions does not come until the age of sixteen and seventeen. The English Catechism is a highly abstract theological and moral treatise added on to the Creed, the Our Father, and the Ten Commandments. In its theological teaching it is not only abstract but also somewhat technical, *e.g.* the matter and the grace of a sacrament. Such teaching therefore would best be deferred until the seventeenth year or even later, when the speculative instinct is becoming developed, that is, if the child has already received simple Sunday-school teaching upon the primary matters of Christian faith and practice.

(*b*) The intensive devotional training ought to come when the capacity for religious expression is becoming active. There are two periods for this—before puberty, and again between eighteen and twenty. But it is a matter in which the wise parish priest must consider individual cases by his own power of observation.

(c) and (d) If the Sacraments are a means of grace they ought to be given as early in life as possible, that is to say, as soon as the child can know what the sacrament in question means. A child of nine or ten is quite capable of understanding what Holy Communion means; and as stewards of the mysteries of God bishops or parish priests ought not to deprive children of their lawful inheritance for a single month beyond the age at which they are capable of inheriting.

In every case first Communion should take place before puberty, for the earlier a habit is formed the more fixed it becomes; and the more plastic the mind, the greater the moulding effect upon character.

(e) Confirmation is also the strengthening and renewal of the bond by which a soul is tied to the Church and to Christ. If first Communion and Confirmation are separated, there is a tendency for Communion to lapse.

To sum up : the " age for Confirmation " in the usually accepted sense of the term must be reconsidered in view of the several elements contained. As a sacrament and a rite, Confirmation should take place before puberty. But the intensive theological and devotional training should be left until the seventeenth year or thereabouts. There is no practice in the English Church so badly in need of revision as the arrangements for Confirmation and admission to Communion; nor is there any document which needs revising more than the Church Catechism, if it is intended for the teaching of young children.

BIBLIOGRAPHY

Adolescence, by G. Stanley Hall. Published by Appleton & Co., New York. 2 vols. pp. 1337. A very voluminous and highly technical treatise.

The Adolescent, by J. W. Slaughter. Published by George Allen & Co., Ruskin House. pp. 100. A small handbook founded upon the above.

The Mind of the Child, by Preyer.

Science of Human Nature, by W. H. Pyle.

Mental and Physical Life of School Children, by Sandiford.

Adolescent Period, by Louis Starr. Mainly physiological.

Compton Mackenzie's *Sinister Street* and Mme Sarah Grand's *Beth Book* give a good picture of middle-class children's inner life, and Morrison's *A Child of the Jago* a picture of a juvenile criminal.

CHAPTER III

PREPARATION IN THE PARISH (1)

By J. F. LOVEL SOUTHAM

I. THE REMOTE PREPARATION OF THE PARISH IN GENERAL

IT is very important, I think, that we should have in mind not only the preparation of the individual candidates but also the preparation of the parish itself. The background of the candidates is the Church fellowship into which they were brought at their Baptism, in which they have been spiritually nurtured and educated, the fulness of which they are going to share as they enter into the communicant life.

It is the life of the body corporate that matters first, its spiritual vitality, its outlook, its worship, the depth and reality of its fellowship in the Communion of the Holy Ghost. The individual is made a sharer of the Holy Spirit through the Body of Christ, and the concrete reality of the meaning of this Body is to be found in the parochial life. It is this which, unconsciously perhaps, has been moulding their individual lives; they will have entered for good or ill upon a spiritual inheritance, imbibed an atmosphere, gained an outlook. Therefore I put first the importance of the general attitude about Confirmation in the parish as a whole. There should be a recognition that through prayer the whole body of the faithful should take a real part in the preparation, and the advent of the new communicants should be looked forward to with interest and expectation, because through them there is to come a fresh dower of the Spirit; they should be surrounded with expectant sympathy, with all the store of faith, hope, and love which the parochial fellowship possesses. Example counts for so much more than precept, and we need to take careful thought as to the interpretation of

our Lord and His Spirit which is being made around them
by the Spirit-bearing Body, and as to the general estimate
of Confirmation that is prevalent. Is the parish Confirmation preparation time regarded as one of the most
important times of the year, bringing a fresh call to all
to stir up anew the gift that is in them ? Are those who
have been confirmed in previous years encouraged to
attend the classes again ? Are those approaching Confirmation age made to feel a spirit of expectancy, to think
how wonderful it is all going to be when it comes ? Are
they made to feel the reality of a fellowship closing round
them to help and support them, and expecting great
things from them ? Are they made to feel that their
lives are wanted at their best by God and His Church in
the comradeship of the great adventure of bringing into
being the Kingdom of God ?

This demonstration of the spirit of fellowship cannot be
produced in a moment ; it can come only as the result of
long years of experience in sharing together the Communion of the Holy Spirit. " The kingdom of heaven
cometh not with observation " ; it is due to the presence
of the Spirit pervading the life of the body corporate,
imperceptibly catching hold of the different members who
are brought up in it and therein " live, and move, and
have their being." It depends upon the manifestation of
the fruits of the Spirit in the lives of the members of the
parochial Christian community ; so that Christian graces
and holy tempers are felt to be the natural thing, and a
desire for them will be planted in the hearts of the younger
members, who will be pointed to their source, the Holy
Spirit.

Confirmation is bound to mean more and more as the
members of the Church come to grasp the fact that they
are committed to a dispensation of the Holy Ghost, praying,
living, walking by the Spirit, ministering the gifts of the
Spirit to one another, providing an atmosphere and surroundings in which these things can develop and grow, the
Spirit having free course and being glorified. It must
make an incalculable difference if " the carnal mind which
is at enmity towards God " is making itself evident rather

than the Spirit of Christ in the main body from which the candidates come.

The fresh soil is really being prepared or spoilt all the while by the spiritual level of the general parochial life. This is one strong compelling reason why the gifts of the Spirit should be sought and the fruits of the Spirit unceasingly cultivated by the Spirit-bearing body : its constant prayer must be " Veni, Creator Spiritus." We know how flowers open out and expand in the sunshine ; and sensitive young souls can easily be warped, cruelly hurt and maimed by not finding themselves surrounded by an atmosphere which is sympathetic and brings the best out of them. The hope for the future depends upon constantly higher and higher levels of spiritual life being reached by the whole body : it will take a spiritual genius of a Confirmation candidate to make any advance when the fellowship from which he has emerged has attained to a dead-level and is content to stay there, resisting any call to further progress.

It sometimes escapes our notice that the spiritual life of the parochial fellowship is the first preparation of the Confirmation candidates, and that that life must be living on into the future, not back towards the past. God is in front of us ; the spirit of faith and hope stretches out towards Him ; we believe that He has ever fresh truths to teach us, new visions to show us, more wonderful graces to give us, bigger things for us to do. And all this because He is making us bigger souls, and giving us more and more the spirit of unity with one another in Him, by which great things are made possible of attainment. It is thus that the first Christians were able to receive the Holy Ghost together at Pentecost ; they were all together not only in one place but in one spirit, they were one in faith and hope and expectation that God would act, and they prepared the way of the Lord by their attitude of faithful prayer. If we consider the meaning of the wonderful words of St. Paul with which our daily Offices end— " The grace of our Lord Jesus Christ, and the love of God, and the fellowship of the Holy Ghost, be with us all evermore "—we shall see that the Church expects all bodies of her people who pray and worship together to manifest that spirit ; only then can it spread outwards to the Church as a whole.

Where the Spirit of Life is there must be growth, movement, development, both in the corporate and individual life ; fresh truths are apprehended, new graces are gained, and spiritual powers bestowed, as by our faith and love expressed in prayer we set God free to possess our souls and so to work through us. People who, unlike St. Paul, " count themselves to have apprehended " are real obstacles to the incoming of the Spirit into other lives. Like the Pharisees of old, they enter not into His kingdom themselves, and they that are entering in they hinder. It is so often the tragedy of Confirmation preparation to see the low level of the spiritual background from which the candidates come, and to find the romantic adventure of the quest for God all but stifled at its birth. " I should like my child to have some religion, but not too much," said a parent to a schoolmaster. This is typical of older people, to whom the thought that what was good enough for them or their parents should not be good enough for their children is almost sacrilegious, covering up something deeper down that it is really a rebuke which they are not prepared to stand. When it gets to this, religion becomes uncomfortable. So they deliberately place themselves athwart the path of the Spirit of Life and incur a responsibility beyond man's power to measure.

It is obvious, I think, how much the background matters and how necessary it is for the spiritual fellowship of the parish to close up around the Confirmation candidates.

There are, of course, many ways, both direct and indirect, by which this can be done. One very excellent way is by some of those who have been confirmed in past years attending the classes again ; and another is by communicants making themselves responsible for praying for one or more of the candidates, and by bringing them in some way into the social life of the communicants. Anyhow, I plead that in our Confirmation preparation we should have the background of the surrounding parish life in view, and that we should see the need for the constant uplifting, development, and progress of that life : it is the general tone, the corporate level that matters. We need to ask ourselves, " Is my parish fit to have a Confirmation, to bear the responsibility of training and developing Confirmation candidates ? "

II. The Preparation of the Candidates

A. *The remote preparation, i.e.* before the time of the classes. Our aim must be to get the Church and its faith really at the back of the candidates' lives. This, I think, is all-important if Confirmation is to take its true place as a perfectly natural and normal step in the Christian life, vitally connected both with Baptism into the Church and the subsequent entry into the full communicant life.

This is the Prayer-Book setting. There is no thought of Baptism apart from Confirmation, of Confirmation being a thing for some and not for others ; the great mass of the unconfirmed baptized that we have with us is not contemplated at all. On the contrary, " Ye are to take care that this Child be brought to the Bishop to be confirmed by him."

Again, there is no thought of Communion being for a few and not the privilege and the duty of all the Church's children ; on the contrary, the normal thing for all is Communion, the very heart and soul of Churchmanship ; but " there shall none be admitted to the Holy Communion, until such time as he be confirmed, or be found in the judgement of the Bishop to be ready and desirous to be confirmed."

Here, then, Confirmation is seen in the mind of the Church to be a normal step in the life of grace, but it can only be felt to be so when that mind is expressed in the Church's life and fellowship, and when this has been woven into the spiritual make-up of the lives of the future candidates. When this has not been done, Confirmation tends to get out of its true place, to be viewed out of proportion. It is not then regarded as a normal offer of a spiritual gift from God, to enable the ordinary growing-up Christian to lead a spiritual life, but rather as a somewhat abnormal act on the part of the individual, the performance of which implies that he is setting out to be an abnormal kind of Christian.

This point of view is, I think, much encouraged by the main stress being so often and so wrongly laid upon what the candidate is going to do rather than upon what God wants to do and to give. We always get into trouble when our religion does not begin with God ; we get it the wrong way round, upside-down, and things that are thus will not work. Great harm has been done to the whole religious outlook of Confirmation candidates, I am convinced, by greater prominence being given in teaching and emphasis to the candidates' " vow " rather than to God's promised and proffered gift of grace.

The " vow " part simply means that the Church uses the opportunity of the Confirmation Service for a public ratification of the baptismal vow, which has been informally acknowledged every time the Christian child has repeated the Church Catechism.

" Dost thou not think that thou art bound to believe, and to do, all those things which your Godfathers and Godmothers then promised for you ? Yes verily ; and by God's help so I will." At Confirmation the child, coming for this especial " help of God," the gift of the Holy Spirit in and through the Church, makes public confession of acceptance of his part of the baptismal covenant, which is primarily, however, a covenant of grace in which God takes the initiative. Such ratification is, however, not an essential part of the Confirmation Service, appropriate though we may feel it to be. When it is over-stressed, the whole general idea gets wrong, and it is this wrong idea, that what we do matters more than what God does (if indeed He really does anything) that lies at the back of the minds of many Church of England people about Confirmation and indeed about the whole sacramental life.

This shows itself in many ways. It has a very distinct bearing upon the question, What age is to be regarded as most fit for Confirmation ? I feel sure, from experience as a parish priest, that, generally speaking, we ought to avoid the years from fourteen to seventeen. The age of seventeen and over obviously has an advantage from the point of view of definite decision being made for God on the part of the candidate; but, on the other hand, there is the great difficulty of providing the life till so late an age with a real background of Church fellowship in order to give what I call the remoter preparation. Sometimes, though in my experience very occasionally, the result of such later Confirmation is excellent. More often, however, one finds it is rather a chance (humanly speaking) coming forward of a young man or woman who has practically no Church background in thought or life beyond occasional attendance at Evensong, which counts for very little. To such, Confirmation is just the strange and abnormal thing that I have described; it is very hard for them to enter into the fellowship of grace and truth, and the life which flows from it.

On the other hand, with those of a younger age than fourteen it is possible to provide the background of the remote preparation through the Sunday school, consciously directed towards that end, up to the age of ten. This means, first, that the children of this age receive special instruction on the Holy Communion Service and how to take their part in it intelligently, and attend the Service, not only that they may become familiar with it, but that they may see the older children and their teachers making their Communion together Sunday by Sunday, and so may thus early enter some way into the fellowship of grace. A "Children's Eucharist" or a Sung Eucharist without Communion cannot do this; the whole outlook and atmosphere is vastly different from that of a parish Communion provided as the chief Service on Sunday morning at which the children are present in an honoured place, becoming conscious of a fellowship in God and learning to look forward to the time when they can enter into its fulness by themselves making their Communion. Here, I believe, lies the secret of bringing the children to their Communion and keeping them there, through their being admitted to some share in a fellowship which is obviously and consciously living by a sharing together of the Body and Blood of the Incarnate Lord: it is through the growth of this and nothing else that that spiritual kingdom will grow, against which the

gates of Hell cannot prevail.   It is only through the power
of a real living membership of a family of grace that the
individual can hope to withstand and to overcome the
world, the flesh, and the devil.   To be confirmed is to be
confirmed into this, and that is exactly where the Church
comes in : it is primary and essential.

Then the Confirmation Service can be studied and an
attitude of mind created that will regard it as the great
privilege of growing up in the Church to receive this
blessing of the Spirit and to go on to the Altar.   So it will
be found that children will begin to express their desire to
their teachers to be confirmed next time quite incidentally
and without any definite urging or even asking.

Children of this age can be taught about the devotional
life and be given much help in it, and this will be invaluable as part of the remote preparation.   It will include
help in their worship-life, through the corporate worship
of the school being carefully thought out with this end
in view, as well as help in their individual prayer-life.
It is very important, too, that they should have some
preliminary training and help in the devotional reading of
the Bible, *i.e.* meditation in an elementary form.

The ideal of the Sunday school for these children should
be to present the Church life and fellowship in its true
meaning, with Confirmation coming as a joyous reception
of power and a means of entry into the fulness of grace
in the Sacrament of fellowship, the Holy Communion,
which it is God's will that all His children should share.

Teachers, too, can do much to influence the homes of
the children by talking with the parents and trying to show
them what they are aiming at, and how greatly they feel
it will help their children if they enter into the full Church
life and gain the habit of Communion before they go out
into the world.   The circumstances of the present day
seem to point to the need of the formation of settled habits
of Churchmanship before the age of fourteen : the world
is pulling very hard at young lives, and there is a material-
istic bias which has not only to be resisted but overcome.   The Church would seem to have more chance of
saving their souls if it really got there first in the formative

impressions of the early years; and it is the intensity of those impressions that matters. It is really a question of God getting the first chance. This, of course, is not seen when the main idea is that the candidate is going to make some special vow and that in consequence the chief consideration is that he should be " old enough to understand what he is doing." When the children in our towns leave Day School other interests of all kinds increasingly crowd in upon them, through evening classes, etc., which makes it more and more difficult to gain either their time or interest for Confirmation preparation. This is a practical consideration in favour of early Confirmation which is forcing itself upon clergy working in town parishes.

It is notoriously hard to get ordinary Church of England parents with only the slightest acquaintance with sacramental grace to see this point of view and recognize the advisability of early Confirmation, because it does not fit in with the religious furniture of their minds and their preconceived notions of the meaning of Confirmation and its place in the life of grace; but it can be gradually done if Sunday-school teachers and clergy work together loyally and patiently towards that end in the school and in the homes. One cannot but feel that ultimately parents will recognize that it is the considered and deliberate opinion of those who have both responsibility and experience that must decide what the Church really means about age when it simply says that candidates must have come to years of discretion, and be able to say the Creed, the Lord's Prayer, and the Ten Commandments, and the Catechism, and also speaks of candidates as " children," that is (technically speaking) past the age of infancy (1–7). It is a big responsibility, surely, to say more about the age of Confirmation than the Church does, especially for those whose acquaintance with the mind of the Church is of the slightest.

I strongly urge, therefore, that we look carefully to the background, the remoter preparation, the surrounding influences in church, Sunday school, and home, out of which the candidates will come. In this not only the clergy, but all communicants, especially those confirmed in the immediate last few years, and the Sunday-school teachers, have a large part to play : the communicants generally by creating the outlook, atmosphere, and spirit of the parochial life, and the latter by direct contact with the children and their homes.

B. *The Immediate Preparation.*—We shall have clearly in mind that the work of preparation has really to be done by God Himself and the individual soul. The work is God's, but He wills to work through us, to the extent that it is left to us to create the conditions which set Him free to work. Remembering this, we shall leave much to God. Often God's workers work too much, they try to go too far, they get in the way, they actually hamper and spoil the work of God, because they try to do the work that only God can do.

We are trying to plant souls in the garden of God's grace ; we only make things impossible if, like childish gardeners with their plants and seeds, we will not leave them to the life-giving forces but keep disturbing the soil to see how they are getting on, and by our foolish but well-meant efforts only succeed in hindering or baffling the slow, silent, invisible working of the spiritual soil.

The following, which is true of all Church work, applies most especially, I think, to this greatest of all works, the preparation of the candidates for Confirmation : " Much of our work, so far from being a witness to our faith in Him in Whose Name we do it, is rather a vast monument to our disbelief in His Power to get on without us." Under such conditions, with such workers, God does not get a chance. We are ministers of the Spirit, who come " to prepare the way of the Lord " and nothing more : it is the Spirit Himself Who really prepares His own way, for He " convinces of sin, of righteousness and of judgement," and He alone can do so. It is not only for Confirmation but for the whole life of grace as communicants that the candidates are preparing, and the whole Christian life is in essence a response to the God of Grace, which we strive in God's Name to elicit. If we bear this in mind, it is bound to affect the whole manner and method of our work.

1. *The Classes*

(*a*) *The Period of Preparation by classes.*—This is normally about three months, if we include the classes after Confirmation and before first Communion. Every year it seems more and more inadequate, and I am led to wonder whether the ideal would not be to start to get the candidates together six months before the first Communion. Classes might then be held for six weeks, which would be mostly concerned with the devotional side of the preparation. The candidates would then learn subconsciously that they were preparing for God to give them something, to do something for them which they were stretching out after in prayer and faith, in expectation and hope, and that, not only individually, but together as a body.

This could be followed by six weeks' break, during which they could be left to put into practice what they had learnt devotionally, and after this would come the normal twelve weeks' classes.

I am conscious that this is rather a counsel of perfection, and that with the growth of night work of all kinds it is probably increasingly impracticable; nevertheless I think it is worthy of consideration : it would at any rate give the final twelve weeks a fair start, where so much time is often lost in getting the classes together. It would also help towards a " weeding out " before Confirmation rather than after, by making a bigger demand at the outset.

(*b*) *Programme of the Classes.*—Our object is to touch and train, to quicken and inspire the whole personality. We must therefore beware of taking up too much time with mental instruction, thus making the class too much like an ordinary instruction in day or Sunday school. We must not go to a Confirmation class with a treatise on the Thirty-nine Articles under our arms. Quite half the time of the class ought, I think, to be taken up with devotional exercises, starting with an act of recollection of God's presence and an introductory prayer for God's blessing upon all the Confirmation candidates as well as upon the individual class. Then a hymn, which would be used at every class and come to be remembered as the Confirmation preparation

hymn. This may well be followed by some of the Catechism said devotionally, sentence by sentence, after the
priest. There is real value in this, as it teaches the text of
the Catechism indirectly and also helps to weave it and its
thoughts, ideals, aspirations, duties, into the devotional life.

Then a short directed meditation upon some words of
our Lord about either the Father, Himself, or the Holy
Spirit, or upon some of the attributes of God's Nature
which have been revealed to us, such as St. John's use of
the terms Light, Love, and Life. In order to vary the
class as much as possible, the candidates might sit for the
preliminary part of the meditation and then kneel for the
spiritual aspirations based upon it. It is most important
that the thought of God should be supreme throughout
the classes and the whole preparation, and this is much
furthered by a meditation upon God coming first : " I
will think upon God."

Then would follow the instruction proper, after which
would come devotions in which we strive to make the
instruction real to the heart and will as well as to the head.

(c) *Subject-matter of the Instructions.*—The instruction
given in the classes centres most usefully round the Creed,
what we believe about God, which is the mainspring and
motive of the whole Christian life. To base our instructions
upon the Creed is a great help towards developing the God-
centred outlook, a religion that begins with God. If
religion does not begin with God, it soon develops into
religion without God, which at its best is nothing more
than the self-pleasing of the ecclesiastically minded, at its
worst the worship of self, which is the basest of idolatries.
We have to guard our candidates against this danger more
than any other, for it is the worst snare for their souls ; a
counterfeit religion is much worse than none at all, and
there are many specious substitutes for God.

I try to have in mind some definite idea about religion,
its meaning and essence, that I want to inculcate, *e.g.*
" Religion is our relationship to God and to one another
in God." God is revealed as Himself Love, and love is
the true spirit of relationship, therefore God Himself and
none else must be at the heart of our religion.

So we think first of God as our Father and ourselves as His children. This betokens relationship and implies that we are made in His image, capable of developing after His likeness, with a mind capable of knowing Him, a heart capable of loving Him, and a will capable of serving Him. The realization of this is the greatest safeguard against idolatry, for if we do not grasp and try to work out the fact that we are made in God's image, we very soon set out to make a God in our own image almost without knowing we are doing it. Present-day idolatry is more dangerous rather than less, in that its images are mental, unexpressed in wood and stone ; we are therefore not so well able to see their grotesqueness.

It is from this divinely revealed fact that God is our Father that the relationships of religion spring : we are children, we are therefore brothers and sisters in Christ, and the relationships springing from these facts go to make up life ; for love, and love alone, begets life.

This means that our relationships must be spiritualized if they are to be alive. Relationships have a formal side, but if they have that and nothing more, they are worthless and dead, without appeal and without power. We can see this only too plainly in the relationships of human life ; it is equally true of the great relationship between God and ourselves. Life comes out of living relationships ; without them we can exist but not live. So, if we would see life, we must spiritualize our relationships, and above all the supreme one from which all others flow, *i.e.* that with the great All-Father " from whom every family in heaven and earth is named," and from relationship with Whom all brotherhood springs. The world is full of talk about brotherhood to-day, and our candidates need to be warned that, apart from the realization of sonship, it is and must remain a barren lie, an idol, a dead and spiritless husk without a kernel.

To attempt to be brothers and sisters without grasping the fact first that we are sons and daughters is contrary to Nature, and it cannot be thus accomplished by grace, for grace is never contrary to Nature, though above it.

It can take nothing less than the acceptance, the entering

into the relationship of sonship to the divine to beget in us a living brotherhood to the human, based upon the eternal divine law, not upon changing public opinion and sentiment. So the divine law runs : " Thou shalt love the Lord thy God with all thy heart, and with all thy mind, and with all thy soul, and with all thy strength : this is the first and great commandment. And the second is like unto it, namely this, Thou shalt love thy neighbour as thyself."

We need to enforce with all the emphasis we can the order in which the Divine Lawgiver gave us these commandments, and the fact that He based them both upon love, which, as St. Paul said, " is the fulfilling of the law." Here is the final and complete answer to those who teach the Christian religion as a mere negation : Love is no more the absence of hate than peace is the absence of war ; relationships do not spring from negations ; negations leave them cold.

It is in the light of this that something of the meaning of sin can be seen ; it is the failure to love God and our neighbour, the spoiling of relationship on our side, the breaking of the very heart of religion, leaving but a dead relationship. It is therefore inevitably true that " the wages of sin is death."

Sin is cutting ourselves off from living relationship with God and our fellows, and the consequence of separation is as obvious and terrible in the spiritual world as in the natural. Sin literally passes into us ; we eat it as Eve ate the forbidden fruit, and we die.

Then we come to the Second Person of the Holy Trinity, God our Saviour. Again we notice a term of relationship to us. The Incarnation, the breaking through of God in a human life into the world, is God on His side taking the initiative, stretching out His hand to renew and restore the relationship between Himself and us—" Who for us men, and for our salvation came down from Heaven."

So the mind, heart, and will of God are presented again to us in our blindness and ignorance, our coldness and deadness, in terms that we can understand, for acceptance or rejection. When God stretched out His hand, He took the risk of its being pierced by human sin : hence was involved the Atonement, the bearing by God Himself of the death wrought by the human sin which broke relationship with Him.

So God would win and woo men back to respond to the appeal of His love, to enter into living relationship with Him. Such response obviously cannot be forced—it must be won ; and it is won as the soul increasingly responds to the attraction of God. The spiritual response on our side must be in essence twofold, the stretching out of the twin hands of repentance and faith, without which, after an act of sin, the relationship on our side cannot be mended and therefore spiritualized : they must, however, come at the cost of suffering, because of the wages of sin in our souls. Both of them must manifest themselves by " confession with the mouth unto salvation," and in neither case is this confession easy : it is the Calvary by which we pass on with our Lord to the new relationship and life of the Resurrection, the relationship and the life of grace. So we are led on to the Holy Spirit, the Sanctifier—once again a term of relationship. The Church falls into its place as the fellowship of the renewed and restored relationship of men with God and with one another in God, through the sharing together (communion) of the Holy Spirit— the Spirit of Light and Love and Life.

The Church, the special shrine of the Spirit's presence and manifestation, is the gift of God to us to-day ; it is what our Lord meant when He so clearly and emphatically committed His Apostles and Disciples to a dispensation of the Holy Ghost, the Spirit through Whom is accomplished the activity of the Divine love.

So the Sacraments take their place as the means by which through the Spirit in the Church the relationship between God and us is formed and fostered, and also as social ceremonies by which is gendered a real brotherhood in God. It is by the sharing of a corporate experience of Himself Who is Love that God means human fellowship to come to life : it must be a thing of the Spirit, it can be so only if it is rooted and grounded in Him.

Prayer, almsgiving, and self-denial, the great Christian

duties, will here be taught as the working out of the relationship on our part, and the candidates will be helped to see
that, like a human relationship, this relationship with the
Divine feeds naturally upon its expression on both sides,
the offer of sacramental grace on God's side, and on ours
the response of the Christian duties and the living out of
the implications of the Christian ideal in the moral details
of every-day life. " Because you are the child of God,
because you corporately are children of God, therefore live
it out, be loving to the tip of your tongue and the tips of
your fingers." This seems to be in essence the Christian
appeal.

A special word needs to be said about each of these
great Christian duties. I would leave Prayer to be dealt
with in private interview, but say a word here both about
Almsgiving and Fasting.

It is most necessary that plain teaching should be given
on the subject of almsgiving, for it is the lack of clear,
definite teaching as to this duty that has led to methods
of raising money for the kingdom of God utterly derogatory
to our Lord, which would be totally unnecessary if Churchpeople had been taught to give, and the Scriptural ideal
of the tenth had been steadfastly held up before them. It
is also the best corrective to the deadly idolatry of covetous-
ness in the individual soul, which is so rife and rampant
to-day. We need to point out that our Lord linked almsgiving with prayer and self-denial in the Sermon on the
Mount, and that therefore there cannot be any true alms
unless this link is kept ; it must be inspired by prayer and
be the outcome of self-denial.

Then it is a natural fruit of the Spirit, having within it
the seed of life; otherwise it is a Dead-Sea fruit, rare and
not refreshing.

Candidates must have put before them their individual
responsibility for God's work at home and abroad, that
they ought to take their place as members of the Finance
Scheme of the parish. To accept privileges without
acknowledging responsibilities, to claim rights without
performing duties, may denote the outlook and conduct of
the natural man, but it cannot be so with the Christian,

because it is an utterly un-Christian attitude, alien to the spirit of sonship. Yet we have it all around us in the Church. The reason must be that there has been something wrong in the appeal that has been made to the young generations of Churchpeople so capable of idealism and sacrifice, that in many indirect ways we have taught them to expect to receive rather than to give ; and such receiving, we have time after time brought home to us, has as a fact brought no blessedness. Sunday-school prizes and suchlike inducements have much to answer for, chiefly in the attitude that they have created and the spirit they have fostered, which is anything but that of sacrifice. It is pathetic to hear people, who have learnt the joy of giving till it costs, say, " Thank God I have learnt to give. Why was I never taught it before ! " Clergy who do not teach their people to give do them a most grievous spiritual wrong, and are untrue to the Gospel as Christ preached it : Christ refused to come down from His Cross ; they take Him down. Self-denial is essential according to the plain teaching of Christ ; it provides the living heart of sacrifice to our almsgiving, it also enables us to gain that self-control which is the hall-mark of sonship and without which there can be no true freedom. It is the only thing that can deliver us from that parody of freedom, licence, which is luring civilization to destruction to-day.

So Christ placed fasting on the same level with almsgiving as an essential Christian duty. All people deteriorate in health and strength both of soul and body when the spirit of discipline does not enter into their lives ; they become spoilt children, the sport of their whims and desires. It is those who lose their life who find it. When worldly people are beginning simply from self-centred valetudinarian motives to practise bodily fasting, it is time that those whose function it is to train the children of light should see what they do if they allow one of the three outstanding Christian duties to be passed by. The Church in the Prayer Book has given us a time-table, and this, we all know, is necessary when unpleasant lessons have to be learnt. The Bible, in Old and New Testaments, teaches us to fast ; the Church tells us when. It should be pointed

out that the three great Christian duties find their focus-
point in the Holy Communion, the great service of love
and therefore of giving, both on the part of God and man.

The fast before Communion should be steadfastly held
up as the ideal ; its appeal should be based not only upon
the fact that it has the sanction of an age-long custom of
the universal Church behind it, but also that it is an act
of self-denial and self-sacrifice by which the body is to be
prepared to receive the fruits of the Sacrifice of Calvary.
The soul is prepared by penitence, the body by fasting,
and both are offered in answer to the appeal of the Cross
and usher us into communion with the Crucified. It
should, however, be carefully pointed out that fasting from
food is by no means the only kind of fasting, which must
include all acts of self-denial ; and that fasting has no
merit in itself, but is a means directed towards the end of
a quiet and disciplined spirit. When fasting is done in a
legalistic spirit merely, so far from generating a gracious
humility in the soul, it most subtly ministers to pride ;
it becomes itself a fetish worshipped for its own sake
because it produces merit ; so easily are we led into worshipping our own religiousness instead of God.

Let us warn our candidates carefully about this snare
in which Satan traps so many unwary souls, who have ceased
to be God-conscious in their religion and therefore to be
truly spiritual in it : we certainly shall not make Christians
if we produce Pharisees, and that in human nature which
produced the Pharisee of old is by no means dead. The
only safeguard is to learn to fast in spirit and in truth to
the glory of God.

2. *Private Interviews*

All parish priests know how much has to be done
and can be done through private interviews alone in
creating the personal touch and so getting at the individual.
It is a very great pity when, owing to the number of
candidates, private interviews have to be cut down, or
the priest is so tired that he is unable to adapt himself to
the needs of the individual candidate.

I feel that here the meaning of the gift of the Spirit to each individual for the true formation of character needs driving home. We must point out that real contact with God makes all the difference to what we are, and that what we are matters eternally. We all want to be our best selves, but it is only with God's help that we can hope to press on towards the mark; and we must want to be our best selves not from any merely selfish purpose, but that we may be fit members of the Body of Christ and worthy instruments to build up His kingdom.

There are, I think, three main things best dealt with in private interviews: private prayers and Bible-reading, social purity, and personal vocation.

(a) *Private Prayers and Bible-reading.*—In these two things lies the opportunity of the soul's constant intercourse with God: God speaking to us, we speaking to Him. It is through such intercourse that the knowledge of God comes, as contrasted with knowing about Him; and it is through such knowledge that the relationship which is religion is deepened and strengthened. Candidates need to be taught to put God first in their prayers. "I have set God always before me." This is the method of the Prayer Book Collects, which almost always mention in the invocation some attribute of God's Nature or something God has done, to be a kind of meditation upon God Himself before we pray. In this they copy faithfully the Lord's Prayer: "Our Father, which art in Heaven."

It is essential that in some way this should be taken into their private prayer life, lest even in prayer self looms larger than God.

Here lies the importance of saying the Invocation and the subsequent silent realization of God's Presence. Added to this, they might find it a help to take some special attribute of God's Nature each day and meditate upon it before prayer, *e.g.* God's Power, Wisdom, Holiness, Truth, Righteousness, Mercy, Love. It is possible for acts of Praise, Penitence, Thanksgiving, Intercession, and Petition to be woven around these, and this is a great help in making the prayer-life, and with it the whole life, God-centred, which is our main object.

In some such way as this, or in making out a skeleton scheme for themselves of Thanksgiving, Intercession, and Petition for each day of the week around certain subjects, it is possible for candidates to learn to pray in their own words as well as by using set forms of prayer in a devotional book. This is essential for freedom of the spirit.

It is also urgent that the habit of reading the Bible should be recovered, not merely Bible-reading, but devotional Bible-reading, *i.e.* in the Presence of God with prayer. The Bible is God's word, the expression of God, the means He uses to speak to us. For the cultivation of our relationship with God it is at least as important that He should speak to us as that we should speak to Him. There must be on our part a listening ear, a spirit of receptiveness—" Speak, Lord, for Thy servant heareth." We have to be prepared to take time and trouble to attune our souls so that they can " listen-in " to God.

Candidates will need suitable prayers and help in drawing out the points in the meditation and in making the response of mind, heart, and will. For some years I had simple helps to meditation stylographed for candidates. These notes have now been published by the S.P.C.K. in their " Little Books on Religion " series. I mention this because this met a need, so far as I was concerned, and I feel it may do so for other priests. I do want, however, to put in a strong plea for definite care and teaching about Bible-reading, for this additional reason, that Grace and Truth must go together; both " came by Jesus Christ " and both are needed for that knowledge of God which is eternal life.

Time was when the Bible was read and the Sacraments were neglected; this produced a personal religion largely pragmatic and individualistic. To-day we have restored the sacramental life, but unless the knowledge of God in His holy word goes with it, I fear the last state will be worse than the first. Sacramentalism by itself is bound to develop into an unspiritual formalism which is the grave of any religion which has not an increasing spiritual apprehension of the mind, heart, and will of God. The open Bible and the Altar must go together.

(b) *Purity*.—It is probably best that the elements of this should be dealt with generally in class, but it is essential that the individual should be taught in private interviews, as great care must be taken to give the amount of instruction needed by each individual life. Here, if anywhere, tact and the personal touch are needed. For girls both the class on this subject and the private interviews should be in the hands of a woman. Indirectly in connexion with this the teaching about the opportunity of sacramental confession provided by the Church of England already given in class can be developed, and the practical need of the individual sounded.

(c) *Vocation*.—The whole question of service needs to be put most emphatically before the candidates towards the end of the preparation time. They must see that they are not God's favourites but His servants, that God calls them because He wants their service for the kingdom, and that it is in that service that they are to find their own salvation—a by-product of discipleship, as it were. They are to receive the lay priesthood of the Body of Christ, and priesthood implies sacrifice. They have to bear witness and to work for God in their daily lives, to be always on the watch for opportunities to extend His kingdom, and this they will find to be a big thing when they start to work it out. They must also be prepared to respond to calls for special work in the parish, and realize that such vocations must imply sacrifice of time, thought, and leisure. They will also understand that the privilege of a life vocation may come and have to be faced, whether in the ministry of priesthood or diaconate or in lay service.

The call of the world in the Mission Field gives a special direction for clear and definite teaching as to vocation in the Church of God. The gift of the Spirit is given that it may bear fruit, and the fruit is not for the tree of the individual life, but for the world. God gives in order that He may give again—through us. "Lord, what wouldst Thou have me to do ?"

3. *Retreats for Confirmation Candidates*

It is of the utmost help if the parish priest is able to take away his Confirmation candidates to a Retreat House and spend a week-end with them conducting a simple retreat. It will develop a sense of God-consciousness and so deepen the relationship between them and God; it will also intensify the sense of fellowship in the great adventure of the quest of the Spirit. It will make a retreat a natural and normal thing to them in the spiritual life, so that they will be far more ready to come for that spiritual refreshing which only a retreat can give in after years. It would be useful to have a few older ones with them also sharing their retreat. A Confirmation retreat will bring them into that spirit of faith and hope and expectation of God's manifestation and working which so clearly marked the first Christians who waited for Pentecost, and on the human side made possible that great outpouring of God, so that " they were all filled with the Holy Ghost." The world needs indeed an outpouring of the Spirit to-day; and the thoroughness with which our candidates are helped to prepare themselves for their individual Pentecost in the Laying-on of Hands may go further than we think in enabling God to supply our need, the need of the Church and of the world, for the Spirit of Light and Love and Life.

CHAPTER IV

PREPARATION IN THE PARISH (2)

By E. Grose Hodge

I. Our Aim

THE essential thing in any effort which is to be really effective is to have a very definite idea of what we are trying to do.

Throughout this chapter I have in my mind candidates of about fifteen years old. I believe that is normally the best age. When these young people come to us with all the splendid and awful possibilities of their lives just opening before them, what is to be our first and greatest hope for them? Surely their *conversion to God*—the definite decision of the will in response to the call of the Holy Spirit—the surrender of faith which accepts the life that Christ offers, and rejoices and rests in the possession of it. This must ever be our goal, the thing we pray for and work for and long for. But we have no right to refuse to present a candidate because we have no clear evidence of his conversion; first, because that would mean constituting ourselves judges of what God alone can *know*; and, secondly, because it is clear that the Prayer Book demands no such standard. We may, and must, demand proof of *earnestness* and of a *desire* for the Holy Spirit's help, as well as of a certain standard of knowledge, but we have no authority to insist upon more.

This standard of knowledge must be our second aim. Nothing could be more fatal than to make our teaching controversial, yet it must be of that definite and positive character that excludes error. The generous mind of the young resents denunciation, especially in the form of attacks on the beliefs of others; we shall save them best from false theology and from all the modern substitutes for Christianity by calling upon them to believe the truth *because it is true*, not because it is the exclusive possession of our own school of thought. Bishop Creighton used to maintain that most of us are right in what we believe but tend to be wrong in what we deny; so our safety lies in building up what is true and leaving the truth to drive out by its own expulsive force whatever is false in our children's religion.

But do not be afraid of dogma. People are afraid of it because they confuse it with dogmatism. Dogmatism says: "You must believe this because I tell you to." Dogma says: "Believe this because it is true." Dogma is only "truth packed tight for transmission," *e.g.* the clauses of the Creeds. It is worth some trouble to get the Catechism rooted in the memory of a boy, even if he does not understand it; and in this part of our work help may be wisely asked from parents and other good men and women.

We must somehow get over that odd conviction of the average Briton that religion is the one thing you can know without learning. Beware of over-subjectivity. It does matter what a boy feels or surmises, but probably not nearly so much as he thinks it matters. Our religion is faith founded on objective facts, and these include the spiritual as truly as the material. It is better to rely upon the word of Christ than upon any feeling we have about it. Aim at precision in your teaching. St. Paul repudiates with vigour the charge of ἄμετρα; he knew that both indifference and superstition thrive on vagueness. Ours must be unhesitating and positive teaching of what is true, that the young may be armed against erroneous suggestions. There is a quite common tendency among really religious people to be content with the moralities of the Gospel without any firm hold upon the great doctrines which are the only permanent basis of Christian morals. Beware of using the spiritual beauty of the religion of Jesus Christ as a means of appeal to the heart of a child, unless you remember that it will affect the child's life permanently only in so far as it has been shown to rest upon historic facts and to possess divine authority.

Lay then a good foundation of spiritual facts; but aim in the third place at making your facts glow—at *Inspiration*.

I believe anyone can teach who loves, and that if he loves he can hardly fail to inspire. It will be impossible for him to give confirmation " lectures " or to regard the young people who come to him only as a " class." The heart of the man who is before all else a pastor of the flock of Christ burns within him as bright young faces look up to him and make mute appeal for the best that he can give. He cannot be content that they can repeat formulæ, that they hold no unorthodox views, that they hope to go to heaven when they die; he must fire them with *love* which outstrips even faith and hope; he must take them out of themselves and so fasten their thoughts upon Christ that they see in Him the glorious Leader whom they long to follow, their Captain in the most splendid campaign in history.

We shall altogether fail if we allow our boys and girls to regard religion as a pleasant path along which they may saunter into heaven, or as an Assurance Society to make them safe for the future. It will not even interest them. But tell them that religion is a call to a great enterprise, that Confirmation is Christ's call to them personally to volunteer for active service, show them that God wants them, that even

> God cannot make Antonio Stradivari's violins
> Without Antonio,

let them see that God's service is not old-fashioned or dull, but always progressive, expansive, with elements of adventure and romance; make it clear that "Church work " will give the widest sphere for every gift and faculty they possess and bring a richer harvest for both them and God than any other work. Let them understand that their very youth specially qualifies them for doing much that cries out to be done; help them to start from their Confirmation with the enthusiasm of soldiers setting out on a great campaign in which, though they may lose a battle, there is no possibility of ultimate defeat.

I dwell upon this because all my experience has taught me that no form of self-interest, even the highest, will satisfy the chivalry of youth. We dare not make little of personal salvation—it is the first and most tremendous question for every individual, but it is purely preliminary ; salvation is not the goal, it is the starting-point of the really Christian life, it is qualification for the highest service.

II. Our Equipment

" Who is sufficient for these things ? " Who shall dare to undertake this most delicate and most precious work of preparing the young for Confirmation ? Surely only he who knows the power of the Gospel in his own heart and has felt it working in his own life. We cannot teach what we do not know, we cannot guide others along paths we have never trodden. All power to help the soul even of a single child must be won out of the conflicts of our own soul in the hours and days that are past.

There is something almost awful in the fact that our influence upon our class will be the influence of what we really are ; not of what the children think we are, not even of what we think we are ; not the influence which we try to exert : it will be simply the influence of the real man—the man as God sees him to be. It is a thought to give us pause, to send us to our room that we may re-examine our foundations and test again the conditions of our spiritual life, which must have so lasting an influence upon the critical work we are about to undertake.

But we must go to this work with a sense of hope and of victory, and our boys and girls must see and feel that that is our spirit. We can have it only by cultivating a very real and practical belief in the Holy Spirit. " Do you really believe," said the captain of the ship which took out Dr. Morrison, the first Protestant missionary to China, " that you are going to make any impression on the three hundred million Chinese ? " " No," said the great mis-sionary, " but God is." There is the secret of success—a distrust of ourselves which cannot make us despondent because we so confidently trust God.

Every time we come to our class let us remind ourselves (in the great phrase of a scientist of European reputation)

" I am here to help God." We shall then remember that these souls are God's, not ours, and that He is going to work in them; that we are here to help God to do His work, not that He is here to help us to do ours. So we are not daunted by dulness or despondent over our disappointments. God will do His work in His own way and in His own time, if we do not hinder Him.

I knew two men who both had the joy of leading not a few young people to definite decision for Christ. One had the highest honour the University of Cambridge could bestow, he had been Senior Wrangler in his year; the other had very little education, he was a carpenter. They were teachers in the same Sunday School; differing in almost every thing else they had this in common—a rather exceptionally vivid belief in the power of the Holy Spirit.

That is the great thing, but there are other things we shall ask God to give us. We shall have great need of a love which suffereth long and is kind; of a patience like His who stands at the door and knocks even when no one openeth; of forbearance which comes of sympathy and understanding; of a very sensitive Christian courtesy. We shall have little consideration for our own feelings, we shall not let them count at all; but we shall be very tender to the feelings of those to whom we speak, who often seem stupid merely because they are puzzled by the rush of new thoughts, and are not a little fearful of the possibilities opening up before them. We shall pray to be delivered from the palsy of custom and of phrases that have lost their meaning, from the dulness of conventionality, from the reserve which calls itself dignity. We shall want to be natural, cheerful, approachable, and very much in earnest, and to let the class feel that it is a splendid thing to be a Christian. Little by little the teacher is turned into the friend, hearts open their doors to admit him, and so the way is prepared for the Divine Friend to enter in and abide.

III. Our Method

I want to claim that the preparation of candidates for Confirmation is peculiarly the duty of the parochial clergy, and if circumstances compel us to allow some of our children to be prepared by others—whether clergy or laity—it should be regarded as exceptional and by no means ideal. Our difficulties in this matter are increasing ; the preparatory school claims some of our children at a very early age, and at thirteen or earlier they are public school boys. The holidays are spent away from home, and when they pass to the university our golden chance has gone. The one precious opportunity the parish priest had—the Confirmation class—when he could win the heart of the boy and make himself his friend for life, is being taken from him. Confirmation classes, of course necessary in boarding schools, are being increasingly held in church day schools, when the preparation is often undertaken by a clergyman from a distance who can have no personal knowledge of the children or their homes and who rarely sees them again when the classes are over.

In the public schools the preparation for Confirmation is much better than it used to be ; in fact in some of our great schools it could hardly be better. But let the parish priest see that he has a share in it whenever possible ; let him *beseech* parents to tell him when one of their children is being prepared for Confirmation, making the request from the pulpit, in the parish magazine, and privately.

He may then write to the boy a kind and cheerful letter, expressing thankfulness that he is coming out on the right side—not enclosing any printed matter on Confirmation. If possible let him tell him he is coming down to the next school match and will want him to give him tea. This is worth almost any effort. If he can get the boy to go for a walk with him, conversation will be much easier and confidence more readily won than in a room ; some of the best spiritual work I have ever done has been done sitting in the twilight on a field gate. With my own boys the request, " Let us sit on a gate, father," was almost synonymous with, " I want to have a talk about something."

There is much preparation to be done before the classes begin.

Arrange to have plenty of time ; it is abundantly worth while to give up many things for a time, even to the extent of giving notice that you must not be expected at committees, and that your regular visiting will be interrupted, so that you may visit the candidates and their parents.

I am writing only of populous parishes where the number of candidates is large. I have no knowledge of any others.

If candidates are to be many we must seek them out, we must cultivate them. I hope to see the day when every Sunday-school teacher will keep Confirmation before every scholar as the great, happy event to which he is looking forward, telling him, "You are a soldier in Christ's army now, but God has something more to give you, and He will give it when, in Confirmation, you volunteer for active service." Make Confirmation a privilege—a kind of spiritual coming of age.

We shall of course be completing a list of possible candidates all through the year; every member of the parish staff, lay and clerical, will have one, and their lists will be compared from time to time.

I earnestly urge that special attention be given to domestic servants in well-to-do parishes. They are often lonely, and have special temptations, and form the pastor's most difficult problem. I always send a letter to the lady in every household, enclosing a list of the classes : " Will you kindly put the enclosed list into the hands of your household staff, if you think it well to do so ? " I find that many are often glad to know of classes when their mistresses are willing to make it possible for them to attend. The response is very considerable, and often gives useful touch with the mistresses as well as with the maids.

Let us have consideration too for the unbaptized, and for the unconfirmed adult. Many are kept back by a sensitive fear of revealing that though they are " Church workers " they really are not members of the Church at all. Let us make it as easy for them as we may ; explain to them individually that the preparation for Baptism is the same as that for Confirmation, that there is a special class for adults only, just about to begin, which will be followed by a Baptism service for adults only, where others will stand with them. I always have this service at Evening

Prayer on a Sunday and take great pains with it ; it is a very moving sight to see quite old men and women confessing the mistake of a lifetime and coming to God openly to get it set right, and it has a salutary influence on the whole congregation, many of whom stand in sore need of its solemn reminder.

Do not fail to preach about Confirmation at both Morning and Evening Services on the Sunday before the classes begin. Take the whole congregation into your confidence as you take in hand this serious piece of work ; let them feel it is their business, and that it cannot be done without their care and prayer ; teach them simply what Confirmation means to the Church, and lead them to welcome these recruits as soldiers welcome reinforcements to an army preparing for advance.

Let the classes be many that they may be small ; serious, but cheerful and informal gatherings, Confirmation "talks" rather than "classes," where constraint gradually dies and the talking is not entirely from one. I am convinced that to a body of uneducated lads or girls a mere lecture is almost wholly useless ; they seem to be listening, but the understanding is not reached unless some mental effort is demanded from themselves. The methods of a good day-school teacher may well be followed. I strongly recommend a young curate to go often to the nearest church school and listen to, and watch, the head teacher as he gives the catechism lesson. He will learn far more (and probably the children will too) than if he always gives the lesson himself, and he will find out how knowledge may be pleasantly and effectively imparted even to the shyest and most stupid.

Let it be well understood that no one coming to the classes pledges himself in any way to be confirmed. He comes only to learn ; the question of Confirmation will be decided when the classes are over, and if he withdraws no one will resent it.

Encourage strongly the attendance of Godparents, Sunday-school teachers, friends—anyone in fact whom the candidate likes to have with him. We can hardly understand the difficulty our young people feel in doing anything alone; they crave above all the support of someone of their own age; let us help them to have it.

I have never been able to see why it is so generally insisted that names shall be sent in beforehand. Many whom we are most anxious to have write with difficulty; to make a formal application on paper is almost terrifying, and they often stay away because they cannot make up their minds to do it. I publish quite definitely that names need *not* be sent in beforehand, but candidates must try to come to the first class. There is plenty of time then for making all inquiries.

Nor is it well to insist that a candidate shall bring his own Bible and Prayer Book. To be seen with these on a week-day would make things hard for some who live very close to others in a crowded district. Let it be understood that you are glad to lend these to any who cannot bring their own.

You cannot expect the average candidate to take notes —he doesn't know how; but insist upon his having a pencil and a large-paged notebook (a lined exercise book is best) and dictate what he is to write. This is laborious work and takes up much time, but it is necessary; let the class read aloud what they have written and commit to memory the parts you indicate; call upon them to repeat them (not individually) at the class, and do not be troubled if some are silent.

I have not found it of much use to set a weekly paper of questions. To the trained mind it suggests school examinations, and is often resented as a task; and to the untrained it is frightening and offers no medium for the expression of their needs or feelings. But it is very valuable, just before the personal interviews, to ask for written answers to one or two simple questions—*e.g.* "Try to say fully why you wish to be confirmed." "Give me your own idea of a true Christian." "What do you undertake to do, and what does God do for you, in Confirmation?" "How are you going to try to witness for Christ and to work for Him?" The candidate brings the answers with him when he comes to see me and we talk them over together— it is a great help to us both.

It is unnecessary to say anything about the syllabus or course of instruction to be taken, because so many outlines of real excellence are published, and it is hardly possible— so widely do we differ in temperament and emphasis—for one man to choose for another. But, though you will probably begin by selecting one of these and keeping fairly closely to it, I would earnestly urge that you should make your own syllabus and take many years to make it. Revise your notes each year with pains and prayer; incorporate the experience gained in last year's classes, let your illustrations be new every year. Let even the foundation facts be reset, and so, while always reasserting old truths, preserve that freshness of thought and language without which you cannot win the ears of the young.

The number of classes will vary—I aim at ten, with one extra on the Communion Service after the Confirmation. Classes after Confirmation are not generally successful; it is difficult to get the candidates to come. Certainly no important part of the instruction should be left till then; it is better to gather them into guilds and clubs and so continue the training with the inspiration of a new start.

Insist upon regular attendance at the classes and advise the culpably irregular to postpone their Confirmation. We are bound to look for proof of earnestness; and to ask that all engagements, all attractive invitations that interfere with the classes, shall be put aside is not too high a standard.

Where there are many sets of classes it is well to keep to the same outline of teaching in each, and to let the same section of it be taught in every class each week; age, mental capacity, education, social position will all require separate consideration as we teach, but the syllabus may be much the same for all. It is a real gain to be able to tell a candidate who has missed his class on Tuesday to come that week on Thursday and to know that the sequence of his instruction will not be broken; it is helpful too for brothers and sisters in separate sets to be able to talk over the subject together.

It is perhaps necessary to refer to only three of the many special subjects about which it is desirable to talk in Confirmation classes.

(1) The sex question is commonly relegated to the private interviews. But if it is spoken of *only* then, is there not danger of it being regarded as a subject that shuns the light of day and is therefore essentially evil ? If it is never dealt with but in private, mystery and secrecy are suggested to the boy's mind and these always excite curiosity. The best way is to deal with the matter generally in class, to speak of it as one of the good provisions of God about which we need teaching as about His other gifts, only, from its special importance and delicacy, requiring reverent and watchful care. Dwell on the positive side as much as possible—the unspeakable gain of a pure mind in a pure body, " the authority of conscience—the blessing of Galahad, the love of parents, the joys of the old nursery life, the hope of some day being worthy to woo and win some good and gracious English girl, and of gathering round one in later life those same traditions of home and family that crown the happiness of the man, and make the strength of every noble nation and build higher the human race." [1]

(2) None will question that our aim should be to call forth clear witness and definite service for Christ—leading each candidate to regard himself as a soldier volunteering for active service and coming to receive his equipment ; do not let us forget that it must be for service *anywhere in the world*. We have to create in the boy's mind an enthusiasm for the Catholic Church as for something great and wide and unselfish, a Divine Society seeking nothing for itself, with no axe of its own to grind, with no self-created limitations—an outflowing force for truth and righteousness from Him who so loved *the world* that He gave His only Son to die that all men might live.

We are without excuse now if we do not make a missionary lesson interesting, the material is so rich and the appeal so compelling ; but we must not be content unless we altogether destroy in our candidate the idea that missionary work is an extra, the fad of a few, the hobby of those who are over-good and perhaps a little odd. He must come

[1] *Confirmation* by H. E. Luxmore. S.P.C.K. I strongly recommend the whole of this pamphlet.

to feel it is the central thing for which the Church was founded by Jesus Christ, and that no one has a right to call himself a Christian in any sense in which Christ would understand the word unless he is doing *something* for the extension of the kingdom of Christ. Such an effort as a necessary part of a young Christian's life is the great safeguard against stagnation, against that merely conventional religion which is more to be dreaded than many a heresy. Let the lad understand something of the darkness of the heathen world and enter ever so little into the wrong done to our Lord by the failure of His Church to let His light shine there—and he will have little patience with the exclusiveness of sects or with the waste and shame of party strife—he will learn to look through it all to the great world issues which wait upon the missionary cause and will rejoice to know he may have a share in this great adventure. Let us spare no pains to make him missionary-hearted, because if otherwise he cannot be Christ-hearted.

(3) We shall probably speak our last word about the Holy Communion at the class. We shall already have taught much about its history and doctrine and benefits, very necessary but not always attractive. I plead that we shall close on a somewhat different note, leaving a picture on the mind that our young people can love. I am accustomed to speak to my own candidates something as follows :

" The classes that have bound us together for many weeks are now closing ; in the nature of things we shall begin to separate, but though oceans may lie between us, we shall always have a divine bond in the Holy Communion. I think the disciples must have realized this aspect of the Sacred Feast keenly.

" They were with their much-loved Master in the upper room ; there was an undefined dread that they were going to lose Him. They watched Him and waited upon His words with particular intentness, they were sitting together at the Passover—that strange memorial of a great deliverance— and He took the passover cake and the wine and made them for ever the divine memorial of that greater deliverance which He was to work for all men upon the cross a few hours later.

"If we could in spirit enter into that upper room and feel as the disciples felt, and hear the Saviour's voice, and let the occasion teach us what His words really meant, I think we should know very nearly all there is to know about the Holy Communion.

"It was all very simple and very loving, and we shall gain from it full help only if we keep our thoughts about it simple and loving too. It was its connexion with the Lord Jesus that made the Holy Communion dear to the first disciples. It brought Him near to them; when things grew dim and shadowy, it made them clear and real again. It brought them the joy and strength of obedience; they loved to think that they were doing as He told them. They knew that He was present with them in that Sacrament, and that His presence meant imparted strength and fuller spiritual life; we do not wonder that very joyfully and regularly they obeyed His command: 'Do this in remembrance of Me.'

"Can you not understand how, when they met to break the bread and pour out the wine, the very action would recall that last never-to-be-forgotten Passover? It would bring back to them the very gestures used by the Lord, the tone of His voice when He spoke, the look upon His face. He had taught them that severed from Him they could do nothing. How thankful they must have been for this bond! It is clearly more than the bond of memory —to break the bread and pour out the wine would suffice for remembrance; but the command was 'eat,' 'drink,' surely to assure us that as bread and wine strengthen the body, so the Lord Christ Himself strengthens the spirit of all who rightly come to His Holy Table.

"So I come back to the thought with which I began —at the Holy Communion Christ is everything—we fix our attention upon Him alone. And as we have Communion with Him we have Communion with one another; we are closer together as we get closer to our common centre. Here all are equal, our differences disappear; we are all the Lord's guests, and that is enough to give us truest fellowship. Let us think of one another. We are bidden to a special audience with our King, let us use the opportunity to ask some divine favour for a friend, perhaps for one who never asks for himself. There must be no selfishness here—no better time can ever be for pastor and people to pray for each other—please pray for me."

The personal interviews. We shall not dare to enter upon these without prayer and self-preparation. No natural gifts will suffice for this solemn and critical work. We may have knowledge and tact, but if we have not spiritual insight and Christ-like sympathy and a patience that is more than courtesy we shall be of very little use. We shall need to remember that we have no right to force ourselves into the inner sanctuary of a lad's heart ; there must be no abrupt questions as if we had a right to demand an answer ; our Lord's personal dealing with the woman of Samaria is an exquisite example of the courtesy of a Christian teacher.

In our arrangements let us carefully avoid anything which suggests the surgeon's or dentist's consulting-room to which apprehensive patients are summoned one by one into the dreaded presence. Let the candidates come singly if possible, not meeting one another even on their way in or out. Give plenty of time to each—half an hour at least, and provide for the possibility of a long extension. I know I am asking what is exceedingly difficult, but it is a sore grief when at last the reserve gives way and the longed-for confidence pours forth, to have to break in upon it with, " I must go now." Never see more than three candidates consecutively ; it is extraordinarily difficult to remain fresh and spiritually alert, with power to throw yourself into another's life and mind if you do. You will find yourself saying the same thing to each, using almost exactly the same words, the mind becoming wooden and mechanical and the heart losing its power of free and natural response. I believe these personal talks are at once the most difficult and the most fruitful part of our whole ministry ; it is worth while to give up much else for a time, that they may not be hindered.

There must never be less than two—one when the classes are barely half over and one as they close. At the first try to get the lad to tell you something about himself ; let him understand that you are not an examiner trying to plough him, but a friend who wants to understand his point of view. Who has not nearly despaired before the dogged silence, the unmeaning smile, the mechanical " Yes " or " No " which is often the only answer to our first efforts at conversation ? I have found it useful to have a kitten in the room, a growing pot of bulbs, some object or picture of local interest to which attention can be drawn ; anything that will set our young people at ease may be used if it makes an opening for the real business on hand.

Try to find out, at this first meeting, about the family, the conditions under which the boy lives and works. Get him to tell you what he does on Sundays ; if he says his prayers, and when and how. Find out if he has been following your teaching, and encourage him to tell you if you have said anything he does not agree with. Do not be too much cast down if you find he does not remember a single word of all you have said ; it is very humiliating, but it is an experience known to the very best teachers ; the mind has not opened yet, but you are laying siege to it in the Master's name and you may find the gate noiselessly opening sooner than you think.

There must be testing in the Catechism of course— though with mercy, remembering that it is being " in- structed " in the Catechism, not saying it absolutely from memory, that is a condition of Confirmation. I have a great admiration for the Catechism, and would re-echo Charles Kingsley's words : " Ponder carefully a certain singular—I had almost said unique—educational document which, the oftener I read it, arouses in me more and more admiration ; not only for its theology, but for its knowledge of human nature ; and not only for what it does, but for what it does not, say ; I mean the Catechism of the Church of England."

The object of the first talk is briefly to find out where the boy is spiritually and mentally, what are the conditions of his life, his strong and weak points ; has he the beginnings of a desire to lead a Christian life ? He may be started on some simple devotion or encouraged to read a book we choose for him ; he may need to be warned to avoid some questionable company, at least as proof that he is trying to do his part. Make careful notes, but never make them in the boy's presence.

The second interview is the time for decision. Let the candidate understand that it is *his own* decision ; his Confirmation is a matter not between him and you or between him and his parents, but solely between him and God. For the first time he must take his life into his own hands and act and decide for himself. He has come to the parting of the ways and must now turn to the right or to the left—only he can decide which it shall be. We must ask, " Now that you know what Confirmation means, do you wish to be confirmed ? " and then we must press for an answer to the further question, " Why ? " Let him see that Confirmation is a real stage in his life, that he receives something that is real, and therefore it must make a difference. He cannot take his stand as a soldier of Christ, by his own will now as well as by Baptism, if he wishes still to belong to the enemy. We shall not be putting too heavy a burden upon him, because we shall point out that the question is not so much what he does as what he really wishes to do. He is not disqualified for Confirmation because he does wrong things—every boy does, often enough—for he is not on their side—he is sorry when he deserts Christ's side, and wants to be strengthened in his loyalty.

If confidences are given, thank God, but do not press for them ; they may bring serious difficulties for you and very likely be of no help to the boy. If you bring pressure to bear, the imaginative child, anxious to please, may even invent something to tell—I have known more than one case ; others are tempted to lie in order to conceal what fear or temperament makes it impossible for them to confess. By all means make opportunities and give every possible opening ; win confidence, if not confidences, by sympathy and understanding, and the tale of difficulties and failure and sin will not be often withheld by those whom the telling will help.

It would be mere evasion if I made no mention of confession in the ecclesiastical sense of the word. If we take the instruction of the Prayer Book at the close of the first exhortation to Holy Communion and keep within the limits of its spirit as well as of the letter, we shall do well. Frankly I find nothing here or anywhere in the Prayer Book or in the Bible resembling the Roman system of auricular confession. That is a highly specialized system, a discipline of absolute obligation, not exceptional but continuous, centred not in the comfort or the instruction of the troubled soul, but in the absolution pronounced by a *sacerdos*. It seems to me that the Prayer Book knows nothing of this, and that therefore it can have no place in our preparation for Confirmation.

It often happens that our advice is sought about the candidates' future work. Is it not part of our duty to turn the thoughts of properly qualified boys towards Holy Orders ? True it is that the call must be by the Holy Spirit—but may not we be the channel through which the Holy Spirit's call may come ? How did the call come to St. Peter ? Diffidence, misunderstanding, often keep a sensitive lad from turning his thoughts to the highest vocation of all. May we not say in some happy hour of confidential talk, " God has given you life, position, education, and you want to use them in the best way. Is there any sphere in which you can do it so well as in the Ministry of the Anglican Church ? It will mean enduring hardness, and sharing perhaps the burdens of the poor ; but there you will find free scope for every talent God has given you. It is a hard life often, but it is the freest, happiest, most expansive life on earth."

But teach him at the same time that he can serve God in any calling. It has often been said that the best missionaries in India are the high lay officials whose shining lives have borne daily witness to their Christian faith. Teach him that there is an intellectual service of the Church, of which there is a growing need. Teach him also that he serves God truly who seeks to remove the hindrances that keep men from Christ. On the bench of magistrates, on county and borough councils, on boards of guardians,

Christian gentlemen are needed to uphold justice, righteousness, and truth. He who will take pains to understand
what we call social questions and will act strongly, fearing
only God, may be helping in a high degree to extend the
kingdom of Christ on earth.

The interviews must not close without an endeavour
to pledge the candidate to definite Christian habits. I do
not mean that we should always extract a promise—I am
a little afraid of promises made under conditions which
might look like compulsion—but that we should enlist the
will and rouse a real intention. The Christian life is a
disciplined life, and Holy Communion and prayer and
services and Bible-reading and Sunday observance are of
immense value even as spiritual discipline. No one gets
any credit for these things, and they do not always seem
to be " doing us good " ; but, when a fall comes or interest
in the things of Christ dies, it will most often be due to
the neglect of these simple religious duties.

Something should be said about the duty of " giving."
We are foolishly shy about this and rarely mention it, lest
a suspicion be roused in the boy's mind that the Church
is after the loaves and fishes and that our object in bringing
him to Confirmation is not wholly spiritual. But we find
no such fears in God's methods of educating His people
in the Old Testament, or in our Lord's words, or in any
New Testament writer. Giving is not a matter of choice
but of obligation, it is an essential part of our religion ;
it is the most practical and often the most real test of our
sincerity. Rightly regarded, it is a sacred and sacramental
thing ; for money is not mere gold and silver ; it is coined
thought, coined work, coined strength, effort, sacrifice.
To give money is to give that which represents much that
is best and worthiest in us, or in our fathers, and is the
direct result and evidence of it. Giving is, to a Christian,
not only a necessity : it is a means of grace, never to be
separated from or counted lower than prayer, and worship,
and sacrament. Many of God's promises are conditioned
by it and, like mercy, it is " twice blessed."

It is not difficult to get a young lad or girl to understand this, especially if we explain *proportionate* giving. I

know a working man's family where one penny out of every shilling that comes into the house goes into what the family call " God's box " ; tips, casual earnings, presents to the children, all are included ; and the children are growing up with the belief that that penny really is God's, it does not belong to them at all, only He trusts them with the spending of it for Him.

It is well before the classes close to relieve the candidates' minds of little anxieties which occupy a larger share in their thoughts than we sometimes know. I always print a paper of " Suggestions " dealing with such things as the time and place of the Confirmation service, dress, the admission of friends, details about the first Communion, how to join our guilds, etc., and what we propose to do in the way of after-care. A copy is given to each candidate, and I go over it with the whole class.

We shall be watchful for opportunities to pray with our candidates. Do not make a rule to begin and end each interview with prayer. Prayer is often more helpful when it is the result of a need particularly and immediately felt. The invitation, " Let us ask God about it," is often the way to a real solution of a difficult point, and shows the candidate that you at least believe that prayer really " does things." Prayer *for* our candidates needs no mention —it is of first importance in their preparation and in our after-care for them.

The limits of space imposed upon this chapter compel the omission of much that might well be said, and necessitate a superficial treatment of much that has been included, but what I have written gives on the whole the line and methods which my own experience has convinced me are best. I do not think they are perfect—indeed, I revise them every year myself ; but I think they form a healthy stock out of which, in the hands of a keen young beginner in this sacred work, a better scheme may grow.

CHAPTER V

PREPARATION IN THE PARISH (3)

By Harold Ellis

Of all the opportunities given to a priest to convert souls, it is probably true that none can compare with the occasion of preparation for Confirmation. Even sickness or the near approach of death is as a rule less favourable, if for no other reason than that in these cases the necessary dispositions are too frequently the outcome of a temporary fear, whereas a candidate for Confirmation usually offers himself not only when he is sound in body, but also at the beginning of his life, before his will has become fixed in the direction of sin. He generally comes forward at the very period in which all that is lovely, chivalrous, and adventurous is beginning to make its strong appeal to his better self. Rarely could a pastor have a more fruitful soil in which to sow his seed, and never again in the history of any given soul will he have quite such an opportunity. Yet in spite of all this we have to confess that we do not manage to retain the active affection of a large number of our sons and daughters who pass through this period under our guidance. In other words, we are quite evidently not using to the full the golden opportunity which is ours during the time of the preparation of our children for Confirmation ; and if we are to remedy this defect in the future it can only be done by steadily facing the facts and learning the lessons which they have to teach.

How is it, then, that in spite of the renewed zeal which the Church has displayed during the last two generations in the matter of Confirmation there is a steady decrease, or, at the best, a standing still in the number of regular communicants ? Making every possible allowance for the general spirit of the age, for the pressing industrial factor and the like, we are in the end driven back to acknowledge that possibly the most powerful cause is to be found in the fact that our methods have been obsolete and faulty. This is not to cast reflection for a minute on all that has been done. Priests have laboured in this matter both zealously and untiringly. The truth is that we have been groping in the dark. We have recognized the uniqueness of the occasion, but we have never been quite clear in our own minds as to what we expected to be the immediate outcome of all our efforts in preparing Confirmation candidates, with the natural result that we have worked along uncertain lines and the issue has been unsatisfactory ; and if we are to advance it can only be by first getting clear in our minds what is to be the aim of all such preparation.

Roughly we may say that in the past there seem to have been three distinct schools working for three different ends. The most common is that school which has had for its object the imparting of Christian dogma. The adherents of this school have set out deliberately during these eight to twelve weeks of preparation to give to their candidates a bird's-eye view of the faith as a whole. For them it is instruction first and last. Yet the very moment we seriously examine this position it is easy to see how futile it must be. To imagine that it can be possible to give to the ordinary candidate in such a short space of time, that is to say, in ten to twelve hours at the most, a course of instruction in the whole faith which he can imbibe and assimilate is to overrate the capacities both of the ordinary priest and of the ordinary candidate ; and to undertake such a task is one of the surest ways to court disaster. Whatever else he may aim at, he is the wise priest who keeps all such instruction at a minimum. Some instruction of course there must be, but to make this the grand aim is useless. The correct procedure is to see to it that all those we are going to present for Confirmation have received the necessary lessons in the faith before they embark on the weeks of intensive preparation. Furthermore, if the Sunday School or Catechism fulfils its true function, it should be quite simple to make certain that those who are likely to be confirmed during the year are grouped together in the same classes for the purpose of hard, grinding instruction in the necessary Christian dogma. There will, however, still be some who present themselves who have not been through any Sunday School or similar institution, and in that case their instruction should come after Confirmation, when they should be placed in a Bible-class which the efficient priest is sure to have for the newly confirmed, and in which his lessons are always doctrinal and not merely hortatory. In such a scheme we need have no fear of our confirmed people not being well grounded in the faith.

The second school to which we refer is that which takes as its chief aim the whole range of Christian morality. To this the main object is merely to ensure good, clean living, and it aims at producing a glorified public school boy. No one can deny that in an age of lax morals teaching of this kind is essential, but to let it be the main plank of our Confirmation instruction is only to invite the candidate to imagine that to be a Christian is synonymous with being a " real white man." Such teaching does not give him a living love for an ever-abiding personal Saviour. To this we might add that, as a matter of fact, our boys and girls are taught very conscientiously in their various schools the need of such practical morality, and it seems hardly necessary to call them together for further emphasis by the priest of truths with which they are perfectly familiar.

There remains yet another and vastly more important school which makes conversion its sole aim. It is true that this must always be the great underlying aim of all preparation, but it is as well to examine it with a little more care. First, there are few nowadays who expect to see in the ordinary normal Christian anything in the nature of a sudden conversion. There are such cases, of course, but it is not usual for the average believer to experience any such crisis. Conversion, for most, is a gradual development spread over a long space of years and even sometimes life-long in its process. In addition, it is not easy to see how in the two or three months of preparation we are to tell that such a conversion has been wrought. What are the signs ? The act of presenting himself can certainly not be taken as such, except possibly in the case of an adult, as such a step is only too often the result of public opinion or of domestic pressure. And, if we see no such visible conversion, are we then to refuse the candidate ? Surely it would be more in accordance with the order of things to look for such conversion after the laying on of hands when the candidate has been strengthened by the outpouring of the Holy Spirit.

The truth would seem to be that none of these is in itself adequate expression of the most desirable aim for our preparation, and we would suggest that it should rather be *the inculcation of the practice of pious habits*—that is, to get the candidate regularly to practise certain pious habits which will enable him to stir up the gift that is in him and so eventually lead to the conversion of his soul. This will mean that henceforward, instead of allowing instruction to occupy the first place, we shall substitute what is vastly more important, Christian practice. Is it not here that in the past we have been so lamentably weak ? Our candidates have received at our hands such plain and careful teaching on the Christian creed as we were competent to give and they have gone from us quite convinced, it may be, of the truth of our Gospel, only to discover later on that they had not been told how to connect it all with their ordinary daily life. They have a confused recollection of the need of prayer, Communion, and the like, but they have not been sufficiently instructed in the wielding of those weapons. They know not how to pray ; they know not how to communicate with profit ; and being so unskilled they gradually give up trying, in sheer despair at their own incompetence. If, however, we have been careful during our preparation period to get them into the habit of prayer, Bible-reading, and worship, then we can claim by the time the Confirmation day comes round that we have at least set their feet on the rung of that ladder whose summit reaches to conversion.

The result of placing the inculcation of the practice of pious habits as the chief aim with which we work throws not a little light on the vexed and important question of the most suitable age of the candidate. When instruction

is our sole aim there is much to be said for a later age ;
but if we are to have the practice of certain habits as our
goal, then indeed it is no longer a debatable point, since
it becomes obvious in such a case that the chance of instill-
ing a habit is better when the mind is young than when
it has become more fixed and has perchance already
formed habits of a contrary nature, which must first be
rooted out before we can sow the good seed.   And this
it is for which we have always contended, that it is far
better to have candidates at a young age than at the
period of adolescence with the vast change it involves for
the individual both in the physical and economic area.
The old retort of, " He's not old enough to understand,"
may weigh when instruction is the ultimate object of our
preparation, but it entirely loses its force when the formation of pious habits is concerned.   The only question
then is :   Is he old enough to pray ?   to worship ?   or to
read his Bible ?   The answer to that suggests the right age
limit, and we know children are old enough to do these
things at a very tender age.

It is, however, of the very greatest importance that we
should grasp at the outset the full significance of what
such a change in the emphasis of the aim will mean to our
methods.   We can gauge it a little if we reflect on the
common procedure of to-day.   When a priest is instructing
a candidate in the faith he usually puts him for that purpose
in a class consisting of others of like age and sex ; but should
he wish to make sure of moving the candidate's will in a
certain direction and of ensuring that he will henceforth
practise a certain habit, he sees him alone, or, as we call it,
gives him a private interview.   For instance, this is almost
universally true of the conscientious priest with regard to
instruction in private prayer.   So, then, if our main aim
is to be the inculcation of certain habits, it follows that
for each of these there will be a private interview.   And
this is eminently true, since none of us can be certain of
moving the will of a given individual when addressing him
in class, as the arguments which appeal to one are impotent
in the case of another, and it will only be by individual
treatment that we can make certain of clinching the will.

This of necessity means that in the scheme of preparation of which we speak private interviews will be both frequent and of vastly more importance than the classes.

What, it may be pertinently asked, is the part that classes play in such a scheme ?   If individual interviews are to have the first place, would it not be wiser to have purely individual instruction throughout ?   Such a policy, however, is not to be commended.   Apart from the fact that, in any case with the young, there is always a very great nervousness about what is going to take place during the preparation—a nervousness which is somewhat alleviated when they find themselves in the company of other " victims "—classes have a very valuable part to play. In them the bonds of Christian fellowship should be formed and fostered.   It is a frequent complaint lodged against the Church that comradeship is unknown in her ranks ; at least we can see to it that our future communicants, by mixing together in classes for Confirmation instruction, do get a fair chance of knowing each other by face and name.   This would appear to argue that one large class would suffice ;   but actually this is undesirable.   While we assert on the one hand that instruction should be kept to a minimum during these weeks, yet there is that minimum to be given, and we must see that it is delivered in the most favourable conditions possible.   A large, unwieldy class does not provide such conditions, which are only obtained by a number of small classes consisting of from eight to twelve members.

To the composition of these classes the most careful consideration must be given.   It is not enough merely to grade the candidates according to sex and age, but there are also other factors for deliberation.   To separate two friends unnecessarily is the surest way to provoke discontent and to cause friction.   Where such separation is essential the parties concerned should be courteously told of the reasons.   If, in addition to all this, these various classes are at different stages in the instruction, much, at any rate in our large cities, is gained.   Frequently it happens that some candidate or other for various valid reasons is compelled to miss his weekly class, but if in the next week there is a class at which the instruction he should have received is being given, he can, by coming to that, be ready to take the proper lesson in his own class. And, too, all of us who have ever prepared Confirmation candidates have suffered at the hands of the late-comer who only comes to a decision when the instructions are well on the way—such a one is easily catered for if there is a class of the kind we have indicated, which, starting after the others, has not progressed far in the scheme.

Classes, then, of a small size, suitably graded, carefully composed, will be maintained and will form the background of the vastly more important work of the private interview which is to be the chief instrument in our hand. Here, however, we at once encounter difficulties. Our greatest obstacle lies in the fact that when we come to the task of interviewing we are left without guidance. In a well-organised parish it is common for the cleric in his first year to attend the Confirmation instructions given by some other able member of the staff, and in this fashion to get the experience he needs for the time when he too must start to instruct. Such a procedure is altogether impossible with an interview. Interviews are by their very nature private and confined to the priest and the candidate, so that we can never witness an interview in actual process. Yet to be left to the promptings of our mother-wit is an extremely dangerous experiment, for while it is quite true that interviews can do an enormous amount of good, it is equally true that misused they can work incalculable harm. An analogous case may be seen in the confessional. Here the priest sits in the dual capacity of judge and physician—his it is to pronounce the sentence of forgiveness and to give counsel for guidance. But it should be noticed that there it is quite possible to allow the office of physician to remain in abeyance. His first business in the sacrament of penance is to give absolution to the penitent and only secondarily to give advice. Yet we know from experience that it is essential that every confessor should have a sound training in the science of dealing with souls in order that he may be ready and fit to guide should occasion arise. In interviews, on the other hand, it is just this rôle of physician which the priest is called upon to fill, and if he is to prescribe healthfully for the needs of the candidate it is more than ever essential that he should have had a careful instruction in his science. For this purpose it becomes imperative that we should decide exactly as to the subjects on which interviews ought to be given.

Usually the sole advice given to the novice is, as we have already stated, that he should interview each candidate on the question of prayer and possibly on morality as well ; and this gives us the clue to the necessary matter. Briefly an interview should be given on every pious habit we are anxious to get the candidate to adopt before his Confirmation, and roughly these are prayer, worship, Bible-reading, almsgiving ; then follow interviews on Communion, service, meditation, intercessory prayer, to be given after Confirmation ; and to these we will return later. These are chosen as the habits absolutely necessary for a confirmed person, because they are the essential foundations of an enduring religion and because they feed and strengthen the love for a personal Saviour ; and if at the end of our preparation we have got our candidates to commit themselves to these practices we can rest happy that they are at the very least treading in the narrow way.

We have deliberately omitted from this list both confession before a priest and the whole subject of personal purity, and we have done so because, owing to the prejudice which still exists with regard to the former, and to the unhealthy secrecy which surrounds the second, we are convinced that the only wise policy in both these cases is to discuss them frankly and openly in a class rather than behind shut doors in an interview. With these we believe more is gained in the long run by public rather than by private instruction.

Even when we have finally selected the topics for interviews and after careful consideration have dovetailed them in with our course of instruction, it is not all plain sailing. Interviewing is a complex science and requires expert knowledge as to how to start and how to proceed. We must know how to set the nervous candidate at ease ; we must learn the difficult art of asking the right question at the right moment ; we must be clear how to deal with apparent irrelevancies which are certain to crop up ; and last, but not least, we must be experts at diagnosing the spiritual condition of our patients. This will mean that as our very first equipment we must be perfectly clear in our minds as to the exact aim of the interview in hand. This entails on our part the most careful and painstaking preparation. It is not the kind of thing we can leave to the last minute or to the happy inspiration of the hour. Failure in an interview is a serious disaster, for it means that we have put forward as forcibly as we can the desirability of the candidate adopting some given practice, and if at the end we have not persuaded him, then it is not too much to assert that his will has become more firmly entrenched in opposition, with less likelihood of its being reached in the future. In the same way, too, it is necessary that anything we say should be living. It must not be a case of enunciating with our lips truths we deny in our daily practice, or indeed we shall either fail to convince, or, being found out in our hypocrisy, we shall alienate the sympathy of the candidate. Personal practice, therefore, will strengthen or weaken the advice that is tendered ; and in a smaller degree, but none the less truly, the place in which the advice is given plays its part. It is not necessary here to discuss the problem of the most suitable place for a Confirmation class, but there is little doubt that those who have experience of the method of interviews would almost unanimously agree that, as far as males are concerned, the study is the most appropriate. Here it is possible, without any feeling of self-consciousness, to talk deeply or lightly, seriously or humorously. At the same time, since a man is always more truly himself in his own home, it gives the candidate a better opportunity of knowing him as he really is. These factors of person and place must be carefully balanced in all our plans for the interview, and equal thought should be bestowed on the frequency with which the candidate is seen. On the face of it this would seem to rest on two considerations—the number of interviews arranged for in our scheme and the number of candidates we are preparing. It is possible, however, to give some helpful suggestions. The ideal is to have as many interviews as classes—that is to say, one a week, always taking care that class and interview never fall on the same day. Failing the ideal, interviews should be given at least fortnightly. It is not necessary that any of them should be of great length, and, in fact, it is wisest to see that none of them exceeds the half-hour. Neither does this mean that the priest will himself be talking for all that time, since in a good interview it will be chiefly a matter of dialogue. Naturally in the early stages, when the candidate is nervous and uncertain of what it all means, the greater burden will fall on the priest; but, as the interviews progress and confidence returns, it should be a case of the candidate having nearly as much to say as the interviewer himself.

These means of the class and the interview are, as we have said, to be the chief instruments in the hand of the priest; and of the two the interview is to be by far the more important. The danger is that in spite of the excellency of our tool we should, through ignorance, misuse it and waste the opportunity. Much depends on how intimately we know the candidate and how we employ the knowledge we have. Assuming that at the beginning the candidate is little more than a name to us, it is obvious that we must set out at once to increase our knowledge of him. Let us repeat what we have already intimated, that the value of an interview is largely in proportion to our knowledge of the candidate, since on this hinges the whole and delicate issue of mutual confidence. It does not require much profound thought to see that any such knowledge is in the first instance most easily and surely gained by a visit to the home. Yet we must be on our guard. Too often the priest imagines that in one single visit he can obtain all the information he needs, and confining himself to that he deprives himself of a very valuable source of knowledge. Rarely is there anyone who has such an insight into the character of children as the parents, and although in the early stages they are tempted to make all their geese appear to be swans, yet if the priest perseveres in his visits, when the strangeness of his coming has at last worn off, they will often give him the very clue for which he has been seeking—some hidden difficulty that the candidate has, known only to those at home ; or some undesirable influence counteracting all his efforts ; or, better still, some new grace he has suddenly begun to display, which, when the priest knows, he will be able to foster by sound advice and practical hints. In short, the truth is he will get his best knowledge of his candidate from the home, and so it becomes an axiom of all good preparation to visit the home frequently, even as much as once a week. Side by side with this he must acquaint himself at first hand wherever possible with the conditions of his candidate's daily work. This is really essential if he is to help him to a practical religion for his daily life. Another valuable means of approach to the candidate's heart is a knowledge of and interest in his hobby. Most men and boys have some one interest to which they turn their attention when free from the claims of work, and if we can only use this, either for the purposes of illustration or even in a more direct way, we shall have achieved a great deal.

In these various ways we shall gradually garner a mass of detailed information, all of it capable of being put to good use, or liable to be lost unless we adopt careful methods to safeguard it. For this purpose we should employ to an extensive degree the ordinary card index system, and at the very first interview make sure to allot a card to each candidate, entering on it there and then his name, the date of birth, and particulars of his baptism. At each succeeding interview such other details as will help us to know our candidate better will also be jotted down on the card. It is of the utmost importance that none of these entries should be merely vague or general, but of a very definite and practical nature. For instance, it is of little use to note down that the candidate has difficulties in the matter of morning prayers, whilst it is of great value to state the number of times they were neglected during one week and how many the next. In fact, our card should be like a patient's thermometer chart indicating his progress and his relapses. The advantages of such a system are innumerable. The priest who makes a custom of reading over the card just before the interview can then be certain that he is dealing with the difficulties peculiar to the person in hand, and that he is not wasting his time in setting up some self-evolved bogy merely to knock it down. Again, anyone who tries the scheme of interviews on a large scale will very soon learn that the amount disposed of in an interview differs with each candidate, and so by entering on the card the point at which he left off he can next time take up his parable just exactly where he should without danger of omission or repetition.

Two cautions of a very important nature must be noted at this point—first, the card should always be entered up immediately after an interview, as the memory is a dangerous thing to trust when we are seeing many people ; and secondly, all these cards, owing to their very intimate nature, must always be kept under lock and key.

The relief that any such system affords when we come to decide the fitness of doubtful candidates is great, for, whatever our final decision, we have the satisfaction of knowing that it is the result, not of a heap of prejudices, but of a very careful observation. To those also who intercede for their candidates by name each day and are anxious to make these intercessions real and living such a card is of inestimable value.

All that has been written so far has been exclusively with a view to the priest who is preparing the candidate ; and, strange as it may sound, it is none the less true, that often, even when he has done his best, there are still doors in the human heart which are locked to him just because he is a priest, which will spring open only to the sympathetic touch of a lay friend. In order therefore that this obstruction may be removed the wise priest will do all that lies in his power to choose for the candidate the necessary lay friend. In very fact we are urged to this policy by our Prayer Book, since in the last rubric but one at the end of the Catechism these words occur : "And everyone shall have a Godfather, or a Godmother, as a witness of their Confirmation." Most commentators are agreed that this direction does not at all necessarily refer to one of the baptismal godparents, but may be, and more profitably would be, some fresh sponsor. It is very strange, when we consider it, how rarely this powerful influence for good is invoked by the parish priest. It is easy to see that as such an office is free from the customary traditions that surround the choice of godparents at Baptism, when it is left in the hands of the parents, who often make a careless if not a bad choice, the priest has in his hands the unique chance of choosing for each candidate a suitable and godly sponsor. And he who conscientiously prepares his candidates will see that at all costs he complies with the rubric. The circle from which the selection of sponsor should be made is obvious—it is of course from our faithful communicants, each of whom should be taught to look forward to the day when he will be chosen to be the godparent of a young communicant. But we must be on our guard against any haphazard choice. In every case effort must be made to pick out from the communicants the person we judge most likely to prove a real help to our candidate. Our selection is surer if during the preceding weeks we have gained a real knowledge of the candidate. Having discovered his weaknesses and his strong points we shall the more readily choose one who will supply his needs. Have we one who is going through life unloved and friendless? Then for him we look for the communicant most conspicuous for Christian sympathy. If we fear for another that he will be hampered by innate slackness, we shall choose for him a man of bracing, energetic character. The selection must be thoughtfully made and every step taken to see that there is never too great a discrepancy in either class or age between the sponsor and the godchild in order that there may spring up in time a healthy, godly friendship.

Confirmation godparents must, however, from the first be carefully instructed in their duties, so that the office shall never become a mere sinecure. Their privilege it is to intercede daily by name for their charge and really to wrestle for him at the throne of God in those crucial early years. They will tactfully and gently shepherd these young lambs, keeping a watchful eye on their religious practice—looking them up when they have been absent from worship; ensuring their attendance at guild or class; kneeling with

them at the foot of the cross confessing their sins ; and in a
thousand other little ways smoothing their path and sharing
their burdens. These also may fulfil the difficult but
necessary rôle of being the go-between 'twixt priest and
candidate, giving to the former many useful hints as to the
best way in which he can supply the help which is needed.
Above all, they will pour out a stream of unfailing encouragement, for lack of which many a young communicant has
given up in despair.

It may be as well in passing to point out that the scheme
we have suggested is not confined, in its advantages, to the
newly confirmed, but is of immense benefit to the sponsors
as well. Frequently we are nonplussed as to the best way
of employing lay help. The ordinary type of church work,
such as Sunday-school teaching, district visiting, serving
at the altar, or the like, does not appeal to all and sundry,
and at its best is confined in its extent. On the other hand,
there are few who will not respond to the definite supervision
of one inexperienced novice, while the very act of under-
taking such a responsibility helps them themselves to live
up to a higher standard than they otherwise would—for
the sake of the younger brother they abstain from acts which
would bring contempt on their religion. In like fashion
the office of sponsor broadens the sympathy of the ordinary
churchgoer and reveals to him the difficulties of those
outside his own narrow circle, and by so doing it tends to
bring back once again into our ranks the lost virtue of Christian fellowship.

As the weeks slip by we shall want our preparation to
become more and more intensive, and for this it is advisable towards the end to hold a quiet day or afternoon
for the candidates. Much will depend on local conditions,
and where it is possible it is undoubtedly best to give a
whole Sunday to this purpose. This would mean beginning
on the Saturday night with a preparation for the Sunday's
worship. The best and often quite practicable arrangements entail providing meals throughout the day in a
church building, and it is possible for one day in the year
to let the Sunday School either have a holiday or receive
its instruction in church, so that the class-rooms may be

free for the purpose of the Confirmation retreat. It is
also wiser to keep the retreat exclusively confined to the
Confirmation folk and not to turn it into a general parochial
one. The main difficulty lies in getting the aim of the
retreat clearly defined. This is best met by concentrating
on the double purpose of letting the candidates have an
opportunity of consecrating themselves to the service of
God and of forming in a practical shape a suitable rule of
life. To ensure this, quietness and silence are absolutely
necessary. Modern conditions are such that life is robbed
of those quiet moments so essential to the growth of the
spirit, and unless for this one day all talking is forbidden
the benefit of the retreat is largely lost. But it is just this
absolute silence which is the great difficulty ; it is so
hard to secure, at least with our younger candidates. It
may, however, be easily gained once the sponsors are
persuaded to make their retreat alongside of their godchildren, as they will then be able to attend to their needs ;
as, for instance, each can be responsible for taking his
charge for the necessary quiet walk. Care must be taken
not to overburden the day. Candidates should take their
part in the ordinary worship of the day—seats can easily
be roped off so that they can sit together—and if both
sermons, morning and night, are of such a character as to
be of particular help to them, they will benefit the rest of
the congregation as well. This will mean that two other
addresses, the first on Saturday night and the other on
Sunday afternoon, will be as much as will be required. All
these addresses must be strictly devotional, dealing with
such subjects as the great privileges which are about to be
conferred on the candidates ; closer communion with God ;
how to keep close to God ; and the encouragement to persevere. In all arrangements it is best, especially with the
young, not to leave them unprovided for in their spare times,
but to see that a cheerful room with plenty of comfortable
chairs and good picture-books is set apart for their use.
It is also a good plan if the priest can see each one separately
before the retreat and draw up a time-table suitable, as he
believes, to the condition of the particular person, containing
such things as times for private prayer, meditation, reading,

and walking. The whole retreat might be summed up at night by getting the candidates at the evening service in the presence of the congregation to renew their baptismal vows in a more detailed way than is done in the actual Confirmation Service.

In those parishes where a Sunday retreat is out of the question, then its place might be taken by a quiet afternoon on the free weekly holiday.

Hitherto attention has been focussed on the preparation of the candidate immediately before Confirmation, but the months immediately following are perhaps even more important. It has been too common in the past for priests to imagine that their work is done with Confirmation, and that all that is required afterwards is to group the new communicants into guilds or similar associations, which meet only occasionally. A little thought will quickly convince us how mischievous is any such idea. The crucial testing time is after Confirmation. We have until now had the candidate under the most favourable conditions, and once the Confirmation is over the candidate has to translate all he has learnt into the terms of every-day life without the bracing atmosphere which surrounded him during the time of his preparation. Not often does he maintain the enthusiasm which was his then, and in any case his ardour is often damped by the sharpness of the conflict and by the experience of many falls. He had hoped for so much as the result of his Confirmation, only to discover that he is not really any better than he was formerly, and with an incredible ease he begins to drop many of the habits he was learning to practise, and gradually but surely slips back into his old self. Ordinarily he no longer meets his priest in that intimate way which he did during his preparation. There is no longer any interview to help him to pull himself together, to encourage and inspire him, and in sheer despair of ever making any headway he finally gives up. It is useless to imagine that of his own free will he will come and tell us of his failures. However intimately we may have known him he is usually too ashamed of his weakness and too uncertain how we shall take it.

The only hope and help lies in the continuance of the

interview. Truly if every one of our young communicants were regular and frequent penitents then indeed we might through the sacrament of penance give the assistance they need ; but as in many cases this ideal does not exist, we do well after Confirmation to continue interviews similar to those we gave before. They need not now be as frequent as formerly. We suggested that during the actual preparation they should be weekly or at the very least fortnightly. Now the need is met if they come once a month in the first year and perhaps once a quarter in the second. If these interviews form part of our scheme they will help to a very large degree to relieve the pressure which is generally felt during the preparation. There will be many important matters which cannot be adequately dealt with then, but which can be expanded and pressed home in an interview after Confirmation. There are always some candidates who are slower of apprehension, who yet, by the very nature of the case, have to keep abreast of their fellows in the class, and these need simpler instruction, which can best be given in interviews after Confirmation. Above all, however carefully we may instruct and interview in the weeks of preparation, there must always be a number of very desirable pious habits waiting to be practised which we have deliberately held back for fear of overweighting the candidate. Assuming that we have already given interviews on prayer, worship, Bible-reading, almsgiving, Communion, and other such matters—and it is as well to state that some of these need more than one interview—we cannot rest content until we have pushed home and got our communicants to practise such things as systematic intercession, ejaculatory prayer, meditation, mortification, service, and similar habits. All these can quite well, and much more profitably, be taught when the Confirmation itself is over. Lack of this kind of post-Confirmation supervision is largely responsible for the leakage in our churches. To leave the young communicant so suddenly to his own devices, and that after a special period of intense enthusiasm, without giving him a helping hand in the hour of reaction which is as certain to come as that night follows day, is the surest way of alienating his allegiance.

Our last word must be concerned with a criticism which is certain to be laid against our scheme. How, it will be asked, can such individual guidance be given in those parishes where one priest prepares single-handed a large batch of candidates? The answer is simple. It is impossible. Gone for ever under this scheme are those sketchy preparations given to fifty or seventy persons by one man. Our plan supposes thirty-five at the outside. But we would ask a question in return: Where are the fifties and seventies to-day who were prepared in accordance with the older method? Not, we venture to suggest, in our thinly filled churches or on our stationary communicants' roll. In places where there are large numbers offering themselves for preparation, the difficulty can be solved by having two periods at different times of the year for classes and interviews—one exclusively for adults, and the other for the young. In any case we prefer at all costs to concentrate on individual and intensive preparation rather than on extensive and mass instruction.

CHAPTER VI

PREPARATION IN THE SCHOOL (1)

By W. W. Vaughan

The writer of this article is conscious that others can speak of Confirmation with far greater authority than he would ever wish to claim. What authority he has has never been conferred on him. So far as it has been won it has been won by stumbling through the school of experience ; it has been learnt from many who never looked upon themselves as teachers ; learnt by mistakes made at times, alas ! at the expense of others ; learnt in those rare moments when there seems to be perfect communion between the human soul and some divine spirit. He is conscious, too, that there is an infinite number of ways of preparing for Confirmation, some good for one boy, some for another ; some possible for one man, some for another. By a blessed arrangement to be met with in the religious as well as in the intellectual world the way must be a very bad one from which the boy can get no help. And perhaps it is well for the pride of the teacher and inspiring to the efforts of the learner to know that the real work is to be done by the candidate himself. No one can prepare him for Confirmation ; he alone can prepare himself, by wrestling with his own temptations, by liberating his own thoughts from all that bears them down, and by groping daily after the light that shines ahead. Help can be given, guidance can be given, but both need more than the co-operation of the candidate. They need his willing and spontaneous efforts, and no greater disservice could be done him than to create the belief that any one or any number of human beings can relieve him of the necessity of making those himself.

This paper has in view boys who are to be prepared for Confirmation and confirmed at their public school when

about fifteen years of age. It is realized that there is
something to be said for Confirmation at an earlier age,
but the arguments for the later age seem to the writer
conclusive. They are, put shortly, that the younger boy
is less able to appreciate the problems that are brought
before him at Confirmation : he has not yet had to face
some of the moral difficulties which he will have to face
later ; he has not yet been taught to stand on his own,
as he is taught later ; his mental development is not of a
kind to enable him to appreciate the problems of faith and
responsibility. All he can do is to accept with docility—
charming docility, no doubt—what he is told. Words of
grave import will have little meaning for him, though he
will be prepared to accept the meaning that is put upon
them by others. The argument that it is important to
confirm boys before they go out from the shelter of the
school does not seem to apply to those boys whose education
is to go on till eighteen or nineteen. It is quite true that
many boys, before puberty, are spiritually inclined, and it
is right that their spiritual needs should at that time be
provided for. But they are spiritual needs of a totally
different kind from those that arise in later years.

If it is to be during a boy's public-school career that he is
to be confirmed, what is the best time then ? It is well
to wait till the first year of his school life has passed, for
two reasons. One is that during his first few terms he has
so much to learn. He is face to face with a bewildering
crowd of new experiences. These distract him and do
definitely make it harder for him to seize the greater
experience that Confirmation offers. Again, after a year
has elapsed he knows where he is ; where he can get help
from his school life ; from whom he can get it. He is
better known to the masters who will be concerned with
his preparation. He trusts them more than he possibly
can do when he first comes. He has made some friends, and
those friends, being of his own age, will probably be confirmed with him. He has, through his letters, by this time
given his parents some idea of the environment in which
he is passing his life. He has also thought more about the
possible future ; he is less likely to be hampered in his

preparation by small illnesses ; he has gained a certain stability of character which comes to boys about the time they are fifteen.

Experience moves me to think that fifteen is the best age for Confirmation. And there is some considerable gain if all the boys who are going to be confirmed are about the same age. Now and then a boy is very young for his age and has to be considered younger than his birth certificate shows. Now and then he is very old for his age, and has to be considered older than the age ascribed to him. But for these special cases special arrangements can be made. In what follows it is assumed, then, that boys are confirmed about the age of fifteen.

The first problem that arises is what is the best way of bringing to the mind of possible candidates the opportunity for Confirmation. Here, and indeed all through, it is right to discard the policy of " safety first." It is better that some boys should miss the opportunity in any given year, or perhaps miss it altogether at school, than that the whole school should feel that Confirmation is part of the school routine from which there is no escape and into which boys are carefully shepherded by persuasion if they are not attracted of their own free will. It is probably desirable that house masters should keep a list of boys who have been confirmed, and it is possible for them to do a good deal by communicating with parents of boys who, they think, ought to be confirmed, but the less pressure brought on the individual the better. One plan is to give out, towards the end of the term previous to Confirmation, that a Confirmation is to be held, and to ask all those who are about the age settled on, and who have not yet been confirmed, to think it over and to talk it over during the holidays with their parents. This gives the head master an occasion for setting forth quite generally the sort of considerations which should influence possible candidates. Boys are sheep. They also want to do what is right, and there is always a chance of some boys deciding to be candidates for no very good reason, though the fact that others that they respect are doing something is not to be looked upon as a bad reason. Almost every year it will be found that there are some boys who are uncertain as to whether they want to be confirmed or not. This may be due to the fact that their parents are not members of the Church of England, or that they themselves feel some doubts about it. In both cases it is advisable to let the boys attend Confirmation lectures and go on with the preparation without feeling themselves pledged to Confirmation. Most, in such circumstances, are eventually confirmed, but even those who decide against it probably gain some good from having realized that there is a problem and having had to make up their mind about it.

The practice as to who is to be responsible for preparation varies in different schools. What is described here has been tried at more than one school. It has its advantages certainly, and probably some disadvantages. It is that the head master, whether he is in Holy Orders or whether he is a layman, should be ultimately responsible, calling in the best help available. Some people are shocked at the idea of a layman being so responsible, but a layman who is head master of a public school must assume some pastoral responsibilities. He generally holds a licence from the Bishop of the diocese, and even if at first he finds it very difficult, and never finds it very easy, to help in the spiritual life of the school, he will, as time goes on, feel how greatly he is himself helped by so doing, and how his power of helping others increases by any effort that he makes in this direction. One great advantage of the head master's assuming this responsibility is that he, presumably, knows more about all the boys in the school than any one other master. He may not know so much about any individual as his house master, but he is, in a peculiar way, in touch with the moral, intellectual, and religious life of the whole school; if he has paid attention to their reports he knows something about the character of each boy, and if he is vigilant he knows something about the attitude of each boy towards religion, so far as an outsider can ever know this. The opportunity, too, that is given him of knowing the school is of great value. He is able to follow the boy for the rest of his school career with added interest. He is sometimes able to help him

because of the bond that has been formed between him
and the boy at Confirmation-time.

But head masters have only a limited amount of time
available, and it is obvious that they cannot do all that is
required for a boy. The house master or the house tutor
should also co-operate, and a form of co-operation which
seems most natural to me is that of making sure that the
boy knows and understands the Catechism. The Catechism
is still a splendid instrument in religious and moral education.
There are expressions in it that want explaining to the boy.
Its attitude wants applying to the boy's ordinary life.
It is good for the boy to learn it by heart, for the intellectual
effort is of some value, but a wise house master knows that
learning by heart in the case of a boy who finds all
memorizing difficult should be interpreted reasonably, and
absolutely verbal accuracy should not be insisted on.
When the head master is a layman, and the house master
possibly one too, it is important that a master in Holy
Orders should take some part in the preparation. The
reasons for this are two : one, that such a master can speak
with authority on certain subjects, where a layman is
inclined to hesitate, and it is well for each candidate to have
an opportunity of consulting the expert over any difficulties
that may occur to him. The co-operation, too, between
the layman and the clergyman on this occasion puts the
whole problem to the boy in its right aspect, and prevents
him from looking upon religion as being in a watertight
compartment separate from the rest of his life, and yet
makes him realize that it has to do with issues wider and
deeper than those which ordinarily concern him.

Assuming that the house master is responsible for the
Catechism, that the chaplain or master in Orders is to be
responsible for the more dogmatic part of religious teaching,
there is still a wide field which the head master can treat in
lectures to all the candidates. The Confirmation Service
lends itself to subjects for such lectures. Short though it
is, it gives just the right and natural opportunity for talking
about conduct, spiritual life, our mutual responsibilities,
our relations with God, our difficulties, Holy Communion,
the importance of religious growth throughout life, and

countless other subjects which must depend to a certain
extent on the individual's choice. In these lectures
difficulties should be faced ; there should be plain speaking
on all subjects. Anything like religious jargon should be
avoided. On the other hand, many boys are offended by
the colloquial treatment of sacred subjects. In little ways
that will suggest themselves to anybody engaged in this
work, the time of this lecture may be made to seem a time of
co-operation. It should, if possible, be given in the
school chapel. Attendance at it should be looked upon
as dwarfing in importance all other engagements. When
a boy misses a lecture through ill-health, the gist of it should
be given him individually on some other occasion. School
work should not be excused for it. It will be found that
boys respond readily to this. Though I daresay they often
find these lectures inconvenient, they are extremely conscientious in attending them punctually, and genuinely
disturbed if from some carelessness—which does sometimes
happen—they miss one.

But the head master should not consider that the work
will be done by lectures alone. He should see each candidate alone in the last month before Confirmation. Of this
interview it is impossible to exaggerate the importance or the
difficulty. Some masters have the gift of interviewing ;
some boys have the gift of being interviewed. Both are
presumably to be envied, but it is possible to be misled by the
facility with which an interview passes off, and an uneasy
feeling has often been left in my mind that the interviews
apparently most successful have left the least impression on
the boy concerned. One thing is quite certain, that almost
every boy has to be approached in a different way. There
are very few rules that can be laid down as guides. One
certainly is that it is far better to have the interview sitting
round the fire than sitting round a table in any formal way.
There should be no sense of hurry, even though for obvious
reasons a fixed time has to be allowed to each interview. Only a certain number of interviews should be held
on each day, as it is so easy for the interviewer to get tired.
When he is tired, he is tempted to be perfunctory and
sometimes, against his will, lacking in sympathy. The

plunge into serious talk is not easy. I am conscious of often having shivered on the commonplace brink too long. But a plunge into the deeper questions very often disconcerts the boy who would otherwise be quite willing to talk. It seems of the utmost importance that in these interviews all attempts at cross-examination should be avoided. Some head masters have boasted that they have found out a great deal about the school at Confirmation times. It is almost a shameful boast. One well-known head master, at an early stage of the interview, always asked the boy what his besetting sin or fault was. It was only when one year he received almost uniformly the answer that it was " smoking on the roof " that he began to suspect that his method might not be the best way of getting at the truth and helping those whom he wished to help. It is better to sit in silence than to make the boy feel that the time is to be used to turn his soul inside-out or to discover his delinquencies. I suppose we are all tempted, when we are pressed, to confess to something, and if we can, we confess to something that is comparatively respectable. But it is not the comparatively respectable things that really trouble the human soul. The interviewer must be prepared to receive benefits as well as to give them. Indeed, he will be a poor sort of creature if he does not think, after all the interviews of Confirmation are over, that he has gained much more than he has given. Surprising misunderstandings often come to light—misunderstandings of the words of the Prayer Book, or the Bible, or of something said in the lectures—and every now and then there are flashes of insight revealed that light up many of the difficulties that always haunt the religious questioner.

It is quite likely that the master will have to do most of the talking. That is not necessarily wrong, as long as he does not talk too dogmatically. It is unnecessary to say that sincerity is even more important at the interview than at any other time. It is probably a mistake to have any definite scheme for the interviews. Boys tend to compare notes, and even to prepare one another, in a friendly and not in an irreverent way, for the questions that may be put. When this is noticed, it is a warning against stereotyped questions. It is advisable to get all the interviews over some few days before Confirmation. There is great gain in the boys having the last few days before their Confirmation free of interviews, lectures, or other special teaching. A period of peace, even though it may be carelessly employed by the carelessly minded, is of the utmost value to those who wish to think. There is a danger of the opportunities of thought, that are bound to occur on Confirmation day, being occupied only by some comparatively trivial question that may have arisen on the eve of the Confirmation, whereas if a few days elapse between the interviews and the Confirmation, thoughts settle down in the mind and things assume their right proportion.

Every now and then the question arises as to how to treat a boy wisely who has been guilty of some fault that indicates disregard of the teaching that he has received, or a carelessness about the importance of the whole question. Each case must, of course, be treated on its merits, but harm is done to all who are being confirmed if any at all shameful fault is condoned and a boy is confirmed in spite of it.

It would not be right to leave the question of preparation without dwelling on the importance of getting the whole school to co-operate to help those about to be confirmed. A prayer for the confirmed is of some use. Those who have already been confirmed should be challenged to prove to the recruits the value of the benefits they have received. All attempts to raise the level of conduct and industry in the school during this term make the task of those who are going to be confirmed easier.

Two details in connexion with Confirmation are worth attention. One is the best time of year for it, and the other is the best day in the week. Experience makes me feel that the Advent term is a better term than the Easter term. Lent gives a natural opportunity for stimulating the religious life of the school, and it is a pity to confuse preparation for Confirmation in any way with Lent, or even a boy's first Communion with Easter Sunday. The Advent term has other advantages, in that it is less often disturbed by illness, and the Advent season seems specially appropriate for the Confirmation itself.

There are, I know, objections to Confirmation being held on a Saturday, but they are outweighed, I think, by the fact that this day is much the most convenient day for parents as a whole, especially for fathers. Further, it enables parents to stay for the Sunday and to accompany their sons to their first Communion. This is of inestimable benefit to the boy, binding him most naturally to his parents at a critical time, and relieving him of a good deal of the strain and nervousness which he is likely to feel on such an occasion. It may be felt by some that the Sunday follows the Confirmation day too closely; but it is worth sacrificing the small advantage of a longer interval between the two to the greater advantage of having the parent and the boy close together at such a time. All arrangements for that Sunday should be made to suit the boy's parents, who are most specially concerned, and to mark the day as one of unusual importance in the life not only of the individual boy but of the school as a whole. If the Bishop of the diocese can stay to celebrate or to help in the administration of the Communion, and to preach, so much the better. His presence at a school at such a time is of peculiar value. The boys recognize that he has spoken to them as a human being, as well as an ecclesiastical dignitary, and that his care for their spiritual welfare is not confined to what he can do for them at the Confirmation Service itself. If he can spare the time to address the parents alone, so much the better. The boys are sure to be moved at such a moment. The parents can be moved too, and very much moved, by even a very short address, which would be appropriate to them as a body and not to the whole congregation assembled for the Confirmation. In the years following the Confirmation the parents' attitude towards it will make a great difference to the boy. All parents wish to help their sons on such an occasion, but we have not all the skill to do so. The Bishop's experience can help us, and has, I know, helped very many. The Confirmation Service itself gains by being short. Boys feel the strain more than we grown-ups know. They want to attend, but it is very hard to attend to long discourses, however eloquent and forcible they may be.

There is no time to follow up the interesting question that arises in connexion with the ecclesiastical side of Confirmation. Perhaps this is well, for its history, the different views held about it now, the historical, archæological, and controversial details might well crowd out more vital but less tangible problems. Still, it is right for the candidate to understand that Baptism and Confirmation were originally one ceremony, that the ceremony is the door to full citizenship of the Church, that there are many branches of the Christian Church, each to be judged by its fruits, that the need for a Church is at least as urgent as the need for government within the State, that the effective and inspiring power of a Church depends on its members, and that all its members must humbly claim and proudly fulfil the privilege of working for it.

It may be helpful, while avoiding controversy, to explain very shortly how this English Church of ours came into existence and how it has been re-fashioned, how in the re-fashioning it lost some of its members, and how, even now, it is divided, sadly divided, into parties, differing in their views of Church government, in their interpretation of Church history, in their observance of ceremonies, sometimes even in their explanation of the Creeds, but united, gloriously united, in their wish to make men's lives more worthy of their Founder, to make His teaching known to other men, and to co-operate in ministering to the material needs of suffering mankind.

The consideration of the Commandments leads very naturally to the facing of many moral questions. To take only a few examples, the Seventh Commandment has no meaning for the boy until he realizes that behind the deed lies the thought, and the thought in this case includes all impurity, with consequent speech or action. Here arises an opportunity for saying something about the sexual temptations that come to boyhood and stay through manhood. And this very difficult subject, dwelt on sometimes too frequently at Confirmation time, can now meet with a healthy, frank, and limited treatment and need not colour too exclusively a boy's ideas of Confirmation.

" Thou shalt do no murder " seems at first very far from

boyhood, but murderously angry thoughts do enter the minds of young and old alike. Unkindness and bullying, against which the commandment warns us, are the special temptations of one stage of adolescence, but they are not unknown in regiment and office, in factory and workshop, in ship and shop, and even in society in a small provincial town. We all need to pray for mercy in this, and that our hearts may be inclined to keep the law of kindness.

It is equally important for us to be brought face to face with the commandment not to steal. In a boyish community few thoughts are more sternly repudiated. None are so relentlessly revealed as the stealing of money. And this same horror of one sort of fault runs right through the lives of men and women. But dishonesty needs explaining in all its hundred guises. Cheating in school, pilfering, the scamping of work, the taking of secret commissions, the outwitting of the tax-collector, the defrauding of the railway company, are widely tolerated, and sometimes even boasted of, and they are all evidences of the ease with which we escape from the obligations of the commandment by giving it too narrow a significance.

All the commandments lend themselves to some such treatment. Preparation for Confirmation thus gives a splendid opportunity for talking over values in a way that cannot be used in the pulpit, of testing them in the light of our Lord's example, of getting rid of those that are false, and of establishing new and merciless tests that would penetrate most pharisaical defences. It should be pointed out that until all the lumber of false values, the obstruction of false choices, be cleared away, the heart cannot be pure enough to see God and to begin to win for itself spiritual communion with Him. Now and again men and women can, even in the midst of sin, keep contact with spiritual motives and spiritual hopes. But these are exceptional people. Whether they are to be called blessed or cursed is not quite certain. Most of us are barred from the spiritual world by selfish, or sensual, or even careless conduct. We need, therefore, to purge our lives, but it is dangerous to purge them to emptiness without filling them with high purposes. And for our purposes to be high we do need religion, the binding force of Creeds and the support they give us in times when the storm of temptation rages, or when for some reason or other we are disheartened. And so, just as the moral issues merge into the spiritual, spirituality itself depends in no small degree on the faith, the Creed, that men may have. And at Confirmation time there is an opportunity, unique, perhaps, but certainly one that does not so naturally recur, of discussing the difficulties and the blessings of the Creed.

The blessings cannot be enjoyed unless the difficulties be faced, and never will the atmosphere be more conducive to facing them reverently and humbly than at Confirmation. A moral effort is being made, and so the risk of diluting the strength of the Creeds, merely to meet the desires that seem to war against them, is diminished. At such a time the hard, and not the easy, path is likely to be chosen. Care must be taken to guard against it being a thorny path, too, and for many it has been a very thorny path that has had to be trodden between Confirmation and, say, the age of twenty-five, when a man begins again to master his doubts by interpreting them in the light of his enlarged experience. Some in disgust leave the path of faith altogether for a time ; not a few never return to it. The plea here is that the mind should be prepared against the stress of later doubts by being told how they have assailed countless men, wherein their potency lies, and on what lines a reasonable faith can be reconstructed.

Perhaps the first task of all is to make clear the history of the Creeds and Articles ; how they were human efforts to meet temporary emergencies ; efforts made by man's fallible mind, under Divine guidance no doubt, but human all the same, and liable to human error, needing to be re-interpreted in the light of enlarged knowledge. In con-nexion with Confirmation it is, mercifully, not necessary to deal with the Thirty-nine Articles. Nor need the Athanasian Creed be any longer a stumbling-block. But certain articles of the other Creeds, perhaps because of our limited experience, do seem to presuppose a view of the universe that has long been abandoned and is soon dis-covered by the intelligent schoolboy, as he gathers knowledge of physics, biology, and astronomy, to be absurd and contrary to truth. Unless this has been faced by his teachers he will receive a shock only comparable to that awaiting him when he first discovers the gulf between Christian teaching and Christian practice.

Out of the history of the Creeds will grow, quite naturally, a discussion of them. Any given explanation may still be far from the truth, but if nothing is said about the Incarnation, the descent into hell, the Ascension, the resurrection of the body, these expressions will either remain meaningless, or will some day soon create a disastrous disturbance in growing minds. It is surely not selfish for the old to wish to spare the young some of the pain they have gone through to themselves, to remove from their path the thorns that have torn their feet. And yet there is a conspiracy of silence that is perhaps excusable in the pulpit, where there is no time for full explanation and great risk of misunderstanding, but is surely inexcusable at Confirmation time, when opportunity can be made and difficulties explored without being dogmatically solved.

Almost as urgent is the need for facing the question of prayer. Without any rigid limitation of its power the selfishness of so many prayers can be pointed out ; the duty of making thought a part of prayer can be insisted on. A prayer for purity does not diminish the stock of purity available ; rather it increases it immeasurably. And so with all moral and spiritual blessings. Prayers for these may fruitfully be compared with prayers for material benefits, of which the supply may be limited. The raising of such subjects only takes the candidate to the threshold of the problem of prayer, but it does set him thinking, and the thought begun may end in his understanding why our Lord's Prayer, with its one simple material petition for daily bread, should be the model for our prayers. So life may be enriched by the use of prayer hardly dreamt of by many.

From this it is comparatively easy to pass on to what is after all the object of Confirmation, being the aim of all religious life—right living according to the will of Christ for us ; not what Christ willed for His immediate disciples ;

not what He willed for the inhabitants of uncrowded Palestine two thousand years ago, but what He wills for us now, at schools in England, and later perhaps in some distant land. The imagination must make some leap, and it needs to be liberated for the purpose, liberated from all sorts of respectable restraints, from the idea of Christ and His surroundings set out in stained-glass windows and religious pictures, helpful so far as they are beautiful, but too often culs-de-sac for our imagination and our thoughts ; liberated from many of the ideas set out in the hymns and in well-meaning books.

Not the least potent argument for holding Confirmation at the public school is that there it is safest to point out where the public-school ideals that persist in life are inadequate, where they need enriching, where modifying. To take one, splendid in itself, but liable to be magnified into something harmful, may we not sometimes lay too much stress on corporate action and corporate feeling, on traditions shared from generation to generation, on membership one with another—all important, but not the only important things of life ? May we not forget that man is also an individual, that he has to learn the stern lesson of not only dying alone, but of suffering alone, of facing his own sorrows alone, in conquering his own weaknesses in daily life, and of training his own conscience, his own heart, his own soul ? The inner voice that we do sometimes hear, chiding or encouraging, is often inaudible because it is drowned by the voices that reverberate around us. Our Lord teaches us that we need sometimes to get away to a desert place, away from our fellows in our religion and in our life. The subtle, sensitive, discriminating, resolute conscience is to be won only by solitary communion with God. And though in very truth it is to be won for our brethren and companions' sake, and to be won with our brethren and companions' help, it is not to be won by their help alone.

It is almost a natural transition from such an idea to the service of Holy Communion. Here again it seems right to give all the help possible by going through the service word for word, pointing out where there are differences of opinion and where the different opinions meet. This common ground should be stressed. It is so spacious compared with the narrow limits within which the differences lie. Our Lord's own words as we have them in the Gospels, and as they come to us through the pen of St. Paul, are surely simple, and yet thought-compelling enough. The child is still too young, and it may be that he will be still too young when old age comes, to decide whether after consecration there is a change in the elements themselves or only a change in their relation ; but he may be told that, though the Church of England repudiates transubstantiation, it does not determine whether the elements in virtue of their new significance are to be regarded as in any way changed in themselves or not, and that good and loyal members of the Church take different views ; and he can begin to learn now that there is anyhow a spiritual change with which should correspond some spiritual change in himself and in all those who kneel beside him with hearts cleansed, with faith renewed, and with all-embracing charity as the Catechism bids.

The fewer rules the service is hedged round with the better. Boys often ask how frequently they should take the Sacrament. It seems best to allow much to their own discretion, to advise them to take counsel with their parents or their friends whom they naturally trust in such matters. There is some danger in the schoolmaster laying down any school custom. Indeed, it is most important that there should be no suggestion that attendance will be observed and recorded. It is better that individuals should be occasionally careless, or even remain careless, than that the whole society should lose its conviction that this is in very truth a voluntary service, attendance at which must be a matter for decision between a boy's own conscience and himself. Experience proves to me that such an act of faith is not in vain. A few more might come if defaulters were noticed and chided, but others would come in a different spirit and the whole congregation might well miss the peculiar blessing that comes to this service Sunday after Sunday throughout the school term. This blessing seems to me to owe much of its quality to the fact that most of those kneeling together within the chapel walls at any given time have made their solemn promise to the Bishop within those same walls, and have prepared their souls to receive the Holy Spirit in the midst of the work, the play, the temptations, the obstacles, the helps, the inspirations of a common life, where they are conscious of having grown from weakness to strength, and for whom the prayer is ever being uttered that they may go from strength to strength.

CHAPTER VII

PREPARATION IN THE SCHOOL (2)

By Arthur Chilton

Archbishop Temple has put it on record that he was confirmed at the age of twelve, that he was asked one question which he could not answer, and that he was then pronounced fit. And there are still some of us who can remember the time when preparation for Confirmation was apt to be meagre and Confirmations were rare. Times have changed. Confirmation is now treated much more seriously both in parishes and schools. Nevertheless there are some who believe that the bad old system or want of system still prevails in schools, and that boys are prepared perfunctorily and by people ill qualified to prepare them. Most of us have heard rude things said about school Confirmations. How far they are deserved it is not the purpose of this chapter to discuss. I would rather start with my conviction of what the school Confirmation ought to be. I believe that the preparation of candidates is one of the head master's most important and solemn duties, and that the school Confirmation should be the very centre of school life. Dr. Moberly of Winchester held strong views on this subject. He recognized that a school is concentrated essence of Confirmation material, and that schoolmasters have it in their power to deal far more completely with Confirmation than the parish priest can do, and he held that Confirmation is the chief instrument put into the hand of the head master with which to deal with boys. He advocated that preparation should begin when a boy entered the school, so that there should be but two classes, those who had been confirmed and were communicants and those who were in training for Confirmation. Confirmation in the parish should be one of the great events of the year ; in the school it should be the greatest.

But if there are some who look askance at all school Confirmations, what do they think of day-school Confirmations ? It must be admitted that the case for the day school is weaker than the case for the boarding school, and it will be convenient to start with a frank consideration of the disabilities of the day school as compared with the boarding school.

At the outset we are met with the fact that most day schools are undenominational. This would seem at first sight prohibitive. But what does this mean ? In an undenominational day school there are many boys who belong to the Church of England. If the staff of masters also contains members of the Church of England able and willing to prepare boys, there is nothing to keep them apart, provided that the preparation classes are held after school hours. There is no danger of interference with other denominations. Similarly, a Jewish member of the staff might conduct a Hebrew class for Jews. But the point need not be laboured, since this chapter is written by one who for twenty years has had actual experience of preparing boys for Confirmation in an undenominational school.

But while the possibility of a Confirmation is not excluded, the undenominational character of the school has an appreciable effect on the material available for Confirmation. There is, no doubt, a large number of boys who belong to the Church of England and who attend the school not because it is undenominational but for other reasons. Nor must it be thought that Church parents who send their boys to an undenominational school are indifferent as to the religious training of their boys. In many cases the reverse is true. They choose a day school because they are unwilling to interrupt the Church life of the home, by which they set great store, and they choose an undenominational school only because of the rarity of Church day schools or because they are attracted to the school of their choice on other grounds and in spite of its undenominational character. Such boys make excellent material for Confirmation, as good as any that can be found in a Church school. At the same time it must be admitted that such a school is apt to attract some indifferent people, who choose a day school not to preserve the religious life of the home, but to avoid the intolerable strain of Sundays at a Church boarding school with its chapel. To such parents an undenominational day school, which since it is open to all denominations belongs to none, seems desirable. An undenominational day school will probably contain more of this indifferent material than a Church day school, and certainly more than a Church boarding school. If the boys were to any great extent of this stamp, the omens would not be favourable for a school Confirmation.

Nevertheless the existence of this element in a school may be regarded as a special opportunity for a schoolmaster who is willing to take it in hand. And the fact that it is easy for any boy to lie undiscovered in an undenominational school is important. There can be no such division of the school into communicants and catechumens as Moberly pictured in a Church boarding school. There a kind of obligation to come forward when the time comes is imposed on parents and boys alike. They may come forward because they are expected to do so. In an undenominational day school if a boy comes forward it is by his own or his parents' declared desire. If he does not, it is probably assumed that he is not a Churchman.

The undenominational character of a school, then, does not make a Confirmation impossible. The school is sure to contain some good material. If some is unpromising, the greater the need that it should be dealt with. And the fact that in such a school a volunteer really volunteers is all to the good. To do what you need not have done implies or begets purpose. Those who come forward in this way take it seriously.

Let us dismiss this point and face a more fundamental disability of the day school. Confirmation belongs to youth as school belongs to youth. But Confirmation also belongs to the whole of life, as some schools do and some do not. To say that a boy belongs to his school and his school belongs to him all his life is to utter a truism to the son of a great public school. He belongs to it as he belongs to his family. He is the son of his school as truly and as permanently as he is the son of his father. He may change his home residence from time to time, and the parish church of his youth may be forgotten. But nothing can change his relation to his school. And it is a great gain if his Confirmation can be associated with that which is a permanent factor in his life, rather than with what was only a passing phase. This is one of the strongest pleas for a school Confirmation in a great boarding school. How far can the day school urge the same plea ? Certainly the great day schools can, especially those which are not mainly local schools. They beget sons of their own and attach their pupils to themselves with the cords of a man, so that they belong there all their lives. The gulf between boarding schools and day schools is less wide than it was formerly. The modern day school with its highly organized games, its " houses," and its old boys' clubs, deals with the whole man and attaches its pupils to itself in no fleeting relation. This is true, whatever the boarding schools may say of us. Nevertheless there still exists a type of day school where a spirit of non-committal is to be found in parents, pupils, and masters. The pupils are mere sojourners, their life is elsewhere. Why should school be anything to them when schooldays are over ? If we are like this, we must not aspire to a school Confirmation. One of the strongest arguments for a school Confirmation is that by it Confirmation is associated with a relation which is intimate and lifelong. Not all day schools, perhaps only a few, can create such a relation. Where it is not found, let us leave the Confirmation to the parish.

Again, for the adequate preparation of candidates there must be on the staff of the school men with the requisite qualifications for preparing them. Day schools do not necessarily attract such men. Not the least qualification is the desire and aspiration to do such work, and there are good men on the staff of day schools, with all the technical qualifications, men who are themselves communicant members of the Church, who have no such desire. I adduce this fact because it is a fact. Perhaps it proves little, since similar men might be found in boarding schools. Nevertheless while the boarding-school system tends to attract and to produce the men required, the day-school system does not. It is possible for a man who is seeking a livelihood, not a life, to survive in a day school. A boarding school will spue him out of its mouth. Too much stress must not be laid on this, since in this matter, as in others, the day school at its best is scarcely behind the boarding school.

It is obvious at a glance that the boarding school can justify its Confirmation on grounds which the day school does not share. The boarding school is the spiritual home of its pupils. Holidays are mere episodes. The school chapel, not the parish church at home, is the centre of the boy's religious life. Parents and parish clergy fall into a secondary position. The complexion of a boy's Church-manship is that of his school chapel rather than that of his parish church. More significant than all, he will make his first Communion and will form his habits of Communion in the school chapel. With the day school it is different. It has no chapel. Parents and priests do not resign their charge—not even during term, for the school is closed on Sundays. Thus the religious influence of the home and that of the parish loom very large, and the day school which prepares boys for Confirmation can do so only with the permission and approval of these parties as well as that of the candidate. In a word, the most cogent reasons for a Confirmation in a boarding school are all wanting. Moreover if the day school is to have a Con-firmation, it will have to face difficulties of which the boarding school knows little or nothing.

Yet there are reasons for a school Confirmation which apply to the day school as well as to the boarding school. Preparation is teaching in the widest sense of the word, and teaching at school ought to be more efficient than teaching by a parish priest. Those who think that know-ledge of the subject taught is the teacher's one qualification will vote for the priest as a specialist in the subject. But it has been observed that specialists sometimes appear as mere bores to their pupils. And those who set much store by experience of teaching and knowledge of the nature of boys and sympathy with their life will vote for the school-master. Individual preparation is generally impossible alike for the priest and the schoolmaster. It is not to be desired, even where possible. And when the priest attempts to organize classes, his troubles begin. There are few hours which will suit all his candidates, and he will have the greatest difficulty in getting them together with any regularity. When he has them, he cannot handle them as the schoolmaster can. The schoolmaster announces the hour of his class and can count on the attendance of his boys. When he stands before them, he has behind him all the traditions of class-room discipline : he knows his boys, he knows the conditions of their lives ; he can speak in a tongue " understanded of the people " ; and he ought to be able to secure the maximum of attention and intelligent interest from his hearers.

This is a great matter, but it is not all. The school-master will teach in terms of school life. School is the battlefield where the boy is meeting the attacks of the world, the flesh, and the devil : at school he will prove his armour ; at school declaring for Christ becomes a real, a difficult, a glorious thing. " Before God and this congre-gation "—the words receive a wealth of new force when " this congregation " is composed of a boy's schoolfellows who will hear him say " I do." And a sense of the great fellowship of school, which they have already, serves as a first lesson in the greater fellowship of the Church, which is not so easy to impart to young people. And then the test of it all : each school Confirmation ought to mean a sensible addition of strength to the school, the result of drafting into it a fresh batch of confirmed men, with the right idea of strength and its source. Unquestionably there is an addition of strength each year after a Confirmation which in the mass must be perceptible even to the boys. It is easier, no doubt, to learn to be a pillar of the State, where there is a State to uphold. The best preparation that the best vicar's study or vestry can give will miss some of these things.

And so, in spite of the disabilities of day schools, and while admitting that in some day schools preparation for Confirmation may be impossible, I would plead for a Confirmation even in day schools, where it may be had. My personal experience may be of some interest. About twenty years ago I found myself at the head of a large undenominational day school, which for seventy years had never meddled with Confirmation. I knew that many of my pupils belonged to the Church of England, and I announced that I was willing to prepare privately candidates for Confirmation. Out of a school of 700 boys, four candidates appeared. For the first few years the numbers remained inconsiderable, but gradually increased. In 1913 the numbers rose to fifty. Since that date I have presented annually from sixty to seventy boys. In the early years the boys were confirmed with others at one of the Bishop of London's public Confirmations at St. Paul's. Since 1913 the Bishop has given us a special Confirmation each year. During these years I have learned many things. The belief that my experience might be of use to others led me to undertake to write this chapter.

In December every year with the Christmas school reports a circular is sent to all parents announcing the date of the Confirmation and of the preparation classes to be held during the ensuing term. At the foot of the circular is a form to be filled up. Parents who desire that their boys shall be prepared are requested to give the boys' names in full, with the date of birth and the date and place of Baptism, and to return the form on the first day of the spring term. If the particulars of Baptism are inadequate, further evidence of Baptism is required. Then each case is considered separately before the boy is accepted as a candidate.

It might be supposed that candidates obtained in this way would all be members of the Church of England, brought up in the ways of the Church, instructed in the Church Catechism, and in touch with parish church and clergy. Most of them answer to this description, though the Catechism has often been neglected. But none of these things can be taken for granted, not even the first.

This means that the day-school master must move warily. We ought to have expected it : we have met the non-committal attitude in other matters ; we were sure to meet it here. Some of those who come forward will have to be rejected altogether, others must be put back till they have acquired habits of Church membership.

Let us consider the parents. First there are the normal parents, who are communicants themselves and have brought up their children in the ways of the Church and desire to see them kneeling by their side at the altar. There are many of these. But there are also those who have drifted away themselves and yet desire what they know to be best for their children. The children of such parents require careful consideration. Probably they would never have been presented through their parish churches, with which they are not in touch. Often they are excellent material : if they are brought to the notice of their clergy, and put back for a year to learn good habits, they become good candidates themselves, likely to become keen communicants, and are sometimes the means of bringing their parents back. Again, there are parents who have no conception of Church membership or discipline and no aspiration in that direction for their children. They do not know, or they have forgotten, that Confirmation is the gate to Communion. They would probably draw the line this side of Communion. But Confirmation—no doubt it is a good thing, and they wish the dear boy to get all the good he can. Incredible as it seems, there are many of this type—ignorant, irresponsible. When you tell them of the discipline of the Church, with its progressive stages, Baptism, Confirmation, Communion, this is something new to them. They are not sure they want their child to commit himself to a system. Why can he not " put in his thumb, and pull out a plum, and say what a good boy am I " ?

If the schoolmaster does not walk warily, he will find he is presenting boys who will never become communicants. What is he to do ? The boy may not have been baptized. This can be remedied. But however promising he is, he will not become a communicant after Confirmation unless he is prepared to steal out of the house on Sunday mornings when others are in bed, and perhaps miss his breakfast or have to wait for it. Not only will he have no encouragement, he will meet with many minor discouragements. No doubt you can teach him that the confirmed life does not lean on outward supports, but is nourished from within by a Spirit given for this very purpose, but you are setting him a hard task when his foes are those of his own household. The only hope is that the schoolmaster can find a strong parish priest ready to conspire with him. If he can, the case is not to be rejected. The boy may well turn out better than some who have not passed through the same fire.

Lastly, there are a few parents who do not belong to the Church of England and yet offer their children for Confirmation. This is the result of ignorance. They do not know the difference between one communion and another. They may be forgiven for ignorance of the Church's teaching, but they are evidently not intelligent members even of their own Churches. There is little or nothing to be done here. Now and again there is another explanation. I have known parents who with open eyes have resolved that they and their children will join the Church. Shyness about approaching a parish priest who is unknown to them is pardonable. It is easier for them to come in the first instance to their boy's schoolmaster, whom they know. I remember one such case in which I prepared a boy and commended his mother to her parish priest. They were confirmed together, and the boy is now vicar of a London parish.

It must not be supposed that the irregularities which have here been so frankly exposed arise in the bulk of the day-school cases. Yet they do arise. A boarding school, which itself supplies all that is wanting and can blame only itself for whatever is amiss, will scarcely touch these things. A parish priest will meet them, especially if he knows all the boys in his parish. Probably he does not. The reason why these cases come to the school is that here is someone who knows the boy and whom the parents think they can trust to do what is right. And so in one way or another it would seem that the day school has special opportunities not to be neglected. This is surely a saner view than the view that because of the many lions in the path the day school should leave it all alone.

But we have yet the parish priest to reckon with. The most guileless and innocent of schoolmasters, who has not even discovered the presence of the lions we have been facing, will recognize that it is his duty, if only as a matter of courtesy, to get into touch with the parish priest of each candidate and to secure his consent and co-operation. Having got thus far, he will discover that a large number of candidates have already directly or through their parents approached the parish clergy on the subject. This is as it should be. When candidates are in close touch with their clergy and secure their approval beforehand, there is no problem. There is no question of the boys being taken out of the hands of the clergy, who are ready to fall in with the wishes of the boys and their parents and even to welcome the co-operation of the schoolmaster.

But he will also discover that in many cases the circumstances are very different. There are the candidates who know their clergy only by name, or not even by name (my Clergy List lives on my table in Confirmation term) ; there are those who have " just moved " (probably six months back), and have not yet sampled the church or the clergy ; there are those whose parents " do not like the parish church " and go elsewhere or nowhere, and are not known to any clergy ; and there are those who are afraid of getting too close to their clergy, who like them well enough at a safe distance, but are uncomfortable at the thought of being drawn into the parish, and who hit upon the brilliant idea of getting it all done at school without anyone's knowing. There is much here for the schoolmaster to correct and straighten out. Until he has done this it is not safe for him to proceed. But he can nearly always do it if he will seek, and is fortunate enough to secure, the co-operation of the clergy. And one effect of this co-operation will be that the hands of the clergy are greatly strengthened and that they gain many potential communicants who but for the school would have continued to elude them.

The schoolmaster, while giving proper weight to the sacramental value of Confirmation in itself as a means of grace, must look further and satisfy himself that there is a reasonable hope that each candidate he accepts will become a regular communicant. He must not take this for granted, as others might do. He will find out from every candidate where he will make his first Communion, and he will arrange that he shall go not as a poor lonely little casual visitor, but as a member of a parochial family, expected and welcomed by his parish priest. Boys readily grasp that this is a thing to be desired, and, odd as it may appear, find in this presentation of the case a new and pleasant light on their relation to the parish. It reconciles them to being introduced to their clergy. And here it should be said that boys are often slack and need encouragement to stiffen them, but they are not stubborn as a rule, and gladly surrender themselves to influences which they can trust. No difficulty as a rule will come from the boy : he is willing to be straightened out. If the schoolmaster and the parson pull together, all will be well.

Can this much-to-be-desired co-operation be brought about ? A parish priest may well regret, not to say resent, that a boy should be taken from him at this crisis which is so eminently his concern, and that he should be deprived of the opportunity, the best he will ever have, of getting hold of the boy. Sometimes the reply of the parish priest to the schoolmaster's letter will contain a pathetic allusion to this point of view. But this is rare, because those who are already effectively in the hands of the priest will never be taken from him by the schoolmaster except with his declared approval. There are cases in which it is obvious to boy and parent and priest that a boy should be prepared in his parish. These cases do not come to the schoolmaster at all as candidates. Those who come to him are either those who have already obtained the consent of their clergy or those whom the clergy have so far failed to enlist or perhaps even to discover. And so it proves that the appeal to the parish clergy rarely fails to produce a satisfactory response. But the schoolmaster must keep this always before him, that he is trying to strengthen the hands of the clergy. Only so can he serve his boys' best interest.

It is not easy to write of one aspect of this matter. When the clergy betray suspicion of a school Confirmation, it is generally because they mistrust the complexion of the school teaching. This is worthy of consideration from both ends. The day-school master who prepares boys for Confirmation has a problem which neither the parish priest nor the boarding-school master has to solve. His boys come from many parishes, of which some are poles apart from others in what I have called the complexion of their Church teaching and practice. At the other end the parish priest of a pronounced school of thought may well feel no confidence in " these schoolmasters." Both schoolmaster and priest deserve sympathy, but especially the schoolmaster. Somehow he must send his boys to their parishes without disturbing the foundations already laid ; or if no foundations have been laid as yet, with foundations which his parish priest will not have to disturb. Some no doubt would say that the task is impossible, unless the schoolmaster's teaching is either too colourless or too glaringly defective to be useful. But others will feel, as I do, that when we are admittedly teaching elementary things it is possible to give sound teaching which is neither partisan nor colourless, and which will send the boys back to their churches with an outlook which is none the worse because it is not narrow. One of the chief difficulties here hinted at would vanish if after Confirmation the schoolmaster could hand the boys over to their clergy for preparation for their first Communion. This would incidentally remove any suggestion that the boys are being taken out of their hands, as well as giving them an opportunity of supplementing the teaching of the schoolmaster in any desired direction. One thing which should always be left to the parish priest is the choice of a Communion manual. The schoolmaster with his miscellaneous class will be well advised to refrain from pressing any particular book on his boys.

Some after-care in the time which follows Confirmation is required. For this, again, the schoolmaster must depend upon the parish clergy. There is little that he himself can

do. Even a school first Communion for all the candidates
at some convenient church is not free from objection. On
the whole, it seems better that each should make his first
Communion where he will make his future Communions.
When formally disbanding my class, I tell them to report
to me when they have made their first Communion. This
gives me an opportunity for a word of encouragement
when they come to report. Other occasions may arise
when Timothy needs an admonition to " stir up the gift."
A final good-bye on leaving school to a boy whom I have
prepared for Confirmation shapes itself almost without
the use of words into " Abide thou in the things thou
hast learned, remembering of whom thou hast learned
them." All this helps, but it is little enough. No doubt
more can be done at a boarding school, where boys make
their Communions in the school chapel. Here, again, the
help of the parish priest is wanted. He should in fact take
charge after the Confirmation is over. If he will prepare
the boys for their first Communion, as I have suggested,
so much the better. I always reserve my instruction on
Holy Communion till after Confirmation so as to make this
possible, and I am always ready to hand over this part of
my task to the clergy. Candour compels me to admit
that I cannot often induce them to meet me here. If
they approve of me, they prefer to leave the whole to me ;
if not, I suspect that they argue that I had better finish
what I have begun. But generally they have a Communicants' Guild to which they are ready to welcome the
boys.

Let us sum up what has been written about the mutual
relations of schoolmaster and priest. At first sight a school
Confirmation seems to mean that the schoolmaster replaces
the priest, whose services are therefore not required. A
schoolmaster who begins preparing boys with this idea will
soon have to unlearn it. Parents and boys who come
forward with the idea that they have evaded the priest
have to learn that the schoolmaster is there to bring them
into closer touch with their parish priests, and not to supply
a substitute for them. The clergy, again, may take the
view that if parents and boys look not to them in this

matter but to others, their responsibility is at an end. This is a view which disappointment or pique might suggest, if the clergy ever allow such things to dictate to them. Unless the schoolmaster can eradicate from his own mind and from the minds of others concerned the thought that he is replacing the parish priest, his good intentions will be defeated. The alternative view is that he is supporting the parish clergy, supplementing their efforts, often introducing to them new and promising material. On this theory a thorough understanding between the clergy and the schoolmaster is required. The results of such an understanding and an active alliance based thereon will be something far beyond what the clergy could have achieved unaided.

It remains to draw attention to a few other features of a day-school master's experience. The right age for Confirmation is a question which has only an academic interest for the schoolmaster. Others may dictate in this matter : he must take the boys when they come. There is room for wide difference of opinion on this subject. If you appeal to ancient practice, you will advocate an early age. If you take Confirmation as it is, rather than as it was ; if you do not quarrel with the accretion of the promises and the instruction, you will incline to a more advanced age. Yet even here there is room for difference of opinion in the interpretation of " years of discretion." Is the age to be twelve or fifteen ? Most of us would compromise at something between the two. The day-school master finds that his candidates are practically all over fourteen, and many over fifteen. This is, at any rate, the age which seems best to accord with the words of the First Prayer Book, which speaks of " that age, that partly by the frayltie of theyr owne fleshe, partly by the assautes of the world and the devil, they begin to be in daungier to fall into sinne."

Parents who are themselves devoted members of the Church often wish their children to be confirmed young. They would not withhold the gift longer than necessary ; and they are ready to accept the responsibility of leading them by the hand during the first years of their com-

municant life. Others, whom nothing will convince that
Confirmation means " being confirmed " rather than " confirming," with less sense of the sacramental character of
the rite and a natural shrinking from imposing on their
children a responsibility which they will have to bear
alone, incline to a later age. Both have reason. In view
of the material with which we deal, it is not surprising that
most of our candidates are old. When boys of twelve come
forward, it is not easy to place them in a class of boys who
are three years older, though on other grounds they may
be suitable candidates. It is thought wiser to keep these
boys back for a year or two than to try to get the other
boys younger.

There is another important consideration, which anyone
who knows schoolboys will appreciate. Schools expect of
their older boys that they shall be pillars of the State ; and
right-minded boys as they grow older gladly and proudly
accept responsibility for the character and conduct of their
class, their house, their school. It is a happy thing when
the call to be a leader coincides in time with the call to
Confirmation. They naturally interpret the promises which
they renew in terms of school life, and the promise not to
follow or be led by the world becomes something real to
the boy who is setting himself against whatever is bad in
the school society and upholding whatever is good. It is
all to the good if Confirmation boys are pillars and pillars
are Confirmation boys. This is possible only if Confirmation boys are those who have reached a mature age and a
respectable standing in the school.

The ignorance of candidates is sometimes deplorable.
This is partly because of the peculiar material of an undenominational day school, and the lack of Church teaching
in the curriculum. The parish priest should fare better,
yet even here I suspect that gross ignorance is not unheard
of in days when it is exceptional for children to be taught
the Catechism at home, and when the practice of regular
churchgoing is so much less general than it was. I have
met candidates who do not possess Prayer Books and many
who cannot find their places. The three Orders of the
Ministry are always a surprise for my candidates. They

are sure there are more than three, since a place must be found for vicars and curates, to say nothing of archdeacons and archbishops. About the Church calendar they have the haziest notions. The boarding-school master should not meet with this ignorance, if the chapel is doing its work well. Indeed, the boarding school seems thrice blessed. Here and perhaps nowhere else can you have regular attendance at divine service, the neglect of which is at the root of the trouble. Yet once again is the day school Confirmation justified by the greatness of the opportunity. The schoolmaster who prepares boys should keep one aspect of his task clearly before him. It is the great opportunity for instruction in the elements. And this instruction must be given now or never. In a few years the candidates will be too old to study elements, and will be content to imagine that they know or even to pretend that they know what they ought to know and do not know. Others may be in danger of taking as known elementary things which are not known : the day-school master will take nothing as known.

The methods of preparation in a day school will not differ from those used elsewhere. Most of the instruction will be given in classes. If a head master does it all himself, his classes will be large. But it may be presumed that he is an experienced teacher, and the boys may be trusted to be at their best in the matter of attentiveness and desire to learn. It is a good plan to delegate to other members of the staff the task of exacting the repetition of the Catechism from each boy. The classes and the private interviews will absorb every moment the head master can spare in the Confirmation term ; but he will have the satisfaction of knowing that it is the most remunerative piece of work in the year. He learns more of boys in general and of his own boys than he knew before ; he has opportunities of helping them, such as he does not find in his other work ; he can get to the root of things. During much of his time he is working on the surface. It is one thing to command, to direct, to punish ; it is another to give motives for obedience and to guide to a source of strength. After master and boys have gone through a Confirmation term together, there is an understanding between them. They have not only looked one another in the face, but together they have looked into the face of God.

What has been here written may seem to some readers altogether too pedestrian. Confirmation, it may be objected, is concerned not with mere conduct or mere instruction, but with a relationship to God which can find expression in other ways than in churchgoing. It is a perplexing thought. Ought we to have more sympathy with the child who knows nothing of the Church's system, and does not desire to know anything, who does not go to church and does not desire to go to church, and yet seeks Confirmation with simplicity, faith, and love, because he can understand kneeling before his Father's throne on the eve of his manhood, and asking for the confirmation of his sonship and the gift of the Holy Spirit? Confirmation is something that God does for us, not something which we do. Ought we to build all on the sacramental rite and leave the rest? On the one hand it sometimes appears as if the old-fashioned ideas of the Church were going, and the doctrine of laying-on of hands must accommodate itself to a new state of things, as it has already done once in its history. On the other hand, if institutional religion is going, why should Confirmation itself survive? And what is the meaning of our sonship, if it is only a beautiful sentiment with no relation to the discipline of obedience? This chapter is written in the conviction that the people must be brought back to the Church, and that Confirmation is one of the chief means by which they can be brought back.

CHAPTER VIII

PREPARATION IN THE SCHOOL (3)

By F. R. GRAY

THERE are many theories with regard to Confirmation, many beliefs, and many shades of opinion. There is at least one aspect which is seen by everyone who has the duty of preparing candidates : we are all agreed that it is by far the greatest opportunity that is given us of bringing before children and young persons their responsibility for the gifts of life, of showing them the source of guidance and strength, and of putting within their reach the means by which guidance and strength are afforded them.

Our first duty is, therefore, to take careful thought that this great opportunity may not be wasted or abused. We should try to form some notion of the content of a candidate's mind with regard to religion before we decide how much we must try to teach. We must find out what she knows, which is an easy task, and, if possible, what she thinks. This is not nearly so easy, for the most talkative girl sometimes shows amazing powers of reticence with regard to her inner life. Happily, a teacher does not depend entirely on the spoken word for her information in such matters.

What does the young girl of to-day think about religion ? Modern conditions which affect the religion of the family are now familiar to everyone and need only a very rapid survey here. There is, in a great many homes, no recognition of any need for religious observances of any kind except the inevitable rites associated with christenings, weddings and funerals. Church-going is altogether neglected by very many ; it is occasionally practised by some ; it is regularly practised by very few. Family prayers, so common two or three generations ago, are almost unknown; outside the homes of the clergy it would not be easy to find many traces of the custom. Nor is it common to find evidence of personal direction on the subject of religion given by a parent. Yet it often happens that parents who never, for instance, go to church, are not only willing but desirous that their daughters should be prepared for Confirmation at school. They are by no means indifferent to the advantages of a training in the principles of religion, even though they seem to neglect it for themselves.

Another feature of family life must be mentioned because it has a very important bearing on our subject. Children nowadays live with grown-up persons. Houses are smaller, servants are fewer, the old-fashioned trusty nurses are hard to find, and the younger members of the family are no longer kept in the seclusion of the nursery and the schoolroom. They hear and, no doubt, often join in, discussions which cause a premature awakening of their critical faculty. Those of us who are engaged in the profession of education are all aware that education of a sort, haphazard and always strangely mixed, goes on unceasingly in many homes. A girl hears open criticism of much that was outside the pale of criticism in her grandmother's time. She knows enough about the questions of the day to enable her to hold an opinion, though she does not know enough to enable her to form one. Among these questions the subject of religion is almost certain to find a place.

We are thus confronted, on the one hand, with widespread ignorance of the Catechism and the Prayer Book as a whole, and ignorance of the Bible, except such parts of it as have been read at school; and, on the other hand, with a slight knowledge of some difficulties of faith which, without any intention to be unsympathetic, we may call popular and superficial. The modern schoolgirl knows very little about the Bible, but she is quite clear that if two accounts of the same event are different, both cannot be literally and historically true. She is, therefore, prepared to put questions to her regular instructors which are designed to prevent them from evading some of the conclusions of modern scholarship. We have to take into account both her ignorance and her knowledge in reckoning up our tale of adverse conditions.

Last of all must be mentioned the present-day conception of the Whole Duty of Man. Side by side with the abandonment of religious observance, there is widespread and deep-rooted interest in social improvement. Young girls are often very ready to give all the help in their power to those who are less fortunate than themselves. The needs of others are systematically brought before them in their schools, and the schools must thankfully acknowledge that they are willingly and generously assisted by the homes. There is an immense amount of truly philanthropic work done by persons who seem to feel no need of joining in the public worship of God. It is only natural that, among such persons, the sense of sin should become altogether dormant, and the average schoolgirl has grown up without thinking about it. She has no sympathy at all with the frame of mind that finds relief in a cry for mercy ; if she were to speak on that point she would probably say that she may be a sinner, but she certainly is not miserable. She is inclined to think that the world is a very good place which would be still better if everybody played the game. She does not use in everyday speech the words " right " and " wrong " so much as the newest equivalents of the phrases, " good form " and " bad form." " It isn't done " is far more deterring than all the commandments of the Decalogue. She recognizes that great suffering is caused by, for example, drunkenness ; but she regards the drunkard's wife and children as the only persons against whom he sins. " Against Thee, Thee only . . ." are unintelligible words to her. We certainly should not wish to go back to the days when Charles Wesley wrote :

> Nothing is worth a thought beneath
> But how I may escape the death
> That never, never dies.

But the pendulum has swung too far. It is good that religion should no longer be used to frighten children ; but that is no reason why children should never be taught that religion has a sterner side.

Together with the sense of sin, the sense of helplessness
has almost disappeared. In the great crises of life it must
assert itself, but in young lives it may well be that no great
crisis has yet arisen. Sympathy with suffering is very
practical nowadays. We are intolerant of pain for
ourselves and others. Medical science and surgical skill
have worked such wonders that it is difficult for many
persons, and especially for young persons, to believe that
they cannot do everything. We do not now seek refuge
from typhoid fever in prayer ; we use anti-typhoid injec-
tions and attend to the drains. This is perfectly right :
no one would dream of neglecting the good gifts of science ;
but there is little recognition among our generation that
they are the gifts of God. Lest we should stop to think
over these things, the world's pace in our country is far
quicker than it was : life is crowded with attractions and
distractions, and children are growing up without the
quiet and solitude in which the still small voice is heard.

In describing the lives of many schoolgirls of the present
day it must not be forgotten that a noteworthy proportion
of them live in homes where they are persons of considerable importance for special reasons. The State now
affords the opportunity of a good secondary education to
many girls who without the help of the State would pass
directly out of the primary school into the world of employment. A great many parents are cheerfully sacrificing
much in order that their children may be better educated
than themselves ; and praiseworthy as this sacrifice certainly is, the effect upon a good many of the children
is not to make them, at least during the years of early
adolescence, conspicuously easy to manage in their homes.
The features thus added to our composite picture of the
English schoolgirl emphasize self-reliance : for a time at
least these girls are conscious of their advantages, and are
confident that they can manage their own affairs and the
affairs of the family as well.

In trying to sketch thus briefly the conditions of the
life of many of our candidates for Confirmation, I am
aware that my outline is very rough. There are all shades
and varieties of homes represented in a large school, and

the girls who are to be prepared show all shades and varieties of aptitude for their preparation. I have tried, however, to show what are the chief difficulties we have to encounter ; and I have in mind a typical or composite portrait of the schoolgirl as she appears to those who know her best. Those who do not know her are puzzled and perhaps repelled ; but they do not see her as she really is. She is merciless to any lack of intellectual candour. She is densely ignorant, but she is also wise in many ways. She is self-confident and tenacious of her own rights and privileges ; but she is also generous and quick to recognize the rights of others. She is not, as a rule, anxious to bestow her confidence ; but once it is bestowed, she will do her utmost to follow the directions of her guide.

The prophet Micah has given to us for all time an incomparable summary of the Whole Duty of Man : the twentieth century in England accepts as an ideal two-thirds of it. In a time of grim conflicts between Capital and Labour, authoritative voices are reminding us that the issue should be not the defeat of either party to the conflict, but the determination of each to do justly. Men and women of goodwill are working in our cities and villages to ameliorate the lives of others ; as a people it may be said of us that we love mercy. But we are, to-day, an arrogant people ; whatever we may say, we pride ourselves upon our success as if it were indeed our own. It is true that when the Armistice was proclaimed we said with our lips and in our hearts, " Not unto us, O Lord, not unto us, but unto Thy Name give glory." But into our hearts has there not crept the vaunt that has been the undoing of so many peoples since the days of Gideon, " Mine own hand hath saved me " ? It is true that we are going through a time when poverty is widespread because there is not work for the workers ; but the spirit against which Israel was fruitlessly warned is strong within those who are prosperous. " My power and the might of mine hand hath gotten me this wealth." We cannot wonder that such a spirit as this has its influence upon the sensitive spirits of our children. As truly as they breathe the common air, they breathe also the spiritual atmosphere

wherein we dwell. It is part of our task to teach them
to do justly and to love mercy ; but as they approach the
day of their Confirmation we shall have failed altogether
in our duty if they have not learned also that they must
walk humbly with their God. We must teach them that
the first and great commandment is, *Thou shalt love the
Lord thy God with all thy heart, and with all thy soul, and
with all thy mind.* The second is like it and must not be
forgotten ; but it is second. With many truly admirable
and highly influential persons to-day the tendency is to
obey the second and to ignore the first.

It may be urged that the first and great commandment
is implicitly observed wherever the second is cheerfully
and spontaneously obeyed. There is something to be
said for this view. Our Lord Himself gives us the test
that He applies. " Ye gave Me meat—ye gave Me drink
—ye took Me, a stranger, in—ye clothed Me—ye visited
Me in sickness—ye came unto Me in prison . . . inasmuch
as ye did it unto one of these My brethren, even these
least . . ." Those who lived lives of service to others have
thus proved that they were true disciples of their Master ;
those who left undone what they might have done for
others are no disciples of His. The life of service is the
proof of discipleship, for the fact is that it is only the true
disciple who will persevere in this life of service, undaunted
by difficulties, unembittered by ingratitude, not discouraged
by repeated disappointment. Our children are ready
to pity and anxious to relieve distress ; but we must give
them a motive which will prevent their pity from deteriorat-
ing into avoidance of any encounter with suffering, and
save them from seeking to buy immunity from personal
service by gifts which cost them nothing. Further, we
must bear in mind that pity is always in danger of arousing
in the minds of children a feeling of condescension ; indeed,
we are none of us exempt from that temptation. It is of
the utmost importance that we should associate a spirit
of humility and of love with the thought of all that young
people may desire to do for others. It is good that they
should wish to serve ; but service is not enough.

We have now to inquire how we are to attain our end.

We have to face the fact of Sin, for there are things to be renounced; we must try in the simplest way that we can devise to show what is the faith of a Christian; and we must lead our candidates to look straight in the face of Duty and to recognize that it is the command of God. In other words, we must lead them to see themselves, their high aims and their sad shortcomings. We must next turn their thoughts to the Unseen Friend who is so close to them and so accessible; and then we must show how naturally follows the wish to serve that Friend and to speak to Him and ask His help. At this point in the preparation I have been accustomed to hand over the candidates to the chaplain, who speaks to them about the Sacraments and, later, sees them in very small groups before presenting them to the Bishop.

I propose to say a little about the general religious teaching in a school before I enter on the discussion of these topics in detail.

The importance of the short daily service with which a school day is opened cannot be exaggerated. It does not matter whether the school meets in a chapel or in a hall where all kinds of assemblies are held; if a reverent spirit is present throughout, there is some advantage in associating thoughts of prayer and thanksgiving with the centre of school work. A girl who has once realized what it is to pray with her whole heart among her companions and with everything that might remind her of daily school life about her, has mastered the secret of prayer. Wherever she may go in later years, however dense the crowd in which she may be compelled to live, she has at her command an inner chamber into which she may withdraw at will and pray to the Father who seeth in secret.

But do girls pray at school prayers? If they do not, I am sure it is our fault in very large measure. We may choose the prayers badly, with no relation to special needs which must arise from time to time. We may choose carefully and well, but by a too conventional or a too hurried utterance we may give the impression that we are only going through a form. We must not permit ourselves to be too prominent ; perhaps the only way to help our children to pray is not to think about them at all at the moment, but to make the prayers our own, merely saying them aloud. Now and then, but not too often, I have found it useful to say a few words about some special prayer which we are going to use. For instance, the words of the Ash Wednesday collect strike strangely upon the ears of a child. To describe God as hating nothing that He has made sounds unattractive. When it has been explained that this is only a very strong way of saying that God loves everything that He has made, and when two or three great words like *God so loved the world*, and *His tender mercies are over all His works*, are quoted, the prayer that we use so often throughout Lent has taken on a new meaning. Again, children accept a fine phrase like *Whose service is perfect freedom* without thinking ; if they are one day shown something of what it implies, it may suggest thoughts that will go on bearing fruit throughout a lifetime.

The hymn at this morning service may be made part of our religious instruction if the girls are taught to sing it well. Nothing is more depressing than a badly-sung, dragging hymn which suggests to the girls that, whereas immense pains must be taken for a school concert, anything is good enough for school prayers. If we have the best hymns we know and the best tunes we can find, and if we take care that every girl has a chance to learn them, we shall not only begin the day with a happy influence, but we shall make upon young minds the impression that nothing but the best must be offered to God.

The lesson read at this time is a very important part of our religious instruction. We have seen that there is little reading of the Bible in the home and infrequent attendance at church. Once a day, five days in the week, our children have an opportunity of hearing it read. How is that most precious opportunity to be used ? I think our audience must somehow be made conscious that we mean it to be used. Our audience know us and are sensitive to our mood. We are teachers, and a teacher is sensitive to the mood of a pupil. In reading to a gathering of four

or five hundred girls at morning prayers it is possible
to be conscious of a general awakening of thought regarding
the lesson that is read aloud. Such an experience is not,
indeed, of daily occurrence ; it may not be very common ;
but when it happens, something must be done to take
advantage of it. Either the lesson must be read very soon
again, or the girls may be asked to learn it by heart, or
some comment may be made arising out of it. The reader
will do as she is guided. The experience is not soon forgotten, and it calls to mind the words of the Psalmist :
The entrance of Thy words giveth light.

Nor need there be any fear that, if no immediate impression has been noticed, none has been made. I think
that all those whose duty it has been to read lessons from
the Bible in this way have been told, often long afterwards,
by one or another of those who heard, of the light that
had entered with some inspired and inspiring words. Or,
perhaps, the words entered first as a passage of exceptional
literary beauty such as young girls often thoroughly enjoy :
it remained in the memory among other passages of the
great literature of the past. At last there comes a moment
of special need : agonizing anxiety, devastating bereave-
ment, perhaps the discipline of abundant happiness—whatever the chance or change that comes to mortal life,
suddenly the divine words glow with light and the way of
God is made plain. Much more might be said about
the daily reading of the Bible in the ears of our children ;
here I am concerned only to point out its incalculable
value in the previous preparation of girls whom we are
going to prepare for Confirmation.

It is to the regular Bible lessons in form that we must
look for systematic religious instruction at school. These
are generally entrusted to the form mistress, if she is willing
to undertake them and is in sympathy with the work. No
one should be coerced into giving these lessons, but it is,
I think, a mistake to confine them entirely to specialists.
Just as the common worship in the school hall brings home
to girls the fact that religion is bound up with the ordinary
duties of daily life, so it may be very useful to make girls
realize that the teaching of the Bible can be committed

to those who teach them their ordinary lessons. If the teacher is really in sympathy with this part of her work, she may be trusted to let some difference be felt.

Every girls' school has its own syllabus of Bible lessons, and within recent years very serious consideration has been given to the subject. As children pass up from form to form it is necessary that those who teach them should be of one mind about fundamentals, or they will have a strangely composite notion of our God. We must read some of the Old Testament stories with them, but we must not fail to point out that in those stories they see God as He was dimly and often mistakenly seen by men thousands of years ago. Then we shall be able to show how the vision of God grew clearer as age followed age. The harm that has been done by the lack of some such explanation will never be known, but it is certainly enormous. If we allow a child to think that at one time the world was so wicked that God could do nothing with it but drown almost all the men, women and children in it, we are making it very hard to believe that God at that time really loved the world. The effect of such contradictory ideas is twofold. Some minds are repelled and disgusted by stories which seem to exalt cruelty and condone deceit ; others, a much greater number, quietly assume that the contradictions cannot be reconciled and they come to regard the Bible generally as a book which has a morality of its own and but little living interest for them.

One of the chief qualifications of the good teacher is to know what not to teach. We must not swamp our Bible lesson with dates which are at best hypothetical and are most likely all wrong ; or with facts which are of some interest perhaps, but are only likely to confuse our pupils, who cannot see the wood for the trees. The teacher of the Bible must be penetrated with the sense that here is a revelation of God to man, and the ultimate purpose of life is this, *to see God*. The historical comments we make must be very few and only such as are absolutely necessary. If the children are interested enough to wish to discuss the bearing of the lesson in its true purport, we shall not refuse to hear and answer what they have to say.

We come now to the special teaching which is given only to candidates. As I have been asked to write from my own experience, it may be useful to give the letter which I send out to parents :

School Confirmation.

"The Bishop of London will hold a Confirmation for the School at St. Paul's Cathedral on a date next term which is not yet fixed.

"This notice is sent to the parents of all girls who attend School Prayers, but it may be well to state that I shall take no action whatever with regard to the preparation of any girl for Confirmation unless on the written request of her Parent or Guardian, and this notice requires no reply unless Confirmation is desired. These requests should reach me not later than   . All Candidates must attend one of the classes for instruction in the Catechism which I shall hold. Those whose parents desire it, will receive further instruction next term from the Rev.   , who has kindly consented to act as Temporary Chaplain for the purpose. Where parents prefer that a girl should receive this further instruction from the Clergyman of her own parish, I shall be prepared to grant such afternoon leave as shall be necessary. There is no wish or intention that the School Confirmation should withdraw the girls from the care of their Parish Clergy ; and no pressure, direct or indirect, will be used to cause girls who would otherwise be confirmed in their own parishes to be confirmed from the School."

(As Confirmations for this school have been held at intervals of three years, I have always given leave for girls to be absent from afternoon school whenever necessary if they were being prepared for Confirmation at other times.)

I have always felt that in a day school it is of great importance that girls should not be in any way influenced by anyone in authority at the school so as to induce them to be confirmed at the school Confirmation rather than at that which would be arranged by their own clergyman. But partly because parochial boundaries mean little in London so far as church-going is concerned, partly because church-going is irregular and infrequent, there certainly is need for a school Confirmation even in a day school.

As soon as the letter is received by parents, many of them wish to ask advice before sending in the names of their daughters. I do not think it is wise to prepare girls while they are too young, but it would be impossible to lay down a hard-and-fast line about age. If I were pressed to mention a suitable age, I should say that few girls are ready for Confirmation before they are fifteen. I think sixteen is the best age for many. We must have some regard to the stage of mental development, though this is not the chief consideration. Some very simple and straightforward natures are ready for the special preparation at fourteen or even younger, while others of a more complex type should wait in order that impressions may be clearer and deeper. I never promise to prepare a candidate without warning the parents that I may feel it right to advise later on that her Confirmation should be postponed. On the other hand, I tell the candidates when I first meet them not only what I have told their parents, but also that if they themselves wish to withdraw at any time before the day of Confirmation, they may come and talk to me about the matter and I shall certainly not press them to be confirmed. If a girl is exceptionally careless or seems to be in any other way especially ill-fitted to co-operate in the preparation, she would naturally be told in the course of a quiet talk that she would be instructed if she wished it, but would certainly not be presented for Confirmation unless she showed some effective desire to do better. There is an element of superstition lingering in many minds which associates what one might call ideas of magic with the rite of Confirmation. The notion exists that some change is wrought by the imposition of the Bishop's hands, without any preparation of the candidate's heart. It is of the utmost importance that this false doctrine should be cleared away at the beginning of the course of instruction, and as it is often present in various disguises, it should be dealt with in very simple and very direct words.

Every teacher knows the importance of the grouping of pupils. Where our subject is one in which the cleverest girls are often the most ignorant, it is best to classify the girls by age and not by mental ability. It is no mean spiritual discipline for a brilliant girl who carries all before her in ordinary lessons to have to ask, or not to be able to answer, very elementary questions regarding religion ; and to recognize that others who take a humbler place in the rest of the day's work are far above and beyond her. If girls are chosen by their age to be prepared together, it ensures that friends will be able to form pairs or groups for reading or for revising notes, and this is often a great help.

I have examined many manuals of preparation and many works on the Catechism. I am sure I have gained much from these ; but I am profoundly convinced that the Catechism itself is the one incomparable and sufficient manual for our purpose. It says what it means and means what it says. Its language is plain : there are only a few words and phrases that need explanation ; and though persons who have not used the Catechism with great numbers and varieties of minds often make the most of these few words and phrases when they wish to find fault, they lay upon the Catechism blame that it does not deserve. I remember my first introduction to the Shorter Catechism of the Church of Scotland. I had travelled all night and arrived in the morning at a hospitable Scottish manse. In my bedroom was hung a great sheet of paper on which this Catechism was printed. I read the first question and its answer, and, at the time, I thought them a far grander beginning than our " What is your Name ? " " To glorify God, and to enjoy Him for ever " does, indeed, open up a glorious vista to the mind ; but our own Catechism arrests the attention of even a little child, and makes every one of us feel that it is in earnest and is concerned with us.

It is a good plan to provide every candidate with a little copy of the Catechism printed in big print. I always direct the girls to take these to pieces and to insert the sheets into notebooks, leaving plenty of room for what I shall tell them to write. About the written work I shall speak presently. Here I must say that I heartily wish that Prayer Books were not reduced to such tiny dimensions and that, for children at any rate, bigger books and much bigger type were supplied. It seems hard to refuse to allow a girl to use a beautiful little Prayer Book which some kind Godparent has given her in view of her Confirmation. There are, however, two reasons against letting her use it. One is that it is very bad for the girl's eyes, and no publisher would dream of asking me to look at a history or a geography book in such type ; the other, still weightier, is that the mind does not readily or permanently take in the meaning of words that are so inconspicuous.

The Catechism was meant to be committed to memory, and I am old-fashioned enough to think that we lose very much by not using it in this way ; but if a girl has never opened it until within six months of her Confirmation, I think it is a pity to insist on every word being learnt by heart. The Creed and the Commandments must be letter-perfect ; for the rest I am satisfied if I find that the words are quite familiar and that the sense is clearly understood. As there is only one preparation in the week for each girl, it is not too much to expect that some work will be done for each instruction. I generally give some passages from the Bible to be read ; and a few explanatory notes and one collect bearing especially on the subject in hand are written out. As a rule, it is easy to see by the questions the girls ask that they have read very carefully. They are not so careful in writing out notes, and very odd mistakes are sometimes made. One realizes how new to many of them are the phrases and the ideas which were familiar to ourselves even at an early age. But as the candidates are almost invariably willing to work, there is satisfactory progress to be noticed within a very few weeks. I have never given more than eight or less than six lessons to candidates on the part of the Catechism that I undertake to teach them. These lessons have been given in school hours, in the afternoon ; and time is found for them by the help of the teaching staff, who are always willing to cut down their demands upon the candidates for the preparation of ordinary work. Preparation for Confirmation is never wholly an additional burden laid upon the girls ; some relief is always given in view of it.

I come now to the preparation itself. I shall speak only of some parts of it in which there may be some difference between the teaching one gives in a girls' school and that which is given elsewhere. I mentioned that among schoolgirls of to-day there is very little recognition of the existence of sin. The Catechism does not ignore sin ; it is too true to the needs of human nature to ignore the one danger against which warning is needed. We are not asked or advised to dwell upon the facts of sin or to reveal all the dark places into which human life may stray. We are shown that it is our duty to let our children know that we see dangers ahead and that we can shed light for them upon the path of safety. There is a good deal of theory abroad at the present time, which, indeed, hardly deserves the name of theory, for it is densely nebulous. This takes the form of an assumption that if children never hear anything about evil they will always be innocent and good. It is not possible for anyone, even a child, with ordinary powers of perception, to go very long without encountering evil. We need not and ought not to dwell in our lessons on special forms of sin in detail. Our candidates should be made to feel free to come and ask us at some other time if they wish us to speak to them about special temptations or difficulties. We need only to accept, as the Catechism accepts it, the fact that there are many wrong things we should like to do and must not do.

In order to awaken the sense of sin, it is necessary to awaken the minds of one's pupils to some realization of God. This is done in a great variety of ways and we must try them all, for we have a great variety of minds to teach. Prayer is sometimes the first, as it is the most natural step towards the Presence, and that is why I have found it a good plan to suggest prayers to be copied out and used as part of the preparation. Reading passages from the life of our Lord often carries forward the thoughts to the loving Father. But I have always found it necessary to make a point of directly speaking about God to the candidates, and of telling them as simply as possible that He is, and that He is the rewarder of them that diligently seek Him. After they have been thinking of Him as a loving Father and a real Person, they begin to understand that it is His pardon they must first seek if they do wrong ; it is against Him they have offended, though they may have offended others too.

We must show very clearly the difference between temptation and sin. The Temptation of our Lord is our safest guide here. We show that He would have been glad to eat a bit of bread after that long privation ; that He had dreams of flinging Himself against Rome as a handful of patriots had flung themselves against Syria ; that in His longing to show men what was meant by faith in God He had imagined some great and spectacular achievement that would compel all men to believe. We must not shrink from saying that these were real temptations ; if our Lord could not have wished those wishes and put them aside because He felt it to be His duty, His example would have been of no use to us.

Among what may prove to be temptations which come to girls are very natural wishes to understand some of the mysteries of life. If they are thought too young for even a partial revelation of these mysteries (and in such cases the mother should always be consulted before anything is communicated), it is generally enough to say that these things are very sacred and in some respects difficult to understand, and that later on the child will be told about them : for the present she must wait. If she is reassured by seeing that we are not shocked by her having thought about such matters, if we show that we think reverently about them and can make her trust to our promise to let her know by and by, and if we take care that she has plenty to occupy her energies in work and play, we do not find that any harm is done. With a girl of rather more mature mind we may recognize that the best course is to give some information. Here, again, we must handle the subject with reverence, saying as little as possible, but taking care not to give the impression that we are keeping anything back because it is too shocking to be told—suggesting, rather, that what may remain unrevealed is all sacred, and we do not speak very easily about the most sacred things.

I am writing of girls at school who have much to occupy their minds, plenty of outlet for their energies, opportunities of every kind for such enterprises as young creatures most dearly love. It is only in very exceptional cases that more than a very few words or a very general statement are needed ; these are perfectly well understood by our candidates, especially when they are helped by the solemnity of manner which our sense of reverence prompts us to adopt. Because every human being knows what it is to encounter thoughts that seem to spring out of an empty background and yet have a character of their own which both attracts and repels, I have always given to candidates early in their preparation the collect for the second Sunday in Lent, and have commended it to them for frequent use. The fact that evil thoughts may (and often do) assault the soul without hurting it is a very good proof, which may be used with the best effect, that temptation is not sin.

Just as one cannot write of preparation at school without considering the previous preparation in religious knowledge, so one cannot envisage the conception of the Christian life set forth in the Catechism without showing how necessary it is that all the discipline of school should be in harmony with this great conception and should lead up to and prepare the way for it. We live to-day in a world which seems hardly to know the meaning of the word " renounce." " Live your own life," " Express yourself," are the burden of the insistent preachers whose pulpit is the novel. Other preachers who deserve respect for their high motives and obvious sincerity give us advice which would come to very much the same thing in the end. " Follow the child along the lines of its natural development " sounds very plausible ; but the experienced teacher answers, " Follow ! to what goal ? " We are older and ought to be wiser than our pupils : it is for us to recognize that those who by and by must rise towards the Christian goal and learn that life is gained only by losing life, should begin that long ascent with some practice of austerity, some training in self-denial.

I have said enough about the want of recognition of religion in many homes to make it clear that in regard to the belief for which the Catechism asks, the school must be prepared to give abundant help. This may be done in part by familiarizing the whole school with the Apostles' Creed ; in my own school it is recited once a week at prayers. But quite apart from any formal expression of belief, the girls are helped to a very simple and natural faith by the simplicity and naturalness of the faith of those who teach them. If we encumber our lessons with difficulties that are not an integral part of the great and true things we set out to teach, if we cannot distinguish between what is material or immaterial, we cannot wonder if the minds of our children are confused ; and here we cannot blame the home—we must take the blame upon ourselves.

Obedience as the Catechism describes it gives no trouble to the candidates. They are amused at the quaint phraseology and are perfectly willing to admit that as far as Duty to one's Neighbour goes the Catechism does not ask too much. They are even a little surprised, it may be, that they are told they are not able to do these things unaided. But before long they realize that the Catechism knows more about them than they knew about themselves.

Thus we come to speak of the aid they must have, and the last lesson I take with the candidates is the lesson on Prayer. The most necessary and the most fruitful part of our preparation is that which deals with Prayer. It would have been impossible to place the subject of Prayer earlier in the Catechism ; it comes most fitly when its need is shown ; but when girls have asked me about the difficulty of Faith I have sometimes replied by telling them to come to me again after I have spoken to them about Prayer. The Catechism has presented Prayer to their minds as not so much a duty as a necessity : thus we have the best introduction to Prayer ; and Prayer is the shortest way to Faith. Children, of course, think of prayer as asking for something ; when they adventure in prayer and ask for something they urgently want, they believe they have really prayed. Then comes disappointment : they do not receive the gift for which they asked ; and they tell us that prayer is not always answered. No difficulty crops up so often as this. We must be careful and sympathetic in dealing with it, for it is a difficulty which often causes great pain and always distressing bewilderment.

Here, again, we must rely to some extent on previous training in school to help us in the special preparation. If by us in school prayers the Presence of God has been felt, if we have been able to lay aside thoughts of all our other occupations, if the children unconsciously but habitually recognize that those who teach them set some extraordinary value on the few minutes that are devoted to the worship of God at the opening of the day, we have established in the children's minds a firm foundation for future teaching about prayer. Sooner or later the time comes when we have our opportunity to tell them that real prayer, though it is not always granted, is always answered ; the spirit that truly endeavours to tell its wants to God does not go empty away. Simplicity, such as children need if we are to help them at all to know what prayer is and what it can do, is not, I am afraid, very easy to attain ; it is perhaps only by the experience of our mistakes that we learn how we ourselves have made the matter complex. We often do not begin as we should begin by following our Lord's teaching. In the prayer He gave His disciples their thoughts were first of all turned to God ; they were not encouraged to think in the first place of themselves and their need. It is this realization of God that makes our prayers not only the outcome but also the great nourisher of our faith. This may be a paradox, but a paradox is not necessarily impossible for a child's mind to receive.

I have always suggested collects that seemed likely to be particularly useful to the candidates, but I also suggest to them that they should try to use their own words at times. A form of prayer helps us to be definite ; but there are many moods and many needs for which no fitting form can be found. The great thing is that our candidates should not be self-conscious and that they should be conscious of the Divine Presence. When they have learned how to pray (whether during their preparation or before it), one may be hopeful that they are ready for the further teaching about the Sacraments.

CHAPTER IX

THE CONFIRMATION SERVICE

By SAMUEL MUMFORD TAYLOR, *Bishop*

IF the first accounts of Confirmation in the New Testament are brief, they are also very clear. The Acts of St. Peter and St. John at Samaria,[1] and of St. Paul at Ephesus,[2] leave no doubt as to " the example of the holy apostles " which, in the prayer of our English Order, the Bishop says that he has followed. " They prayed for them that they might receive the Holy Ghost. . . . Then laid they their hands on them, and they received the Holy Ghost." And yet it would hardly be true to say that this is the idea of Confirmation that is foremost in the mind of every member of the English Church to-day. With not a few it is rather the renewal of the baptismal vow that stands out as its main purpose. The public confession ; the promise ; the words of the hymn with which the service so commonly concludes, " O Jesus, I have promised,"—this is echoing in the minds of the candidates as they go away.

And although the question and answer in which the baptismal vow is acknowledged and ratified were no part of the Confirmation Service till 1662, no one can deny how useful and impressive this action of the candidate can be made. It was implied indeed in the days when it formed no part of the rite. But when it comes to be the predominant idea, it has got out of proportion. Confirmation is a means of grace. And it is dependence upon God, both for good desire, and for help to fulfil the same, that should stand out in prominence. And although generations of candidates have been told that they have come " to confirm " " what their godfathers and godmothers promised for them," yet the very title of the service lays emphasis on the greater fact that they have come to be

---

[1] Acts viii. 14–17. [2] Acts xix. 1–7.

confirmed—" The Order of Confirmation, or laying on of
hands upon those that are baptized." It tells of God's
act rather than their own—His blessing. " Our help is
in the name of the Lord " is the first note struck when the
introduction is over and the office itself begins.

It could hardly have been foreseen that to add to the Confirmation a renewal of the vow of Baptism, which though
it could take place at any time was specially appropriate at
this time, would be in any way misleading. Nevertheless,
it has become clear that there is need now, both in the
preparatory instruction and in the ordering of the service,
for placing the emphasis where it should be—not on the
suitable introduction, but on what is essential in the rite.
Sometimes the very insertions and additions which are
intended to enhance its solemnity have in fact tended to
obscure the simplicity of the laying on of hands with
prayer, which is the Confirmation.

The Revised Order of Confirmation, recognizing this
need of readjustment, makes two provisions.

(1) The present Preface (" To the end that Confirmation . . . assented unto ") is restored to the position it
held in 1549, and becomes a rubric again. Its place is
taken by an address beginning with, " Dearly beloved
in the Lord, in ministering Confirmation the Church doth
follow the example of the Apostles of Christ. For in the
eighth chapter of the Acts of the Apostles we thus read " :
There follow verses 4, 5, 12, 14–17 ; and then two brief
paragraphs set forth (i) the outward sign and the inward
grace of Confirmation, and (ii) the intention of the Church
in ordering that those now to be confirmed shall openly
acknowledge themselves bound to fulfil the Christian duties
to which their baptism has pledged them. It is that the
congregation may be certified of their steadfast purpose.

(2) The actual Confirmation is to proceed from the
words, " Our help is," etc., down to the end of the prayer
following the Lord's Prayer without any interruption by
preaching or other instruction, or by the singing of any
hymn or anthem, " except that a hymn may be sung, if
needed, in the course of the laying on of hands."

Taking then the revised form as our basis, let us see

how the service may be ordered, so that its meaning shall
be clear, and that those who are to be confirmed shall have
the most help in realizing it.   It may be treated in four
parts: I. Introductory. II. The Renewal of Baptismal
Vows.   III. The Confirmation and Conclusion.   IV. The
Address.

I. The bishop, on entering, goes to the chair at the
entrance to the chancel; or to the sacrarium.   One advantage of the latter is that it marks off the introductory
part of the service from that which is central.

A hymn at the beginning is useful, and will be followed
by the Preface (" Dearly beloved in the Lord ") read by
the incumbent of the Church, if appointed to do so by
the bishop, the candidates standing.   At the end may be
sung, kneeling, a hymn addressed to the Holy Spirit.

II. The bishop now moves from the sacrarium to the
chancel entrance, and, the candidates and the congregation
being seated, he will probably think it well to explain in a
few words that he is about to ask the question, and why. He
tells the candidates, in substance, how they were pledged
at Baptism to certain duties before they were conscious of
it ; that now they have been under instruction they know
what those duties are ; and the question, in other words,
is this—Now that you know what it meant, do you acknowledge that you are bound by the vow which your sponsors
made for you, and are you resolved to stand by it ?

Before the question (" Do ye here . . . ? ") is asked, it has
been found to be very valuable to spend a few moments in
silence, all kneeling ; the candidates being bidden to remember the answer they are about to make, and the grace
that they may expect from God in order to persevere ; and
the congregation being reminded that they are there not
as onlookers, but as helpers with their prayers.   It is unusual to have any silence in our services, and this helps to
make it the more impressive and solemnizing here.   Indeed,
from that moment there should be a spiritual tension that
is not relaxed in what follows, to the end.   After the silence,
the bishop bids the congregation to remain kneeling, and
the candidates to stand.   It helps to maintain a reverent
quietness that the congregation should continue kneeling,

instead of rising and seating themselves, and in little more than a minute having to kneel again.

Then follows the question. The division of the question into three parts, which is offered in the revised Order as an alternative, will hardly be preferred. It lays more stress than is necessary here on the Renewal, which, as we have already seen, is to be avoided. And after the instruction on the Catechism that has been given to the candidates so recently, a reference to the " solemn promise and vow " should be sufficient without any further explanation of it.

Sometimes the question has been asked individually of the candidates by the bishop, holding the list in his hand and saying, " N., do you . . . ? " But this seems rather to minister to that mistaken view of Confirmation as consisting primarily in a public profession, instead of the receiving of a divine blessing. If the Christian name is inserted anywhere it should be, as of old time, at the moment of the laying on of hands.

III. After the answer follow the versicles and responses, which are often said by the bishop and candidates alone ; and at " Let us pray " the candidates kneel, and the bishop, extending his hand over them, offers the great prayer, the invocation of the Holy Spirit, with solemn deliberation.

In the Sacramentary of Gelasius (seventh century) " Amen " was said after the petition for the Holy Ghost the Comforter, and after each pair of the six gifts of the Spirit, as well as after " the spirit of the fear of the Lord " at the close. This must have added greatly to the impressiveness of the prayer ; and a brief pause, at least as long as the saying of " Amen " would require, may well be made at these same points, or at least after " the Comforter." We have been told that the words of our Common Prayer go too quickly for a real concentration of thought upon them. Here is a case where that may be remembered with advantage.

After the prayer the bishop, as a rule, sits ; and the candidates are brought up to kneel before him, the men and boys coming first.

Where the rows of seats are not open at both ends each row of candidates should be brought a little down the church as they come out, so that those who sat farthest from the middle of the church may go up first to the bishop, and thus they will come back in their right order, and be able to go to their seats without crossing one another.[1]

The rubric directs that the Bishop " shall lay his hand upon the head of every one severally, saying, Defend, O Lord, etc." Our great town populations have made difficulties that were never contemplated in the days when this direction was given.[2] Confirmations have been largely multiplied since the time when William Wake, Archbishop of Canterbury (1724), confirmed about 1,300 persons at Cranbrook ; or when at Leeds Parish Church, in Dr. Hook's time, upwards of 1,000 candidates were presented at once, in 1837, and again in 1840 a like number ; or forty years later, when Bishop Thorold confirmed not far short of 600 at Newington Church, and it took exactly three hours and three-quarters. But there are still frequent occasions when the number is over one hundred, and at times two hundred.[3] A literal obedience to the rubric must then make the service of intolerable length. There have been various ways of meeting the difficulty. Some bishops limit the repetition of the prayer to fifty times ; which means that three or four candidates may receive the imposition of hands while the prayer is said once. It is not at all uncommon that two at a time should be confirmed, and in this case " Defend, O Lord, this thy child with thy heavenly grace " is repeated, with the laying of the right hand on the head of each of them, the remainder of the

[1] Dearmer, *The Parson's Handbook*, p. 458.

[2] When Henry VIII came to the throne he found in the whole of England and Wales no more than twenty-two dioceses. To these he added six, and proposed to create nine others. He contemplated a total of thirty-seven dioceses for a population of from three to four million souls—that is to say, for about the present population of the diocese of London. Yet for a population nearly ten times as large the Church has seemingly to content herself with only forty diocesan bishops. (Wilfrid S. de Winton, *Reform in the Church of England*, p. 232.)

[3] Bishop Creighton would never confirm more than two hundred at a time.

prayer, from " that he may continue " and onwards, being said once for both.

Sometimes the parish priest asks that the candidates may come up two at a time, as they feel less nervous, and more able to think and pray, than when they come up alone. This is worth considering. We probably under-estimate what the prominence and publicity of approaching and kneeling down alone may cost the candidate when, as often happens, Confirmation has been delayed to an age more self-conscious than childhood. It does not prevent the use of the full prayer for each, though two are confirmed side by side.

It seems clear that whenever it can be done without undue delay—and this is in the majority of cases—the rubric should be literally observed. But it is not a point to be settled lightly, and as a matter of course, for in many a Confirmation the time spent in the coming and going of the candidates is too long, and the reverence of the service suffers. Those who have gone back to their place, and those who are awaiting their turn, both find it difficult after a while to keep their minds in the attitude of prayer, and the congregation, many of them without experience in acts of devotion, tend to drop into the mere sight-seeing mood, and help to lower the spiritual temperature. All then that can be done reverently to ease the strain, which is inevitable, should be done in this matter of the Confirmation prayer. The question is not disposed of by the suggestion that there should be no address. That is a subject for separate consideration; but even if there be none at all, it does not meet the difficulty of the wearisome length of time that must be faced at large Confirmations if the present direction is strictly carried out.

It has been proposed that the organ should be played during the act of Confirmation, and this may be very solemnizing and helpful, if you can ensure that it be done very quietly and with real taste and feeling. This cannot always be reckoned upon. A safer use of music is the singing of a metrical " Litany of the Holy Spirit," if it can be kept very quiet. The congregation may, in our larger churches, be depended upon for singing it.

Experience teaches that it is best, on the whole, to be without a choir. The difficulty of the length of time taken by the laying on of hands is great, whether the choir be kneeling or sitting. And it is no help to the candidates, young or older, to be looked at by the choristers as they approach and kneel. Nor can we expect of the boys that they will be absorbed in their books, or remain with closed eyes, all the time.

In the first English Prayer Book the candidate was named by the bishop. This is sometimes done still ; "Defend, O Lord, this thy child X. with thy heavenly grace." And it is so fitting and full of meaning, both in connexion with Holy Baptism, and in its impressing on the candidate the love and care of God for him individually, that it may well be done whenever there are but few candidates, and the priest presenting them and standing by can quickly name them to the bishop as they approach. But this would hardly be possible, or might lead to delay or confusion, in the circumstances we have to bear in mind.[1]

The name may however be specially inserted in the prayer when it is desired, for some sufficient cause, to change that which was given to the child at Baptism. The decision of Lord Coke, supported by all the judges in the case brought before him, and after the practice of addressing the person by name was discontinued, was that a bishop might so change a name, as the common law of England.[2] When a child has been named, at some time of popular excitement, in memory of a battle-field, or a jubilee, it is a charitable work to free him from bearing this burden any longer.

Again, in the first Prayer Book of Edward VI the bishop is directed to sign the candidate with the cross when he confirms him. The direction was omitted in the book of 1552, but the practice seems to have continued. Bishop Jeremy Taylor says : " I do not find it forbidden

---

[1] In the Scottish rite the candidate is addressed by name, before the prayer. " N., I sign thee . . . and I lay my hands on thee. . . . Defend O Lord, etc."

[2] See Blunt and Phillimore, *The Book of Church Law* (pp. 60–1, 9th edn.), where instances are given.

or revoked. And therefore it may seem to be permitted
to the discretion of the bishops." And in 1636 Bishop
Montagu writes : " It is a frequent practice to make the
sign of the cross in the Name of our Lord Jesus Christ,
both in baptism, and in the confirmation of those who
have been catechized."

The use of the word " servant " in the prayer " Defend
O Lord, etc.," has been condemned on the ground that even
the oldest of adult candidates may rightly be called a " child
of God." Which is perfectly true. But does not the
objection leave out of sight the fact that there is some
ambiguity in the use of the word here ? At most Confirmations some are presented who have reached, or passed,
middle age. It requires a serious effort, in the face of
many who have long known them, to come forward with
the children of the parish, for a rite that is naturally
associated with children, and it seems to add to the difficulty
that they shall be spoken of as the " child," which in
one sense they are, and in another they are no longer.
Practically one is sensible, at the moment, of its adding
to their difficulty, if they were not referred to as
" this thy servant." Moreover, in the prayer of Invocation immediately preceding, all the candidates,
young and old, have already been spoken of as " these thy
servants." [1]

After the laying on of hands the service proceeds, without
break, with " The Lord be with you," the Lord's Prayer,
the two collects, and the Blessing. The word " them " in
the rubric before the blessing has taken the place of the
more explicit direction of 1549 and 1552 : " Then shall the
Bishop bless the children, thus saying."

IV. Complaints, or perhaps good-humoured grumblings,
appear with a certain regularity in the church papers, as
to the length of the addresses given at Confirmations, and
sometimes as to their character. It is an important matter,

[1] The " half-ashamed sense of doing now what ought to have been done
long before, and sometimes a slight irritation or annoyance " has been
adduced as making either some alteration in our present Order, or an alternative one, desirable. This would not assume that all adults who offer themselves for confirmation have been baptized as infants. See Hardman, *The
Rite of Confirmation*. p. 22.

and is worthy of the fullest consideration. Three different opinions have been expressed.

(1) First, why should there be any address at all ? Nothing was said about it in the " Order of Confirmation," until in the revised Order reference was made to it in a new rubric. And have not the clergy been instructing the candidates for months past ? One might suppose that this preparation had not been carefully leading them up to the Confirmation day. In days past, it is true, this might not have been, in certain places, an outrageous assumption. We are told of one Bishop who habitually acted upon it. His custom was to expound with much care every sentence of the Catechism as far as the questions on the Sacraments, before the laying on of hands ; and the remainder, with the same deliberation, afterwards. He could probably have justified himself by instances, in his own experience, of what had counted for preparation. But that was long ago. It is not because of any deficiency in the preparation that the bishops of to-day think it desirable to give an address. Their desire is to reinforce the efforts that have been made by the parish priest, who, despite the most careful and earnest teaching, is never, by his own confession, perfectly satisfied. There are always among his candidates various degrees of interest and of understanding ; some have seemed much more impressed than others. From time to time he makes improvements in his methods. But even when the understanding has grasped the outlines of Christian doctrine and practice, he will be uncertain in many a case how far it has penetrated in feeling and will, and a foundation for sincere resolutions and for perseverance in well-doing has been really laid. Has the beauty of the ideal that he desired to set before them in all its attractiveness even dawned on some of his candidates ? Has some generous loyalty to the Lord who died for them risen up in their hearts at the invitation, which is also a command, " Follow Me " ? Have they realized that to " follow " Him means the life of service, of God and their brethren ? In proportion as he has tried to make the most of his opportunity, the true pastor will be grateful that, on the Confirmation day,

when they may be supposed to be most sensitive to spiritual impressions, a final word to them by another voice, and that the voice of their " father in God," shall press home the counsel that has already been given. Some practical advice as to method in prayer, preparation for Communion, the importance of public worship, and so forth, will come like the final stroke of the hammer that drives the nail home. " The kind of address that I like," said a homely but truly pastoral parish priest, " is one that sends them away thinking—then our Vicar was right, after all." Endorsement by another authority, and by one whom they regard with special respect, lifts some things out of the region of the well-meaning, but possibly individual and peculiar, into that of assured and important fact. So are they helped to be " willing in the day of His power."

(2) Another opinion is this. Probably it is right that an address should be given, but why two ? To this there seems to be a twofold answer.

The first in the shape of a further question : if only one address, at what point should it be given ? Granted that it should not be inserted in the " Order," it must be either before or after it. Suppose it is given before. There is still to come the asking of the question. It is at once to follow. In any words spoken at that moment will there not be a tendency to dwell emphatically on the meaning of the promise ? It is easy to pass from this to the thought of the grace that is needed to keep it. But in the mental picture it will be likely to take a position that, as we have noted already, needs to be corrected, for its over-prominence in the common view of Confirmation. It will tend to confuse the preparatory and additional feature of our rite with its essential purpose, man's part with God's part. And, on the other hand, the enforcement of a life in accordance with our Christian faith and the grace given to us comes with more point after we have been strengthened by the Spirit, when the sense of responsibility is sharpened, and some readiness to rise to our calling and ministry towards God and man, in the " royal priesthood," has been stirred. But if the one address only is to be at the close, the bishop may well think that he should not have omitted a serious but heartening word in preface to the solemn renewal of the vow. A word on what the Baptism of a Christian must mean in a world whose standards and aims are far lower; that as Christians they are called to endure hardness, as opposed to the softer way, which goes with the stream; that this confession before witnesses is no light matter, harder than they now know, and yet of no doubtful issue, God being on their side. It need take but a very few moments to impress this, but it will be in place, and will meet with response.

It seems likely then that, for the sake of clearness and proportion, it will be well to divide what there is to say on these two subjects, though less need be said in the first case than in the second.

And there is this further support. If two points, connected yet different, such as the renewal of the vow, and the strengthening of God's Spirit for His service, are to be treated, it is better, though no more time be taken in doing so, that the teaching should be divided. We have the experience of the mission preacher. He tells us that when two important points are to be handled, it will be better to separate the words spoken about each by an interval—either of silence, or an act of devotion, or a hymn—than to go straight on without break. If this be true at any time it is specially applicable here, for the laying on of hands has conferred, in the theological use of the word, a new " character " or status in between.

(3) A third suggestion is this: that " if the bishop wishes he should say a very few words about Communion to the candidates after the Blessing, and then depart "— nothing more in the way of address being required at the service.

Certainly such words may fitly be spoken, but why not something more also ? We wish them to leave as expectant communicants. To our counsel on preparation, and on regularity, we may well add something on the practice of the presence of God, daily prayer, and reading of the Scriptures, which are the only security that the communicant life will be maintained. Something more is needed to support it than the knowledge that it is both a

duty and a privilege. Nothing that will help towards the
level of life that makes it natural for them to come must
be allowed to drop out of sight. Nothing that will help
to avert what is a far too common experience, that they
come to a first Communion, and perhaps for a few times
after, and then no more. This all must feel who are aware
that only too poor a proportion of the confirmed are
added year by year to the regular communicant members
of the Church.

To sum up these thoughts :

(i) The reasons in favour of an address at Confirmation
seem to be overwhelming. The bishop will naturally
feel at such a time the responsibility of his pastoral office,
and will desire to make full use of the opportunity. As
Bishop Creighton said : " It is a great privilege of my
office that I am brought into contact with many young
lives in my Confirmations." [1] There is also much to be
said, and this was his practice, for giving two short addresses,
one leading up to the vow, the other on prayer and Holy
Communion, with a view to perseverance and growth.
Never are there more attentive hearers; none are more
likely to remember what is said to them.

(ii) Brevity is essential, lest the good effect of the
words spoken should be lessened or destroyed. Something
like five minutes for the first address, and fifteen for the
second will be wise. This means taking some pains. But
the pithy, epigrammatic style of Bishop Thorold—to
refrain from illustration from the practice of bishops still
living—is an art to be coveted. One of his addresses is
given in full in Simpkinson's *Life*, p. 203, and cannot have
lasted much more than ten minutes. The Confirmation
was at St. John the Divine, Kennington. There were 189
candidates. An entry is found in the Bishop's diary that
" the congregation was immensely attentive." [2] It is said
that the custom, once usual, that the candidates should
stand while the bishop speaks to them is still found in
some places. This must surely add to the apparent length
of the address.

[1] *Life and Letters of Mandell Creighton*, p. 32.
[2] See also *Life*, p. 400.

(iii) It is maintained by psychologists that for the average churchgoer an hour is about the longest that a service should last, if attention is to be fully engaged. And an hour will give abundant time, including two addresses as above, with an average number of candidates. This is not too much to expect, even with the fifteen minutes in church before the service begins, which is apt to be forgotten in measuring the demand on strength and attention.

Experience shows that it is best to speak to the candidates immediately after the Blessing. When a hymn comes between it seems to relax the tension, and in a measure to break continuity. But a hymn should follow the address. While this is sung the bishop goes to the altar, and after a Collect for Perseverance, gives a blessing to the congregation present, and so brings the service to an end.

It is not sufficiently recognized that the truth of the priesthood of the Christian Church as a whole,[1] which is admitted in a general and figurative way, has practical consequences which go to the root of some of our shortcomings and difficulties to-day. For example, the taking part regularly in public worship is only too commonly regarded as depending in the case of the laity upon inclination or temperament. It is thought to be part of the duty of the clergy to provide frequent opportunities of worship, for those who wish for them, and to discharge this duty reverently; it is mainly their affair. Whereas the Baptism that admits each member of the Body is followed later by a laying on of hands which consecrates to a priesthood that belongs to all the faithful; and that priesthood has an aspect towards God in the service we call worship, as well as an aspect towards man, in service that is ready to meet any of his needs, but takes its highest form of ministry in leading him to God. Offering is the fundamental idea in worship, and in this the whole Body is concerned. " The bread that *we* break," St. Paul says. And " we offer," " we present," is the language of our liturgy.

[1] I St. Peter ii. 4, 5, 9, 10; Rev. i. 6.

Dr. Robert Moberly has expressed this with his accustomed precision in his *Ministerial Priesthood*. " The priesthood of the layman is no merely verbal concession. It is a doctrine of importance, essential for a due understanding of the priesthood of the ministry " (p. 92). " The ministry represents the whole Body, and wields, ministerially, authority and powers which, in idea and in truth, inherently belong to the collective life of the Body as a whole " (p. 72). " We shall, I believe, approach the truth in this matter by insisting, in no metaphorical sense, upon the sacred character and the solemn responsibility of the priesthood of the Christian Church as a whole, and (apart from its ministerial and executive sense) of every individual lay member of the Church " (p. 258).

If this be understood, it will be felt that an ordination to the priesthood and a Confirmation may appropriately show some resemblance, and indeed that such resemblance should be evident and impressive, if ceremonial is to express clearly a doctrine that needs to be much more firmly grasped than is usual at the present time.

(i) The imposition of hands is central in both cases.

(ii) At an ordination the bishop sits for the laying on of hands : a position of ministerial authority. " No direction is given as to the position of the bishop during the act of Confirmation, nor is there any uniform tradition on the matter. The analogy of ordination suggests that he should be seated for the imposition of hands if the candidates are brought to him." [1] In the American Church the bishop passes along the rail, as when administering Holy Communion, and to Bishop Hall it seems unmeaning to sit, and even inappropriate.[2] But if the responsibility of their ministry rests on the lay members of the Body, it is desirable that this should be emphasized at the time when their consecration takes place ; and this is done by the bishop assuming a posture like that which is used in ordination. Such misconception as that which is crystallized in the misleading phrase, " going into the Church," when what is meant is " receiving Holy Order within the Church," is

[1] Dr. Frere, *Principles of Religious Ceremonial*, p. 125.
[2] Hall, *Confirmation*, p. 214.

connected by this ceremony, which is " neither dark nor
dumb," but eloquent and clear of a passing to the full
exercise of the spiritual privilege of a Christian. It has
become almost universal in the English Church.

(iii) The use of the " Veni Creator " at the ordination of
a priest is found in certain Pontificals from the twelfth
century. And at a Confirmation, where the central
petition of the prayer before the laying on of hands is,
" Strengthen them we beseech Thee, O Lord, with the
Holy Ghost, the Comforter," the custom that is widespread of a hymn invoking the Holy Spirit, and sung
kneeling, is very suitable. It should not be inserted in the
Office, but, as suggested above, will be appropriately placed
before the renewal of the baptismal vows. Nor is it necessary to use the " Veni Creator," which to some may seem
too closely associated with the Ordinal for this purpose.
The " Veni, Sancte Spiritus," the Whitsun sequence (attri-
buted to Stephen Langton, Archbishop of Canterbury)
may well be used.[1]

(iv) The use of Unction, which has been added to the
imposition of hands from a very early time, was discontinued in the first English Prayer Book. As it was the
symbol of consecration,[2] and especially of consecration to a
priesthood, this was a loss from the point of view of the
recognition of the priesthood of the laity. It was a supplementary ceremony, but as time went on it went far to
efface the original outward sign, and so in accordance
with the purpose, in this as in other matters, to return to
primitive rule, it was dropped.

[1] *Hymns, A. & M.* (complete edition), 156. But see also the translation
in *The English Hymnal,* 155.
[2] Dr. Chase, *Confirmation in the Apostolic Age,* pp. 67–8.

CHAPTER X

THE AFTER-CARE OF CANDIDATES (1)

By H. Lovell Clarke

Our adolescent Churchmen and Churchwomen deserve as much detailed and scientific study and care as, for instance, the children, who have received so much attention during the last half-century. Owing to the relative neglect of this, the good work begun in a child has too often been allowed to evaporate when childhood is over. Not only are young people always of great consequence, but they are doubly so to-day, when, throughout the world, they are in the van of all manner of world-movements. In times of comparative equilibrium the people of maturity are masters of the situation. In times, like the present, of restless change, the significance of the young becomes emphatic. It is imperative that the contribution of young people to the life and work of the Kingdom of God be given its full scope.

The problems of adolescence have already been handled in a previous chapter, but the wise after-care of adolescents newly confirmed is so closely connected with psychological knowledge and experience that a brief survey of the characteristics of youth in its changing phases is desirable here.

Childhood is hungry for experience, impressionable, absorbent of ideas, without much capacity of criticism. It draws no very clear line between the real and the imaginary. Childhood is the irresponsible age of the uncritical accumulation of materials. It is as natural for a child to collect knowledge, facts, and experiences as it is for it to collect butterflies, wild-flowers, or postage stamps. Childhood is as absorbent as a sponge, but its critical faculties are latent ; its egoism is ingenuous and unthinking ; it lives from day to day.

Life moulds the child : the adolescent, at the age of fifteen or thereabouts, begins to seek to mould life. Then begins the age of idealism, the quest for a life-purpose. This age of adolescence ought not to be unduly prolonged. Many ills of the personality in later life are traceable to retarded development, to unwillingness to enter upon a new psychological phase. Adolescence must give place to maturity when the latter is due. It is not sufficient, in the directing of the life of a parish, to have bridged the gulf that separates childhood and adolescence. A similar bridge must be built between adolescence and maturity. Where the problems of adolescence are clearly understood and the parochial organization is evolved to meet the instinctive needs of its young people, the problem becomes, not, how the Church can keep its boys and girls of fourteen, but, how it can make its adult organizations sufficiently true to the needs of young maturity to keep its young men and women who are leaving adolescence behind.

Adolescence seeks for an ideal whereby it may find completeness. It is a strange, critical, tempestuous age, which views all things in heaven and earth with mingled criticism and veneration. It is attracted to all manner of social, religious, and political idealisms, but it is completely committed to none. It is often distinguished by an arrogant outward sureness, which conceals an inward uncertainty. It is apt to ignore children as being foolish and the middle-aged as being petrified.

Normally, the adolescent is deeply interested in the opposite sex, but is not committed to any member of it. Guidance is needed and welcomed, but dictation is resented. Exaggeration is instinctive. Things are " ripping," " topping," " beastly." Adolescents are capable of idealizing, almost indefinitely, older people whom they admire and trust, and the success of their organizations is therefore conditioned by the wise choice of older persons who are appointed to be their leaders. It would almost seem that the tribal habit is instinctive at this age, and that a tribal leader is a necessity of the case. The Church must needs deal with its adolescents by means of a certain segregation of them into young people's organizations. If it fails to do so, it will fall between the two stools of childhood and maturity, and it will not keep its young people.

But there comes a time when the quest for a life-purpose should be completed, when the exploratory by-paths of adolescence should be exchanged for the one straight, hard highway of maturity. Youth likes to delay the making of the decisive choice ; for to settle down to one plain way of life means the eliminating of choice. To have made the decision is to be in the position of the man in the Greek proverb who held a wolf by the ears. The age of irresponsibility and indecision is over. The work and the life chosen must be held firmly, or they will turn and rend you.

Those responsible for the after-care of adolescents will need to shape the life of the parish with a view, not only to maintaining a continuity of loyalty to Christ and His Kingdom during the age of transition between childhood and adolescence, but also, with as much care and wisdom, to holding that loyalty during the passing from adolescence to maturity.

It will be well to define certain limitations in the scope of the section of the book for which the writer is responsible. The after-care of older Confirmation candidates presents special problems, which are not here considered. The majority of young Churchmen and Churchwomen fall within the category of weekly wage-earners. Their circumstances and their inclinations make them markedly social by nature, and they require the provision of organizations of which they become members, and to which they are ready and desirous to devote much of their leisure time. It is to the problems of the after-care of young weekly wage-earners that the writer addresses himself.

The personal factor is naturally, and in all cases, of great importance. To prepare candidates for Confirmation with any effectiveness demands a close spiritual relationship with the candidates during the time of preparation. Every priest must experience some regret when the classes are over and the newly confirmed become merged in the general body of the communicants of the parish. He

should endeavour to maintain some real spiritual relationship with those whom he has prepared and must be ready
to be at their service freely and for an unlimited period.
A practice which is keenly appreciated by young communicants is the summoning of all one's personal candidates,
year by year, for at least ten years, or till the earlier ter-
mination of one's ministry in a parish, to come together to
Communion on the nearest Sunday to the anniversary
of their Confirmation. A general invitation is not sufficient.
A personal invitation is necessary by means of a letter,
worded in some such way as follows : " I do not forget
that —— is the anniversary of your Confirmation——.
I am therefore inviting you and all those who were confirmed with you to meet at the Altar on —— that we may
all pray together for the renewal of the gifts of the Holy
Spirit that were given to you at your Confirmation." In
a large parish this becomes a laborious task as the years
go by and the numbers and the dates increase, but it is
keenly appreciated and it helps to maintain that personal
spiritual relationship which is most fruitful.

But all this has its obvious limitations. The aim is to
build up a habit of regular Communion and the practice
of a spiritual life which is not too much dependent upon
the support of one particular priest. Otherwise the
departure of a priest to another parish may mean the
falling away of numbers of communicants who have been
insensibly depending upon his support for the continuance
of their life of devotion.

The after-care must somehow be put into commission.
It is therefore necessary that young people's organizations
should be developed upon lines calculated to ensure this
end. Psychologically adolescents differ so widely from
people who have attained maturity that separate organizations seem almost a necessity. Separate devotional treatment, with a view to their spiritual needs, seems to be as
much advisable as separate provision for their social needs.

There will be described below, in some measure of detail,
not a theoretic system, which might or might not be
practicable, but one that is in full operation. There is
no attempt to exaggerate its success, or to shirk the diffi-

culties it raises. It is the belief of the writer that its problems are such as arise out of a plan that has life, and that, while demanding thought and decisions, they are fraught with hope and encouragement. The writer is the more at ease in commending the plan in general in that it is not his invention, but something that he inherited from his predecessor.

The age-limit of the Sunday School is fixed at the thirteenth birthday. As soon as boys and girls have attained that age, they are immediately transferred to Bible classes. It is important that they should be solidly settled into an older organization before they go out into the world of older people. If they are still in the Sunday school when that important event of their lives takes place, they will be ill at ease, and they will tend to resent the action of the Church in continuing to class them with the children. We find that there is eagerness to make the change. They become members of large Bible classes, with interesting syllabuses of instruction. In the parish in question, with a population of 18,000 to 20,000, there are more than 600 adolescents in such classes. Besides the usual instruction, there are frequent addresses by outside speakers.

The aim is to train good citizens, as well as good Christians and good Churchmen and Churchwomen. Care is taken to give the chief emphasis to religious teaching, in the more limited sense, but, with that emphasis maintained, the range of subjects is very wide, from personal devotion to anything that helps towards enlightened citizenship. Such an objective, undertaken and carried out on a large scale, as a deliberate policy, can command the voluntary services of speakers of specialized knowledge and of distinction in their subjects. The general formula is : Religion, Fellowship, Citizenship, Education. The largest of the boys' Bible classes is developing its own orchestra. It is officered by its own older members, who do all the work of registration and carry out the details of management. The problem of discipline has never, in the experience of the writer, arisen. The whole thing is so completely their own affair. They take a great pride in it and it is an important factor in their lives. No outside speaker would be invited unless he were competent to talk to boys and young men. This class meets in its own hut, which was purchased by the parish ; and, over a term of years, the lads are repaying the capital outlay. This is made possible by means of their annual sale of work. An essential feature of all the young people's organizations is the Mothers' Committee. It is formed from among the mothers of the young people of the particular organization. They elect one of their own number as chairman (the technical term survives, though she is strictly chairwoman). They work in close co-operation with the head of the organization, and are not only of great use in an advisory capacity, but also render much financial aid. Only the largest of the organizations needs a yearly sale. Not one of the organizations is subsidized by the parish. They are, and prefer to be, self-supporting, and the Mothers' Committees make this possible by holding working parties, and, where necessary, organizing a Sale of Work Club and arranging for the regular collection, at the houses of the subscribers, of money to be spent at the sale.

The above lads' club meets throughout the week in its own club-rooms and hut. Under the Fisher Education Act, certain of its activities are conducted by teachers provided by the Education Committee of the city. Gymnastics, singing, and various sports are some of its activities.

A boys' organization on this scale and with so wide a scope needs special leadership. In the parish in question it has hitherto been possible, in spite of the prevailing shortage of young clergy, to secure a succession of men, newly or recently ordained, with special aptitude for the work. It has an attractiveness which is obvious, and it appeals to principals of theological colleges as a field for men of promise in leadership. Having been chosen for some special aptitude, the leader is accorded much freedom in the application of the principles underlying the work.

Attendance at the Sunday Bible class is obligatory, and also, of course, conformity to all the rules of the club. Confirmation is kept before the members, but as a matter of personal decision, not as a matter of obligation. As a

matter of fact, the response is fairly general, and the subsequent attendance at Holy Communion on the whole
regular.

All the young people's organizations together, of both
sexes, have their own Sunday in the month for their corporate Communion. They are not omitted from the
general Communicants' Roll, and, as well as the older
communicants, they are invited to the general devotional
service of preparation which precedes another Sunday in
the month, and some of them avail themselves of these
general facilities. We think it important that these cards
of invitation to the general preparation should be regularly
issued to them, with a view to the time when they have
outgrown the adolescent life. But in practice their
devotional life is treated as a separate problem. This is
probably sound, as their devotional attitude and their
devotional needs are not likely to coincide with those of
older people.

The above Bible class and club was developed later than
the Church Lads' Brigade company. It was felt that,
while the quality of the C.L.B. was excellent, it was almost
necessarily limited as far as numbers are concerned. A
successful company cannot be extended indefinitely, and
the question of the supply of suitable officers imposes
limitations upon the number of companies in a parish,
whereas such a Bible class as has been described above is
capable of almost indefinite expansion. The C.L.B.
company of the parish has also its own club-room, and,
according to the regulations of the Brigade, its own Sunday
Bible class. Its strict discipline and its detailed order
make a strong appeal to many lads, and its influence on
them is far-reaching ; but there are many to whose temperaments it does not and will not appeal. The general
familiarity with the principles and methods of the C.L.B.
render it unnecessary to devote more space to it.

Yet another type of boy is attracted by the ideas and
the spirit of the Scout movement. There are accordingly
two groups of Scouts, to which a large number of boys
belong, many of whom are adolescents. As with the C.L.B.,
the general scope of this movement is too well known to

need detailing. All must belong to a Bible class or to one of the Church Sunday schools.

There are no tests for admission to membership of the young people's organizations. They are open to all who are prepared to abide by the rules. The conception is not that they are a suitable means of dealing with young members of the Church. They have a distinctly mission scope. They are concerned with the adolescent life of the parish, not merely of the Church.

The leaders of the girls' organizations are nearly all professional teachers, who give their time and their services voluntarily. The principle is that they shall have a real control and initiative. It appears to us that psychologically young people fall most naturally into groups and have a natural disposition to follow one leader. In consequence, while there are most valuable committees of mothers behind each organization, the leadership is designedly autocratic. The support of the clergy is offered and welcomed ; they have an authority by reason of their general position in the life and order of the parish. But this is not strained to imply that men are competent to arrange the normal workings of a group of girls. If committees are needed, the procedure is that they are formed of girls themselves under the chairmanship of the leader. Much depends upon the ability and devotion of the leaders, but the scope of the work and the freedom of leadership have attracted the best type of leader.

The same general principles are aimed at in the case of the girls as in the case of the boys : Religion, Fellowship, Citizenship, Education. Less frequently than in the case of the boys are outside speakers invited to address them. The main group of girls' Bible classes all meet in the same building ; but, for the purposes of instruction, they are normally graded according to age, each group under its own teacher, under the general supervision of the leader. To emphasize fellowship, they are all assembled together for prayer and for receiving general instructions. All manner of activities are undertaken during the week. These are mainly within the organization of the Girls' Friendly Society, but, in order to allow for different types of girls, there are alternatives in the form of clubs, gymnastics, country dancing, needlework, singing, occasional lectures—one has recently been requested on the subject of the New Psychology. Such are some of the weekday activities.

Besides the normal individual church attendances, the organizations are encouraged to attend church corporately from time to time at Mattins or Evensong. No pressure is brought to bear upon any organization to this end. The initiative must be theirs.

It will be seen that the identity of the organization is emphasized and that the team spirit is encouraged. It is true that this creates a problem, that of a limited loyalty. It may well happen that an organization becomes so attractive and its membership so engrossing that the larger issues of church life may be missed. The difficulty must be incurred, if there is to be successful enterprise in young people's work. Psychologically, adolescents need to be dealt with by means of some measure of segregation. The alternative is an unscientific and almost certainly unsuccessful attempt to deal with people of widely varying ages and of differences of outlook as a single large group. The strong probability in this case is that the group will fail to be large. A further segregation is necessary as between the sexes, which must obviously have separate organizations and a variety of choice in the alternatives presented to their own sex.

Co-ordination is attempted with considerable success. The aim is to create, out of the various groups, each with its own strongly marked characteristics and its own widely developed life, a young people's consciousness, a sense that they form an element in the whole corporate life of the parish, with a common outlook. Many measures are taken for the development of this consciousness. First, the Young People's Corporate Communions are for both boys and girls together. In the consideration of various parish affairs, conferences are held of representatives of all their organizations. It might be advisable to form a Young People's Council which should meet at regular intervals, for the surer unification of their various activities.

This was done in one parish within the writer's knowledge, with good results. Joint social gatherings for both sexes are frequently held. They support each other's enterprises. For instance, the girls equip and staff a stall at the boys' sale of work.

Throughout the whole of the young people's work the need of efficiency is emphasized. Whatever is undertaken must be carried out wholeheartedly. A young citizen of the Kingdom of Heaven must abjure slackness. It is the note of a Christian to do with energy all that is undertaken. Such is the general principle enunciated, and it corresponds with the best facts of young life and gives them a respect for religion. We expect, and in the main we obtain, efficiency and sometimes outstanding success. We hold, too, that the young have a capacity for spiritual adventure which is essential to the corporate Christian life and a buoyancy of body and mind which is needed for the continual recruitment of the vigour and enterprise of Church life. Anyone having the spiritual oversight of adolescents will do well to note that the renewals in the history of the Church of Christ seem normally to have originated among young people. The traditional portraits of the first disciples suggest maturity, if not old age. Their lives and actions suggest otherwise. St. Francis of Assisi, St. Clare, the Wesleys, Joan of Arc, and innumerable others were adolescents in the literal or broader sense when they set their hands to their momentous Christian enterprises. This point will be treated in more detail when the devotional life of the adolescent is considered.

Loyalty must be built up from its foundations. There will probably be no vigorous young life of a Church unless there are first separate young people's organizations. Great care must be exercised to develop, out of these, a general, united, adolescent consciousness. Rivalries will spring up, jealousies perhaps, which will be difficult to overcome. But the risk must be undertaken, if it be true, as I believe, that the adolescent naturally and instinctively seeks to be identified with a single group under a single group leader. It would appear that such is the inevitable unit.

To organize otherwise is to court failure and narrow accomplishment.   The problem of creating a unity out of the different units is always present.

And when a considerable measure of this unity is attained, there remains yet another critical problem, that of unifying youth and maturity.   The psychologists speak of an agelong conflict between the young and the old.   The wise handling of the adolescents bridges the gulf between childhood and youth.   You are delivered from the disappointment of seeing young people drift away from the Church in large numbers when they go out to work at the age of fourteen. But you are still faced with the problem of being able to command their loyalty and devotion to the Church and the Kingdom of God when they arrive at maturity.

It is not easy to say when this change takes place.   The psychologists state with considerable unanimity that the decisive ages, when a rapid change of outlook and of personality takes place, are between three and four, when self-consciousness originates, at about sixteen, and at about twenty-one.   The use of the word " I," at the first of these ages, is the sign of a vital development.   At sixteen, or thereabouts, comes mental adolescence, which is later than physical adolescence by a year or so.   At twenty-one, or near that age, according to their theory, should come mental maturity, when the age of restless questing ends and the settling down to a life-task and a life-aim should take place.   With regard to the last of these three changes, it might well seem that, under modern conditions, it is generally several years later.   Marriage, a natural stabilizer, is deferred to a later average age than in former generations. Economic uncertainty of employment, and the monotonous nature of much of that employment, which is almost inevitable in many departments of an industry organized on a basis of machinery and mechanical processes instead of individuality, have almost certainly a tendency to defer the age of settling down.   It is not difficult to perceive, on the part of many young people of to-day, an inclination to hold back from maturity and to cling to adolescence.

Such hesitation brings its nemesis.   Retarded development is as injurious as accelerated development.   It is difficult to say at what age membership of adolescent organizations should cease. Perhaps a hard-and-fast rule is impracticable. But it is imperative, first, to establish such adult organizations as shall appeal to the maturing adolescent, and secondly, to establish such contact between the two as shall bridge over a gulf which may otherwise be hard to cross.

Part of the policy of Church life should be a watchful care to secure that in the councils and responsible actions of the Church there should be a due proportion of young people of proved leadership who are between adolescence and maturity. Observation will disclose how frequently this representation lapses and how often it has never been put into operation.

Sections of the work of the parish may wisely be entrusted to organized youth. For instance, an auxiliary choir of young people of both sexes can be formed for use on special occasions. Many other pieces of work will readily suggest themselves.

Psychologically there will come an age at which the stage of adolescence is left behind and maturity will supervene. As we have seen, this would normally be earlier than it is, if it were not for modern conditions of industry and economics. When the point arrives, it is necessary that there shall be ready to hand adult groups which will prove congenial. Such groups have a way of lapsing into a membership of which the average age is too high, and care is needed to counteract this. Soberness and gravity, and a certain repose and fixity of thought, may be congenial to people whose adventures in life are far behind them and who value peace and tranquillity highly. But a group in which these characteristics are predominant will not have much attraction for men and women of twenty-five or thereabouts. A proportion of people, in any community, ecclesiastical or otherwise, is tired, and, after life-experiences which have taken the zest from their minds, are not likely, if their number and spirit predominate, to commend their organization to those who, in the first flush of maturity, are full of physical and mental vitality. Among all adult groups which seek to recruit themselves from the ranks of maturing adolescents, a vital spirit, a wide outlook, and a concern with the essential issues of life should be most deliberately developed. The programmes should embrace, as in the case of the young people's groups, a range of interests both wide and significant. In the management of these adult organizations, the newly mature should have representation in office. The same formula should prevail: Religion, Fellowship, Citizenship, Education. The study of the programmes of such bodies as the Student Christian Movement, when they are met in conference, is illuminating. They disclose an international outlook and membership, a preoccupation with issues that are world-wide, and an audacity of enterprise which throws a flood of light upon the type of Christian spirit which appeals to the young. A careful consideration of them will guide those responsible for the policy, life, and development of the adult groups which the young people of the Church will be invited in due course to join. At a recent Student Christian Movement Conference the mind of the assembly wavered between abolishing war and purifying commerce. They finally decided upon the latter course. Commerce will remain in need of yet further treatment after all their efforts, but the episode reveals their generous mind and is a useful indication of the type of adventurous Christianity which can hold the loyalty of the young. A study of the mentality of the present students at, for instance, a Chinese University will give a wholesome, if exaggerated, picture of the adolescent mind.

Unless care is exercised, the young people and the older people of a Church will naturally live their social Church life too completely apart. Animation and probably a certain amount of noise will distinguish the former, whereas it is likely that tranquillity will be a feature of the latter. In the sequel, they will remain apart, and there will be mutual reproaches of want of interest in each other's life and work, unless the relations between the two are carefully thought out. The principle needs to be established of visits between the two as part of the essential organization of the common life. Practical experience shows the wisdom of such a policy and its fruitfulness where it is sustained.

While we have been considering the necessity of bridging the gulf between youth and maturity, we have not yet approached a factor in the case which is of profound importance—the factor of courtship and marriage. The Church will naturally be sympathetic and will endeavour to be wise. Part of that wisdom may well take the form of arranging frequent joint social meetings between adolescents of both sexes.

The writer has little sympathy with the point of view which holds that the purely social life of a Church should be reduced to a minimum and which frowns upon the meeting of the youth of both sexes under the ægis of the Church.

The early essays in courtship are generally tentative. That being so, they may be viewed either with sympathy or with disapproval. The former attitude is surely wiser, and it gives the Church the right, willingly granted, to make its own conditions with regard to the conduct of such meetings. The general attitude of disapproval will lower, in young people's minds, the ideals of the relations of the sexes and will certainly tend to alienate them from the Church.

The serious courtship which ends in marriage presents a real problem in the matter of the continuous, active Church membership of young people. Courtship and the early years of married life quite rightly and quite naturally tend to desocialize, for a time, the two concerned. The Old Testament enactment to the effect that the young husband was to be exempt from all liability to military service for the first twelve months of his married life was wise and understanding. A happy and successful marriage depends to a considerable extent on freedom from interference from others during courtship and early married life. The Church should quite frankly recognize these things, and might well grant a kind of leave of absence, at any rate with the exception of attendance at worship. Wisdom and understanding at this time will probably be repaid by a lifelong loyalty. The return to active participation in the common life of the Church will develop naturally through the Font Roll and the Sunday School.

Some organization, to include the engaged and the newly married, might well be considered and attempted in parish life. Its meetings would naturally be infrequent. Such an organization would require careful thought in the determining of its aims and methods, but its results would probably be of much value.

The form of youth-organization frequently adopted is one which has its headquarters in London, which is ruled by a fixed constitution, and has as its unit the parochial branch. The adoption by a parish of young people's organizations of this type interprets to the members that principle of a wide brotherhood in Christ, that common membership in the Church of Christ, that citizenship of the Kingdom of Heaven, which it is our duty to teach. This extensiveness of membership has also its naturally strong appeal to youth. A boy scout, attending an international jamboree, is exhilarated by the sense of belonging to something which is wider than class and transcends nationality and race. All that conveys to our young Churchmen and Churchwomen that we stand for brotherhood as well as for consecration draws out the best in them and appeals to their loyalty. But, beyond such wide organizations, there is sometimes the advisability of forming youth-organizations in a parish which are not branches of a larger association, but stand alone. Where this is done, the utmost care is necessary to avoid the sense of isolation or narrow interests. This can be effected by the arrangement of mutual hospitality between the young people's groups of different parishes. Distance need not be an obstacle. It may indeed be an additional inducement. An outing in motor-charabancs can add to the enjoyment of Christian hospitality. Visits to the parishes of former clergy revive the memories of former pastoral relationships and spiritual experiences.

The adolescent, engaged upon the quest for life, readily responds to all that appeals to his or her imagination as a vital issue and a wide vision. What is static repels them, what is dynamic attracts. The widest field for their vision

and enthusiasm is afforded by the world-wide expansion
of the Kingdom of God. The phrase " the Kingdom of
God overseas " is used deliberately. " Foreign missions "
somehow strikes a false note. While the Church is engaged
in the winning of converts in foreign lands, the real scope
of her endeavour is far wider and more appealing. In a
real sense the word " foreign " is obsolete. In Christ we
are " no more strangers and foreigners." We think of the
non-Christians, not as foreigners, but as potential fellow-
citizens of the Kingdom of God. What the Church has
realized, or should have realized, is also being felt by the
best secular thought with respect to humanity. The
Kingdom of God, in all its breadth and depth—that is
the real task of the Church overseas : the saving of Society
as well as the saving of souls ; the sweetening and purifying,
through faith in Christ, of all phases of the common social
life in all lands, as well as the purifying, through repentance
and the grace of God, of individual lives. No presentation
of Christianity to the young which omits or understates
the vital issue of the expansion of the Kingdom of God
throughout the world is likely to meet with a notable
response.

Conventional representations of the first disciples depict,
grouped round our Lord, a number of middle-aged and
elderly men, with the exception of the youthful St. John.
It is probably nearer the truth to imagine them as youthful.
The mother of Zebedee's children comes to our Lord
with a request in the interests of her two sons. There is
a certain instability, combined with a generous enthusiasm
which, to reflection, increasingly gives the impression of
youth. It has been said that Christianity first came as
a young people's movement and that, ever since, people
have been trying to appropriate it to the middle-aged and
the old. It is hardly too much to say that all the subsequent renewals of Christianity have originated from youth.
There is a strong suggestion of the turbulence of youth
in the little band which was hauled before the magistrates
of Thessalonica under the accusation, " These that have
turned the world upside-down have come hither also."
St. Francis was locked in a cupboard by his father and

released by the compassion of his mother. But it needs no argument to prove the youth of the Franciscans.

Francis himself founded his movement when he was about midway between twenty and thirty ; St. Clare was seventeen when, after having made a first unsuccessful attempt to identify herself with the movement, and having been fetched back home by her brothers, she at the second attempt established her decision.   The Franciscan brethren, with their self-chosen title " Joculatores domini," with their unconventional doings, bear all the evidence of youth, which indirect evidence is reinforced by some more precise information. Joan of Arc was treated by her father as a naughty girl who was telling lies when she disclosed to her family her spiritual experience of visions and voices. Her age at the time is not in question. The Wesleyan movement was the product of undergraduates. These instances may be paralleled by others. The general evidence establishes the proposition that in the main the renewals of Christianity originated from adolescents.

The word " organization " has occurred frequently in this article. It has been used for convenience, not with any emphasis on the strict meaning of the word. God is the Lord of Order, but more essentially He is the Lord of Life. Life must underlie order. The Church is more essentially a living organism with the life of the Holy Spirit within it than an organization. Organization suggests, and suggests truly, human effort and contrivance. Organism suggests Divine life. The control and ordering of an organization requires the wisdom and the experience of the middle-aged and the old. To contribute to the developing life of an organism is the function of the young. Organization had become almost a fetish in the Church during the last two generations. It has its rightful place. " Governments " is a concise word in St. Paul's list of the gifts of the Spirit. But a generosity of spirit and a recklessness of adventure are characteristic of the New Testament and correspond with the temper of youth.

In her adolescents the Church has a wealth of spiritual capacity. In the opinion of the writer, besides the ordered and grave sequence of the parish devotional life, there should also be a devotional movement, directed by the priest personally, to correspond with the spiritual outlook of the adolescents. Others will also be attracted and will find a place quite naturally in the movement, giving it, indeed, stability. But the modes of it will be designed primarily for the young.

It will be found to correspond closely with the underlying principles of all the youth-movements which have renewed from time to time the life of Christianity.

The first principle is that of prayer. Many sides of the Church's work have been rightly organized on the basis of committees and the procedure of a constitution and of voting. The wise priest welcomes the developments of this principle which have taken place in recent years. The democratic principle is based upon our Lord's high estimate of the possibilities of the human personality and of the social life. But the sphere of devotion and of spiritual experience does not lend itself to the machinery of committees. Any spiritual development must begin with the ascertaining of the will of God, and prayer is the avenue, and it must be enabled by the grace of God, for which prayer forms a channel. The priest himself must take the lead, believing in his Ordination commission, and renewing his own private devotion. The group for prayer must be small at the outset, the smaller the better. No decisions must be taken, no expansion attempted, unless, in answer to prayer, God's will thereto is indicated. Spontaneous prayer rather than the use of set forms would seem to be more congenial to the spirit of the movement and more in accordance with the spontaneity of youth.

The second principle is that of sincerity. Illumination is one of the most emphatic of our Lord's promises. There must be a single-minded desire to know God's will at first hand. Our Lord stresses the single eye. The beatitude which has as its reward " they shall see God " has as its condition that they shall be " pure of heart," which phrase contains a strong element of purity of motive and single-mindedness of spiritual inquiry. Sincerity, then, is the second principle. It is a characteristic of youth to be impatient of formulas which it has not explored for itself.

The pledge of sincerity is not only closely related to the Gospels. It is also psychologically congenial to the adolescent.

The third principle is that of obedience to the will of God as disclosed in answer to prayer. Youth resents an enforced obedience, it is true. But an obedience that springs from spontaneous loyalty is in close accordance with its generosity of spirit. The obedience will manifest itself in service of Christ and His Kingdom. Such pieces of service should be offered to the Prayer Fellowship rather than to the individual member. The director of the movement has the responsibility of defining the tasks in general, but the acceptance must be spontaneous. The task that is undertaken as the result of choice is likely to be carried through with a spirit which may be lacking in a task undertaken under dictation, however wise and however benevolent. Youth has a way of welcoming a leader and of resenting a dictator.

The fourth principle is that of comradeship—love and trust of one another. A real fellowship is essential, the conception being alike basic in the New Testament and according to the best idealism of the present day. Man is gregarious. He has innate instincts which must be directed wisely and turned to high purposes, but which must not be merely thwarted. Among these is certainly gregariousness, and loyalty to the groups to which he belongs.

The fifth principle is joyousness. " The disciples were filled with joy and the Holy Ghost." The Church has been tempted at times to substitute gravity. Gravity has its place. But joyousness lies deeper. St. Paul was content to be a fool for Christ's sake. In their early days the Franciscans were viewed as irreverent. But they were wiser than their critics. Joyousness is the most convincing proof of the reality of the working of the Spirit. It is unmistakable and it is infectious.

On some such lines as these, not in any sense to the exclusion of the normal, ordered life of a Church's prayer and praise, there is a fruitful field for the development of adolescent devotion. The whole movement can, and probably should, be quiet and restrained, and the elements of it will prove to be closely related to the needs of youth. There is scope for spontaneity, loyalty, adventure, large projects and originality.

How far is all this practicable in parishes other than the one described ? The question is very much to the point. It has been developed in a large industrial parish. In such a parish the resources of the home are limited. Opportunities are welcomed for social life on a large scale when the work of the day is over. The great numbers which can be drawn upon and the large numbers which can be got together in such organizations as have been described give a vigour and a largeness which certainly owes something to the gregariousness of the human being, whether young or old. For the leadership of the largest of the boys' groups young clergy, in succession, of special aptitude have hitherto been secured and are probably essential. But there has never been more than one ordained man detailed for the adolescent work. All the rest of the leaders have been laymen. I see no reason why the whole of the principles should not be applied in most parishes, certainly in town parishes. Having had no country experience, I hesitate to pronounce upon the case of such. Much of the detail seems to be practicable in any town parish. It will demand unceasing thought and psychological study. It adds a vivid interest to work which otherwise might readily degenerate into routine and become burdensome, tedious, and disheartening. The whole aim and issue of the work of the parish becomes living and the sense of life communicates itself to the Church community. A solid adolescent organization, or organism, is created which holds the interest and the loyalty of the young during critical years of their lives. Confirmation need not be pressed prematurely, and there is the strong probability in any case of a number of years during which the devotional habits of the newly confirmed can be consolidated. Failures there are, and many ; but there are also unusual opportunities. Above all, there is always the encouragement of working along lines which appear to correspond with the broad psychological facts of young human life in its development from childhood to adolescence and from adolescence to maturity.

CHAPTER XI

THE AFTER-CARE OF CANDIDATES (2)

By R. C. JOYNT

I

THIS chapter has in view one of the Church's gravest problems. Leakage from her communicant membership is taking place almost everywhere. But it is proceeding so noiselessly that it is noticed only by the keenest observers on her watch-towers. Minute-guns often proclaim much less significant tragedies than the lapse of souls from the sacrament of their redemption. Yet this is occurring on a great scale before the eyes of those who care. The decadent process is not precipitous in speed; it is gradual. But a falling away from regularity in communion normally ends in an entire abstention from sacramental worship, and this is what is befalling a large proportion of the confirmed, especially in the years immediately following Confirmation.

The extent of the relapse, inadequately realized, calls loudly for a great recuperative effort, and for a revision of the after-care methods which have so poor an account to give of themselves, if the flow of life from this bleeding wound in the Church's side is to be checked; still more if it is to be stayed.

To attempt this at least is surely one of the most imperative of all obligations. But such an attempt, even when it is seriously proposed, seems to be given a much lower place in the Church's organized activity than other more spectacular enterprises; though these are often less urgently called for in the best interests of the Church's work, indeed of her very life. In a time which makes much of processions a pageant of the lapsed communicants of a county, or of a great town, would be an impressive spectacle. Such a display would bring home, could it be given, to the parochial conscience, and especially to the official keepers of that conscience, the heavy guilt which lies upon us all for the crime of neglecting to shepherd Christ's sheep so as to retain them within the fold.

Streams of fresh young life, " crammed with " possibility, pour inwards every year through the gateway of Confirmation ; and day by day other streams flow outwards through gates carelessly left open, or at best only sleepily guarded by their responsible watchmen. For such a dreary and depressing depletion effective remedies ought to be zealously sought for, and sought for till found. But this ebbing away of the younger communicants, alarming as it is, is yet possibly not more lamentable than the fact that so sinister a phenomenon stirs little apprehension in the Church's average mind. Almost paternally gentle, rather than peremptory, are the demands in authoritative quarters that she should give herself to the prayer, sacrifice, and self-searching on an entirely higher level which would inspire adequate efforts to hold back this persistent drift of young lives from the highest of their privileges. And even when these demands are made by the councils, chapters or the synods of the Church, they are uttered on a note of unexpectant despondency, as if the grave evil was entirely incurable. The truth, probably, of the matter is, that the pain of this sore in the Church's heart is not acute. She feels much more deeply about other things of much less gravity.

Possibly the Confirmation Register is the most pathetic of all a parish's official records. So few names entered there, and these all that were won (in many cases) out of a great population ; and of the few so many to be written off, after a brief interval, as ineffectives. In explaining these figures we of the clergy should take full account of all the facts, without dealing gently with our own failure in love, diligence, prayer, winsomeness, watchfulness. We brought them with high hopes to be confirmed, and then perhaps left them—beyond what is fitting—to their own efforts in the culture of the soul. How near the clergy were to them in the happy weeks of preparation and first communion ! How fully they opened their secret hearts to them ! *But now ?* Well, while much remains to rejoice over, many

have folded their tents, and almost noiselessly and unob-
served slipped away from the " ordered files," as Keble
calls them, which partake of the " royal dainties " of the
sacrament. That this is not an over-statement of facts
which challenge our methods of after-care, official figures
prove with an impressive certainty.

In the thirty-eight English dioceses there were 2,294,190
Easter (season) communicants in 1922 ; 2,413,874 in 1923 ;
and 2,444,483 in 1924. These figures show an increase
of 119,684 in 1923, and in 1924 an increase of 30,609 over
the previous year ; and of 150,293 in the two years combined.
That is to say, 150,293 more persons were at the Holy Table
at Easter in 1924 than there were at Easter in 1922.

But there were confirmed 218,196 in 1922, and 233,427
in 1923 ; or a total of 451,623. In other words, while an
influx of 451,623 communicants was added by Confirmation in the two preceding years, the actual increase of
Easter communicants in 1924 was just over one-third of
that number. If it be said that many of those who communicated in 1922 were confirmed before Easter in that
year, the same might be said of 1924. Over three-fifths
of the gain of the preceding years had disappeared from
visible fellowship, so that even after generous allowance
has been made for uncontrollable losses, as by death, the
figures are very disquieting. It is as if jewels were being
placed in bags with holes, through which many were being
dropped, to be very rarely found again. It may be added
that in 1924 Easter Day was April 20th, a very late date.
(*N.B. Later figures were not available when this was written.*)

II

After-care of the confirmed is closely connected with
what precedes Confirmation in the ingathering and the
instruction of the candidates. Such a great falling-away as
is deplored may have some relation to the methods used
in forming the preparation classes, and also to the manner
of life of the children and their homes. It is found that
relapse is not so frequent amongst those who were before
their Confirmation fairly well rooted and grounded in the
faith of the Church, knew something by experience of the

fear of God, and were fitted a little by the spiritual atmosphere of their earlier days to appreciate the meaning and privilege of communion with Him. On the other hand, most of those who slip through the weak meshes of the Church's net are they whose conversion was indefinite and uncertain, and who had but slight experience, or even understanding, of the Spirit's sanctifying grace. They were " joined unto the Lord," but the links were mechanical or ecclesiastical, not vital.

After-care, then, presupposes a prolonged preparation before Confirmation. This is at once solemn and joyful work. Severity, censoriousness, and exclusiveness are painfully out of place in it. But if they are, so, too, are laxity and a deficient standard, and the desire to make " a fair shew in the flesh " by bringing goodly numbers to be confirmed, when this means the inclusion of the unready. To hold back young people from this great means of grace, and from subsequent communion, is a serious course, even where little assurance of the preparation of the heart is available ; but a low standard is even more dangerous, when it sends forward, that they may become temples of the Holy Ghost, those who are palpably unready to receive Him in the laying on of hands.

One example of this may be offered. It is almost an invitation to subsequent relapse to present for Confirmation persons who have not already regularly practised Sunday worship in church. Yet this risk is often incurred, and attendance at a Sunday school or a Bible-class is reckoned as an adequate substitute for Morning or Evening Prayer, where the habit of church attendance has not been formed ; forgetting that it is only through such previous training that the confirmed can profitably pass forward into the use of the highest worship of all. An elementary condition of permanence in the communion life is normally the familiar and regular previous use of the ordinary means of grace. It is not in one part of the land only that thronged Sunday schools, adult classes, and popular men's services are found flourishing in parishes where there is but a sparse and fitful attendance at the Holy Communion. The reason for this curious contrast is simple : the school and the class are in the main designed for teaching ; the Church Services are mainly for worship. " My house shall be called *the house of prayer.*"

The present writer's estimation of the average Sunday school as a training-ground for the soul is not high. Noise, irreverence, careless handling of holy things, deficient provision for kneeling, inadequate equipment in material and *personnel*, and (too often) the absence of the clergyman's impact upon the souls of these crowded and restless groups —these are not uncommon features, and they give no support to the beautiful ideal that the school is the nursery of the Lord's family and the porch of His Church.

" I do not go to church ; I attend Sunday school." This is familiar to the ear of the parish priest as he inquires into the religious habits of those candidates for Confirmation who are drawn from the school. The average youth of suitable age is not found in strength at the Church's regular services. They do not go there normally of their own accord. In many places they are marched to Morning Prayer, and then herded together in crowded pews in remote corners of the building from which they can be conveniently piloted out again when the Good Shepherd's servant appears with food—it is hoped—for " the hungry sheep." Hence *After-care* does force us to think searchingly of the days and the ways which precede Confirmation. When will " great preaching " make some room for more simple, carefully prepared exposition of the Bible, such as would shew the beauty and glory of our Lord's redemption and of the service of others for His sake ? When it does, two things will happen : the tired or resigned look will vanish from the faces in the pews where the righteous go, and the younger people will find that the ways of worship are ways of pleasantness. Then, too, will there be some approach to truth in their lips when they sing that the joy of God's house excels all earthly joy. Present conditions are the seed from which a goodly share of the lapse from communion springs. A garden treated in the spring-time on the lines of much of what is called spiritual training of younger people would not be clothed in perfect beauty in summer.

III

After-care implies very much : as that new communicants require special care ; are the sheep of Christ, and as sheep apt to go astray ; are the jewels of His diadem, purchased with His life, and precious to Him, and as such entrusted to the Church's keeping.   They are also the Church's own children, entitled to be individually tended, watched, and fed by her pastors, from whom the Owner will require a strict account of their stewardship.   They nearly always respond to love and care, and they can be retained by faithfulness within the green pastures of the Church's domain, if the weak places in her hedges are made secure.

The Communicants' Union (or Guild).—Many experienced men find this a useful part of their pastoral machinery. Conditions of membership vary, but commonly there is given to those who join the union a card containing a few simple rules of life, as methodical prayer and Bible-reading, and regular attendance at Holy Communion.   There are often a motto text, the member's name and sundry details of the hours of the Church Services, and the like.   The writer is one of those who question the value of such a union.   He sees some real danger in it, and has found very few instances of its having realized its promoters' hopes. For the genuine communicants' union in a parish embraces all the confirmed, and its meeting-place is properly the Holy Table itself.   There is real risk in setting up within artificial boundaries a union inside this complete circle— whose rules are quite clear in the Prayer Book.   It forms an inner community which might—though often incorrectly —be supposed to be governed by higher ideals than those which the entire body of faithful people seek to reach, or on whom special obligations might seem to lie, and from whom a higher standard of worship and service might (in virtue of their inner membership) be expected.   This is not good.   The communicants of a parish are all one in Christ Jesus ; they are all bought with His precious blood ; all of His grace partake ; and on the love and loyalty of them all has He the fullest claim.   This wide fellowship has no room *as communicants* for a specialized class.   No privileges can be given, or obligations imposed, which do not belong to all, merely on the ground of membership in a more restricted body. The true communicants' union comprises all who have right to the sacrament of union.

The habit of private devotion, constantly inculcated and fostered by counsel and help, arms the new communicant and the older alike with the most robust defence against the spiritual declension which is both a cause and a consequence of intermittent, and ultimately of forsaken, communion. But sympathetic and suitable guidance must be provided if Bible-reading and prayer in secret are to be effective ; and there is a wide field open for the best kind of printed helps to Bible study (in magazine or other form), in which one of the daily Lessons might be explained, with devotion and good sense combined. It is certain that the private reading of the Scriptures is given up by hosts of young communicants, with incalculable consequent loss, because they know neither how to read nor to understand them. They need much help, and it is a plain duty to give it. For the Bible is in many parts deep and difficult, and even the New Testament, in Dean Church's words, " is a severe book." At any cost of effort to their spiritual guides they must be encouraged and helped to accustom themselves to the daily use of it ; for nothing can take its place in establishing, strengthening, and settling the spiritual life of the communicant. Much of the forsaking of the Holy Table can be found to have its beginnings in the growing weakness of private devotion in the confirmed.

Prayer.—Bible-reading and prayer are the mainstay of the soul's life. They are the *Jachin* and *Boaz* of the temple of the Spirit of God. To help the prayer-life in the earlier stages of the pilgrim's way is to render the highest service. There are manuals with this end in view in great numbers, and books of this class best serve their purpose when they foster the free flow of the soul's sincere desire in the self-taught words which good desires inspire. Self-expression has its greatest exercise in prayer. But the best manual of all for private (as for public) use is the Prayer Book itself, *e.g.* the Litany, Psalter, and the Collects and other Prayers. Hymns, too, greatly help private devotion, and it is most seemly that the pulpit and the class should shew how these two mines of spiritual wealth may be explored and used. The parish minister who determines that the young communicants shall know how to read the Bible with profit and pleasure, and to make much of the mighty forces released by prayer, and who *teaches* his people to pray, will be spared much of the agony of a dwindling attendance of the confirmed at the sacrament, where God rewards openly the souls that habitually seek Him in secret.

At this stage a few suggestions may come in. *After-care* is composed of many ingredients. These are chiefly personal to the " sky-pilot "—*a grand title.* Reverence ; sympathy ; genuineness ; generosity of outlook ; the shepherd-heart ; the shepherd-memory for faces, names, and dates ; spiritual methods ; devotion to our Lord ; approachableness ; a patient ear ; graciousness ; simplicity. If these flowers, so to speak, grow in the parson's personal life, the hold he has on the confirmed will be strong indeed. They are to be had by prayer, and they cannot be done without. They spring up from heavenly seed, and need careful cultivation. Consider now only three of them :

Reverence.—Irreverence is unreality's ugly sister. The young communicant is incalculably hindered by both. To celebrate sacred mysteries and to speak holy words as if our Lord was only a few feet away *tells*, while the opposite *repels*.

Sympathy.—To have tears for all woes ; genuine joy in another's joy ; understanding in difficulties ; to have a heart at leisure from itself, and a wing ready to receive and shelter a troubled soul ; to have a hand free to pluck from another's heart a rooted sorrow, or to apply with the faithfulness of a trusted friend the knife to some bad thing in a guilty conscience : these are only some of sympathy's ways. The prophet in the dead child's room is a perfect parable of sympathy ; for he " put his mouth upon his mouth, and his eyes upon his eyes, and his hands upon his hands : and he stretched *himself* upon the child." One need not be a master of exegesis to see the exquisite symbolism of that scene in the desolate home at Shunem. Nothing can take sympathy's place, for it has no equivalents. It flows out at any call of sorrow or joy or sin. The man of sympathy has great rewards. The child was sure of him when she shewed him her broken doll; so it was to him that she turned when as a disillusioned bride she had a broken heart.

Spiritual Methods.—The contributors to this book are to say what they know, or have proved. Susceptibilities on some subjects are acute, and this is one of them. But the writer has a conviction, which has survived the after-care, such as it was, of between two and three thousand candidates for Confirmation, that there is a deep cleavage between the secular and sacred in human life, and that many things which belong " to the world "—in St. John's meaning of that word—are incongruous and perhaps hurtful when they are called into the service of the Church. It is not, he believes, by them that young life is won and kept for the Redeemer. His shepherds are commissioned to feed His flock—" with the word, with their life, with the fruit of holy prayers," says a great Father of the Church. They are not called to amuse them by doubtful, if not positively sinful, expedients on the plea of " keeping them together." There are great fields of untainted recreation which they can encourage without turning the sheep into pastures where poisonous weeds predominate. Should these phrases offend against the generosity of mind extolled above, forgiveness is pleaded for on the ground that, amongst the Church's great perils to-day, the greatest is the eating out of her life by the world and its spirit; like the slow, silent destruction wrought by the death-watch beetle in some venerable temples of prayer. *Non tali auxilio. Be spiritual ; be spiritual ; be spiritual,* said a Lord Chancellor whose son and grandson are loyal Churchmen as well as eminent in the service of the State to-day.

IV

In what follows I must pass out of the impersonal and speak direct in the first person to those who read it, and especially to my own brothers in the Church's service.

Confirmed at School.—These are a most important but elusive element in residential parishes. They stand apart largely from our local ways and organizations. So their after-care is a special problem. Its difficulty is plainly seen by us all. It demands special treatment. Nothing can quite take the place of the close contact established between the incumbent and his own Confirmation classes. But much can be done, and cumulatively the following suggestions have been found fruitful : (1) During their time of preparation at school send them a brief letter each week, with no merely professional taste in it. (2) See much of them in social and other friendly ways during their vacations. Encourage them to " drop in " on you. (3) If possible, be present at their Confirmation. This is really valuable. (4) Make sure that they prefer to be confirmed at school. This is often not so, and head masters and mistresses have been effectively approached on this vital point. (5) Enter their names in your Confirmation Register, and do not forget the anniversary when it comes round. (6) Write them a brief note now and again of an informal kind. (7) The supreme essential is that they should love and trust the parochial *padre*. They will do so when he deserves it and is not a mere purveyor of the pieties. (8) Remember that printed communications are all but useless. The personal touch is the only touch that *really touches*.

" *Godfathers*."—The Godparent in these inverted commas is not the ecclesiastical counterfeit who " denounces them all " in Holy Baptism and is an unspeakable person. The Confirmation godparent or super-godparent is an experienced, and sympathetic, and human individual of either sex who loves young people and will naturally care for their state. Every new recruit admitted to the Sacrament after Confirmation should be placed in the care of such a guardian. The ties that unite them should be those of pure friendliness—the big brother watching unostentatiously the younger one's interests, spiritual and otherwise. I have in mind several of these to whom young communicants as naturally gravitate as bees to certain flowers. Their price is above rubies, and you realize it when you see them together, *e.g.* in games on week-days, and side by side on Sunday at the Holy Communion.

Visitation.—It is all but useless to " visit " young men communicants in their homes. In a small crowded house it is inconvenient ; in a big one it often evokes shyness, which in a boy is next neighbour to fear. No, they must be encouraged to *visit you,* or to share a ramble with you, or a bicycle ride, or a visit to a cricket-match. *This tells.* It strengthens fellowship. The Confirmation godmother, too, will devise her own suitable means of meeting her *protégés'* needs, and of holding them in the leash of love.

Servants.—This great class is worth far more of definite after-care than it usually receives. I take for granted their admission to the G.F.S., Y.W.C.A., and other similar fellowships. But they also need and deserve the personal touch of the shepherd of the parish. In residential districts especially they form a considerable proportion of the communicant body. Visit them regularly. Greet them as valued members of the flock when their employers are visited. Follow them up with letters of commendation when they leave your parish. Encourage them to feel that their clergyman is their friend. Attach the new-comers to a class or guild, and introduce them to some experienced members of their own calling. Pray *with* them, when it can be conveniently done.

Church-workers.—Amongst the best safeguards against their backsliding is the fact that the new communicants have some definite work to do for the Church. In an active parish-life there is much room for many varieties of employment. Experience shews that responsibility ministers to stability. So every possible effort should be made to get these recruits to wear the yoke of service in their youth. Clubs, guilds, schools, choirs, classes, scouts, guides, brigades, bands of hope, mission services, open-air campaigns, Children's Church, missionary unions, temperance work—all provide doors of opportunity which they can enter, and if they know that they are trusted to be faithful they will not as a rule be found to fail. In every large body of sidesmen obviously there should be several genuinely (as distinct from *quasi-*) young persons, and in children's services, such as are a prominent feature in well-worked residential places, the officers should all be in the stages of early adolescence.   In recommending these methods, it is experience, not theory, that is speaking.

Letters of Commendation.—This essential of a watchful ministry is widely honoured in the breach rather than in the observance of an obvious duty.   It is pitifully wrong to let barely fledged communicants pass out of the family life of a parish into a new environment, where all things and all people are strange, without care being taken to graft them into the home-life of the Church there.   In this way many of the tragedies of spiritual relapse occur. Cold indifference at either end is really a guilty negligence. With many young people removal to new scenes means leaving the loving light of a warm hearthstone to go out into a starless night.   Nor should interest cease when the roots are well established in the fresh community.   An occasional letter of encouragement, however brief, from the spiritual parent of a young soul is an effective factor. All young things love warmth, and more things are wrought by letters—*not circular*—than this world dreams of.

Letters.—These are ordinarily a great burden to the perfunctory or over-busy official.   But their yoke is easy, and their burden light, when they are *love*-letters.   Their power in the relations of the parish priest and the confirmed—perish the word " confirmee " !—is hardly to be over-estimated.   Few things give the average boy or girl more pleasure than a letter.   Not a dilution of last Sunday's sermon, but a *letter*.   It may be short, but if it is natural, simple, loving, wise, it goes far.   Some men have this gift of writing in remarkable measure.   To others it is denied. The right kind of letter, sent spontaneously now and again, makes a wonderful bond between the minister and the receiver.   The physical and mental toil of correspondence is a great strain on a heavily burdened life ; but there is no department of the outside-of-the-Church ministry more useful in after-care.   One letter of this kind written on an average every day would effect incalculable consequences.   But the official, and perfunctory, and patronizing blemish must be entirely missing, if there is to be any *bind* in it.

The vicar's letter received on special occasions, such as

sorrows or successes, or new departures, or on anniversaries of Confirmation, of first communion, or of birth, is now a fairly general institution ; and just in proportion as it is known to be a fixed part of the parochial system does its influence diminish in volume. Any reminder is good on such occasions, but two or three lines in familiar hand-writing is a more fruitful ideal in after-care than a deluge of printed cards of greeting poured under halfpenny postage into the nearest pillar-box. One is personal and warm, and the other official and printed, and, therefore, less warm. Both have been tried, and there is no question about their relative values. Some of our own dearest possessions are brief notes in the sender's handwriting—but who keeps a printed card ?

Speaking generally, the best after-care is given when the conventional and the customary give place to something which enables your heart-beat of sympathy and interest to be heard.

Classes, Services, Clubs.—No young communicant is fully provided for who is not linked up with some grouping for instruction, recreation, or self-improvement. A stalk of wheat cannot stand alone. Union is strength and safety. The united are twice blessed. They give support, and they receive it. So the newly confirmed are to be carefully placed in classes under the helpful leadership of those who love our Lord and who sympathize with the ideals of younger life. A well-graded system of Bible-classes is indispensable, if the right teachers are in control. Bible instruction of the wise kind, as was suggested above, is a very urgent requirement. Emotional and uninstructed churchmanship will not stand the buffetings of life. Nor will any scheme of ceremonialism if unsupported by Scrip-ture. " *Tolle, lege,*" should be supplemented by *rationem de ea quæ in vobis est spe.* Clubs for recreation, limited to regular attendants at the church services, conducted on definitely spiritual lines ; classes for instruction in great subjects, such as botany or astronomy ; Saturday rambles, with someone in charge who knows the notes and habits of familiar plants and birds ; Sunday evening sermons for young people, avoiding far-fetched titles,—all these have been found contributory to the great ideal of losing " not one of them " who have been admitted through the wicket-gate of Confirmation.

The Value of One.—The corporate view is now in much favour, and this is well. But a body has many members, and the good health of the whole is dependent on the condition of each ; and not least on the health of the smaller members. " If she lose one of them, does she not light a candle, and sweep the house, and seek diligently till she find it ? " Such is our Lord's manner of teaching the value of one soul. How easy to think that all is well when a great total of membership has communicated on some high festival of the Church ! When we have more of His Spirit we shall perhaps not ask only how many communicants there were present at Easter, but we shall ask ourselves how many of those who were confirmed last year, or in recent years, were *absent* from the Sacrament. The mother-heart aches badly when one chair is wilfully vacant ; but mother Church's heart seems to be not very deeply concerned when her children fall out of the family fellowship one by one. A hunger of heart that yearns over, and follows the steps of, the straying ones is the mark of the true shepherd. He may test the reality of his entire ministry not best by his fervour in preaching righteousness in the great congregation but by the patient, loving, and inventive persistence with which he tracks down some poor tempted lad, or a girl drawn back again from the sacred board into the worship of dress and the world's vain show. " Where are the nine ? " Where is *the one* ?

> " Lord, whence are those blood-drops all the way,
>   That mark out the mountain's track ? "
> " They were shed for *one* who had gone astray,
>   Ere the Shepherd could bring him back."

Indeed the shepherd of souls whose pastoral tracks have no marks of his sacrifice on them is a long way off from his Master. He is also by a long way short of the spirit which has pangs of pain for the loss from communion of one of those little ones who believed in Jesus as Saviour, and sought the gift of His Holy Spirit in Confirmation, but has now gone out of the household of faith into the night of indifference or perhaps worse. Hirelings do not go into the streets and lanes of the city or search life's highways and hedges for the homeless—and to be homeless is to be away from God. No, hirelings do not this. They do not work overtime. But shepherds do, when a lamb or a sheep is missing. They put a great price on the weak brother for whom Christ died. True after-care, in the last resort, means that the shepherd *cares* and watches, works and prays, and has no skill in counting the cost of these to himself.

Some Brevities

(1) A card containing the name, date of birth, dates of Baptism, of Confirmation, and of first communion, is given on the first Communion Sunday (S.P.C.K. 109), signed by the incumbent. This is to be framed by the receivers and hung in a conspicuous place in their rooms, and the prayer on it regularly used. It is found to be a successful reminder. A book of definitely practical counsel is given at the same time. This small volume contains suggestions on Bible-reading, prayer, hours, and frequency of Holy Communion, and urges the importance of rule and method in the cultivation of the soul's life.

(2) Leaders in parish work, such as teachers, scout-masters, secretaries of clubs, are exhorted and expected to come (at agreed times) to the Holy Communion with their young communicants, and also, which is equally valuable, to invite them to sit with them at Morning or Evening Prayer where this can be done.

(3) The preparation-service before communion is useful in theory, but in practice is often disappointing.

(4) The affectionate relations which are established in the preparation period before Confirmation may well be fostered in every possible way afterwards, and attachments of the most intimate kind are thus maintained. Thus these inexperienced young lives feel that in any kind of perplexity or difficulty they have in their clergyman a real friend to

whom, if he is a whole man of God, they will turn at such times, rather than to any other, except the right kind of mother.   This is one of after-care's most precious fruits.

(5) The writer has not tested it, but it is said that something on the lines of the " class-meeting " in which experiences are exchanged, in a reverent spirit and under experienced leadership, has been found fruitful.   Whether this be so or not, it is certain that groups or " wards " gathered, under a safe guide, where common difficulties are handled, are of use.   Experience shows also that in every large communicants roll there are those who will welcome a class for deeper Bible study, and for even (elementary) Greek, and generally for the kind of pursuits which used to be encouraged in mechanics' institutes and the like. These suggestions have been worked with success.

(6) It is good to send for anyone who is known to be growing slack in his religious habits.   Firm, wise, friendly, affectionate words with a closing prayer are found to restore such a one if he is dealt with in a loving spirit. There is a wide difference between merely fussy anxiety and manly, tender interest.

(7) The personal touch, it may be repeated, is the most powerful touch of all.   The touch that is only official, or perfunctory, or reproachful, is like the prophet's staff which was duly placed by Gehazi as ordered on the dead boy's face.   But his report was that the child remained dead.   " There was neither voice nor attention."   There never will be the response of returning life to mere priestly propriety.   When, however, *the man of God* measured himself on him, and came down to the boy's level, " the flesh of the child waxed warm."   That touch of love, sacrifice, interest, still requickens the dead and revives the drooping soul.

(8) Every Confirmation day should be made a great day in the parish.   On the previous Sunday evening the whole body of those confirmed during the preceding ten years should be in the most urgent way, and at any cost of effort, gathered for a reunion service.   At this the vicar himself should pour out his soul to them.   Where the Confirmation is in the afternoon of a week-day this service

is often held the same evening. A stranger preacher should not be invited to intermeddle in this domestic and family function. Such a congregation wants to hear the voice that prepared them for the great event. The very tenderest emotions are stirred in such a service, and the irregular who have taken the first step backward are found trooping to the Sacrament on the following Sunday.

(9) Steady, plodding, pastoral care in visiting (anointed every day " with *fresh* oil ") and in personal interviews by the parish priest who never forgets that he is a shepherd, and who can " pass the time of day " with heaven in his voice—where has this been known to be unfruitful ? or to have failed in keeping the precious flock of communicants intact ? A great ideal truly, but their Lord and his is able to make *all* grace abound towards both him and them.

Final

The Man who cares and after-cares.—It is not wrong to cry out at the end of these paragraphs—" Who is sufficient " for this big thing ? The self-complacent, the man of narrow view, the comfortable person, the late riser, the servant of low ideals, the self-seeker or self-indulgent, the slave of either arm-chairs, tobacco, or self-esteem—none of these is " sufficient " anyhow. But there is a sufficiency available. It is " of God." It is sought in constant prayer ; and those who seek find, whether they seek for souls that have strayed, or for confirming blessings to rest on them. This pen writes with confident certainty that he who has his Confirmation Register always near at hand, who often goes over those beloved names, one by one, and again and again mentions them to the Listener, and passes out from such interviews with Him on his after-care rounds, with His love in his heart, His skill and wisdom in his head, His notes in his voice, and His touch in his hand, will prove that successful after-care is not an unattainable ideal to pursue.

CHAPTER XII

THE AFTER-CARE OF CANDIDATES (3)

By W. P. T. ATKINSON

THERE are two temptations threatening the parish priest as he approaches the difficult problem which is the subject of this paper—the after-care of those who have been confirmed. The first is to aim at quantity rather than quality ; the second, to concentrate upon those who are now called " adolescents," to the detriment of other sections of his congregation. These may well be dealt with by way of introduction.

(*a*) In theory the worship of numbers is renounced by all speakers and writers. In practice it is a snare to all of us and its traces are to be found in many quarters, often the most unlikely. It appears in many schemes of re-union for the Church. Its cloven hoof is manifest in annual papers of statistics. Many are obsessed by the parish lists of communicants, collections, and the like. Above all, and most pertinently to the matter in hand, it is evident on the part of those in charge of bands of young people, in the ceaseless comparisons between register and register, numerical result and result. An evident instance appears in this question which has frequently been asked : " Do the methods used by those known as Anglo-Catholics save the few at the expense of the diffusive influence on the life of the district which is claimed by other methods ? "

About twenty years ago a book called *Our Lord and His Lessons* was written by the Rev. Spencer J. Jones on certain aspects of this very question. It is well worth reading. He pointed out that every system claiming to be Catholic must be based upon our Lord's own methods. Among other things, this implies concentration on the few, not at the expense of the many, but that the few may be missionaries to them. That which was true of the training of the Apostles should be true in religious training to-day. Indeed, the principle may well be traced to the pre-Christian era, for the doctrine of the Remnant is a foundation of all Old Testament interpretation.

Therefore there must be long and patient education of all disciples, young and old, that in them may be gradually formed the Christ-character. Certainly many will fail to persevere towards so high a standard. There will be heart-rending decisions for the teacher between losing, at least for a time, some of his boys and girls, and lowering the general standard in order to retain them all. He must be firm, if gentle, in clinging to the former alternative, in "saving the few"; but it will not be at "the expense of the diffusive influence on the life of the district." A small band of well-trained and practising Churchmen is far deeper in its spiritual influence and a far better foundation for the true work of a parish than vast but semi-worldly clubs and institutions, which could do their excellent work equally well if conducted by agencies professing to be no more than social and philanthropic.

There are indeed more real dangers for "the few" themselves—the ever-present perils of spiritual pride in an unspiritual world, and over-preoccupation with the paraphernalia of religion in an irreligious one. These, however, become proportionately less as the teacher increases in experience and the parish becomes accustomed to his methods and ideals. He must not turn back because there are lions in the way.

(b) There has lately appeared a new Mesopotamia for the educationalist—the blessed word "adolescent." Would he be up-to-date, he must use it on every occasion, until it has become a byword to his hearers. "Adolescent" missions and campaigns are held. We are told of people who are "good with adolescents." We have adolescent clubs and services. Now, the word itself is dangerous. Young people called by it in this way will inquire as to its meaning. Harmless in itself it may be, but any explanation must tend to awaken an unhealthy interest in personal development, physical as well as spiritual, and will lead to undesirable introspection. Nor must a more far-reaching result of this practice be overlooked. The popular over-emphasis of one section of the race will be at the expense of the whole unless it is carefully counteracted.

We are told of the " adolescent problem." Many declare with praiseworthy honesty that they lose from their congregations an enormous percentage of their children, even as many as eighty per cent., at the age of fourteen. In the case of some of the clergy this problem is often created by the fact that they have hardly known their children until that age. Overwhelmed by their own multifarious duties, they have committed the youngsters to the charge of more or less efficient teachers, until the time of the least spiritual moment of their growth, which is also the traditional English age for Confirmation. Then the priest comes in, and his task is almost hopeless—a problem indeed. It is surely obvious that he should strive to know his young people in infancy, in childhood, in adolescence, in youth, and after marriage—a gradually growing knowledge demanding real patience and perhaps less personal satisfaction than the transitory hero-worship which the boy and the girl are so ready to give to the new-comer who knows them in their teens only. He will still have his failures and his losses, but in far less numbers, and these by no means in overwhelming proportion at the age of fourteen. For there must be losses at each transition from stage to stage, from school to class of senior organization. Undue emphasis on adolescence has made many overlook the perils of other ages, while the exceeding attraction which these young people exercise over a sympathetic teacher is a real peril to the next generation. He does everything for the adolescent or with the adolescent in mind, forgetting that in a year or two there will be none left unless the infants and children are being trained to take their place. This temptation will tend to grow unless it is resisted at the start. Surely it is right to remember that a priest's aim must be the development of perfect Christians ; that the growth must begin with infancy and continue to old age ; that each period will have its own problems, which, if duly dealt with, will lessen those to follow ; that development must be in part physical, though this is mainly outside his province ; that his own special sphere will be the religious development, intellectual, moral, and devotional ; that he will therefore need some knowledge of moral and ascetic as well as of dogmatic theology. Here is a problem which will need all his patience and all his skill, but if he has the whole in view, there will be some chance of dealing adequately with each section as it arrives.

We are led by such considerations to a threefold division of the after-care methods which are at the disposal of the Church : (1) the use of the sacraments, (2) ways of prayer, (3) instruction in the faith. The discussion of these three subjects, with a fourth section on some additional points, forms the main part of this chapter.

I. The Use of the Sacraments

(a) *Confirmation* lies beyond the scope of this article, but so much that follows assumes that the child has been confirmed at a suitable age, that it is pertinent to insist on the ages of ten and eleven as by far the most hopeful when they are possible. This is particularly true in two cases : the first, of children whose homes are good and whose parents are practising Church-folk, where there is every likelihood that they will be helped in the performance of their duties ; the second, of those whose circumstances are the very reverse, whose homes are poor, whose parents care not at all, and who have to stand alone. Of course, in the latter case even more than in the former, the greatest care must be taken to ensure that the child is himself really anxious and eager, and he must be very carefully guarded and encouraged from stage to stage. Granted this, it is, humanly speaking, his only chance that he shall have formed regular habits of Communion before the age of testing arrives.

The battle for that which is at once the more scientific and the more Catholic age for this Sacrament is being

won, but still there is much parental ignorance and hostility
to combat. It is necessary to insist and insist again on
God's grace being the essential thing, and not man's act,
and that a suitable amount of understanding only, not
complete knowledge, is requisite. Confirmation is not
the end of learning, but the beginning of further instruction. With the best of intentions it is possible to teach
too much in the preparation time, and thus to leave an
impression that only the complete theologian is ready for
the bishop's hands. It is probably wise to circulate a
year or so beforehand a letter to the fathers and mothers
of future candidates emphasizing briefly and clearly the
true facts. In this way it may be possible to avoid at
least some of the disturbing and unseemly disputes with
which every priest is familiar when the time for enrolling
the names of candidates arrives.

(b) *Communion.*—Everyone would agree that here we
touch the heart of the whole question. If the young
folk have learnt to find in it the centre and inspiration for
their lives, our work is done.

There have been many failures in the past through
treating the reception of the Blessed Sacrament as a sort
of appendage to Confirmation. A great deal will, on the
contrary, have been gained if through all the earlier years,
Communion, our Lord Himself, has been quietly but
constantly kept before the children as the great coming
privilege for which they are getting ready. Therefore it
is essential that they should be taught from the first that
it is an obligation to be present every Sunday at least at
the Holy Eucharist, primarily, it is true, that they may
know the meaning of worship, but also that they may gain
a true impression of this wonderful Thing, this Holy
Communion for which they are already beginning to
prepare. Nor is this end completely attained if they
have only been accustomed to be present at a Eucharist
at a late hour; regularly, even if only occasionally, they
should be present at an earlier hour, so that they may
see others make their Communion. They will thus learn
to consider it a normal experience, thereby losing any fear
that they may have of it as of the unknown. If this had

been the practice in years gone by, less would be heard to-day of that entirely English anomaly, the non-communicating Churchman.

It should be noted also as of real if secondary importance that the immediate preparation for the sacraments should be spoken of as preparation for Confirmation *and* first Communion, or, if this is too long a phrase, for first Communion only.

These last paragraphs, regarded from our present standpoint, have, it is true, been in part retrospective, but they cannot be omitted, inasmuch as they emphasize again the vital need of treating life as a whole and avoiding a few strenuous weeks of religious enthusiasm with their introduction to a whole world of unexpected spiritual treasures, weeks which will normally be followed by a fatal reaction in the growing child.

Granted some such gradual and increasing familiarity with this greatest of Sacraments, there are three special points on which progressive guidance will be necessary—frequency of, regularity in, and preparation for Communion. The three are interdependent; especially must regularity and frequency react upon each other.

(1) The Church's ideal of *frequency of Communion* has varied from one extreme to the other. In the Eastern Church to-day, as also during the long periods before and after the Reformation in the West, Communion is made very seldom, and the minimum rule of the Roman and Anglican Churches is still very low. On the other hand, there has in practice been a great increase, especially during the past fifty years. What rule of frequency must be recommended to the beginner? Some authorities would aim at making Communion a great and rare privilege during the first few years, others encourage reception every Sunday, or more often still. Bearing in mind the principle of growth, which has been insisted on so often, it would seem that monthly Communion—probably on the old-fashioned "first Sunday," as being the easiest to remember—is the best for a start. Those who are regular and careful in this may be led on step by step to greater frequency, using such periods as Lent and Advent for

temporary experiment. In any case, emphasis must often be laid on the soul's *constant* need for food in order that there may be within it that Life which is eternal. There is also the still greater and mysterious urgency of our Lord's desire for the soul. Often this appeal to a more heroic instinct will succeed, when that of the individual's own need is of small avail.

(2) *Regularity* is an even greater and more important problem. It is better that the children should communicate regularly and comparatively seldom, than more frequently in a spasmodic manner. It is easy for a child to continue a practice for a month or two and then so very easy to forget. This is partly due to the need of the grace of perseverance, but partly also to a lack of the sense of time. Few young communicants can say without much thought when they last made Communion, and even then as often as not they are wrong. Consequently there must be some form of reminder. Canon Peter Green's book on *The Care of Lads* recommends monthly post-cards. He would probably agree that there is grave peril in this of causing growing lads and girls to rely entirely on another's memory. In any case, this method should not be used beyond the first year, and after that only on special occasions or at difficult times like the holiday season. Little by little they must be weaned to depend upon themselves for reminders, or there will be a calamity in a few years' time. Guilds or classes that meet each month may be more safely used for corporate reminders, but even here the day must be kept in view when they will not be available. A voluntary register of Communions has been found helpful, in which members of a Guild may record their Communions month by month. It must, of course, be a confidential book, seen only by the members and the priest in charge. Its voluntary nature will help to foster the much-desired growth in personal responsibility.

(3) If *careful preparation* were assured, the frequency and regularity would look after themselves. Much modern English Churchmanship has tended to increase the frequency, but has lost the awe-ful care in preparing which

was common to our fathers. Mission priests have often been alarmed to discover, in parishes where the number of communicants was impressively large, an almost entire absence of any sense of sin or unworthiness in approaching the Divine Mysteries. On the other hand, there is a real peril in multiplying forms and prayers of preparation for Communion to such an extent that the burden becomes too heavy at least for youthful bearers. As in the case of Confirmation, so here with every Communion, the remedy lies in remembering the fact that it is *the whole life* that makes the soul ready for its Great Guest, and not a few evenings of additional devotion.

If the young soul is living a healthy life of regular prayer, short daily self-examination, and gradual instruction, the immediate preparation for Communion need only be quite brief. The Catechism gives the framework for this as a threefold act : (*a*) examination and repentance, which is of such great importance that it will be dealt with in a separate section, (*b*) faith, and (*c*) charity, which essential virtues can best be encouraged and exercised by special short acts of the will and simple reminders of their implication. Sometimes also, in the case of the last, there will be need for some form of restitution. So will follow naturally what many would agree to be the best and safest means of preparation, sacramental Confession, or the Sacrament of Penance.

Before passing on to consider it, reference must be made to the importance of insisting upon the primitive rule of a strict *fast before Communion*. Much of the laxity of which mention has been made would be checked if this ancient act of reverence were regarded as essential, and not merely as desirable if sufficiently convenient. There will, of course, be hard cases for which the Church as a whole will be able to provide. Some communicants may be allowed to come late and leave early, or may be encouraged to sit during the greater part of the service. However this may be, the essential fact is that the preparation of fasting is a unique witness to the solemnity of the great spiritual act of Communion, the centre of the Christian life.

The Sacrament of Penance.—It may not be out of place to summarize the great advantages which this Sacrament possesses in the training of the penitential side of the spiritual life, more especially as it affects young people. More than a summary is forbidden by lack of space. (1) The care in self-examination with a view to repentance and confession, which are far more likely if that confession is to be made in the hearing of another. (2) The effort and discipline involved, which form an act sufficiently definite, but not so hard or long as to be wearisome. (3) The certainty of forgiveness through absolution, which is " a means whereby we receive the same, and a pledge to assure us thereof." (4) The consequent relief from the sense of sin, which is often so marked a reality in the hearts of boys and girls. (5) The gradual growth in repentance and in perseverance, which regular use of the grace of this Sacrament supplies. (6) The opportunity for obtaining counsel and advice under the best conditions.

Granted the above, it is desirable to consider the best methods of bringing young people to their confessions. This may be done before, at the time of, or after their Confirmation and first Communion. The second will probably be most general, but in any case it is of the greatest importance in their after-care that the priest should study in detail the whole question. The following are practical considerations :

(*a*) *The instruction given must be absolutely definite.* Everyone knows how useless it is to teach young people great truths or practices by innuendo. In speaking of confession it is no good to use vague phrases which seem to imply a special private interview and no more. Nor must any knowledge about it be taken for granted.

(*b*) In my opinion the Sacrament of Penance must be treated as a *normal part of the Christian life and system,* not as an extraordinary thing to be used only by those who are either very good or very bad, and only to be mentioned *sub rosa.* Unfortunately the prominence which has been given to it by the disputes with which it has been surrounded for the past century make this extremely difficult. How often have the days before Confirmation been made a turmoil for some unhappy child by the sudden intrusion of an angry parent who has taken no interest at all until he has heard the word " confession." What it means he has not the least idea, except that once he knew a Roman Catholic, etc. etc. On the other hand, it is hopeless to begin by asking the parents' permission, as though all the rest was the usual thing and this was only an exception. Perseverance must be exercised, perhaps for years, until it is recognized that all children and young people who attend the church in question will be taught and encouraged to go to their confessions as a simple and natural part of their religion. It is this very simplicity which commends it to the common sense of young people, to boys even more than to girls. Nor can anyone conceive of its corporate value until it is unquestionably used by all in a group or congregation who wish to be worthily prepared to receive Communion.

(c) " But *it cannot be compulsory* in the Church of England." No. Yet there is the compulsion of the individual conscience which young people, left to themselves, will always recognize, when they have been clearly and definitely taught this way of proving their contrition and completing their repentance.

There is a good deal of confusion of ideas on this matter. Communion at least three times a year is compulsory in the Church of England, which does not mean that anyone is driven to receive Communion, but that anyone who recognizes the Church to be the one " Ark of Salvation " is morally compelled to use her covenanted means of grace. So, too, the Bible makes it compulsory for Communions to be made worthily, though here only the individual can know if he is obeying the condition. But if once the priest teaches clearly the scriptural doctrine of absolution, if once he obeys the whole Church and the Prayer Book, and urges or " moves to " confession as the relief for mortal or serious sin, then the moral compulsion to use the Sacrament of Penance for one who has any real sense of sin is overwhelming. Young people left to themselves hardly ever fail to see this. In present conditions, however there are cases in which the influence of an ignorant home or friends is such that an escape from the Church's discipline is suggested and confession is refused. This is more frequent after the first one or two confessions than in the first instance, and can only be met by insistence on the gravity of sin and the evangelical message of forgiveness.

(*d*) *A minimum rule* should be recommended of not less than every one or two months, subject of course to a need of increased frequency in the event of serious sin or general slackness. It is not desirable to wait for the great festivals, though they are most valuable as starting-points. As an impersonal reminder it has been found useful to send a list of special confession times before Christmas and Easter to all young penitents, regular and irregular. It is not uncommon to find that special help is needed in preparation for second and third confessions, even when the first has been perfectly understood.

(*e*) *The Direction* given should be of the briefest, and where possible confined to one point only. The act or prayer given as a penance should bear on the same point, and should usually be such as can be said or performed at once, before leaving the church. Periodically some question may arise which demands longer discussion or advice. In this case it is often best to ask the penitent's permission to talk it over apart from confession, with fuller time at disposal.

(*f*) For *self-examination*, papers and lists of sins should be avoided. Rather instruct on the principal spheres of the Christian duty, for example, Religion, the Home, Work, and Friends, the inner Self. By careful catechizing, corporate or individual, the implications of each can be made clear so far as is natural for the child or young person at his present age. Obviously they should increase and deepen in proportion as the conscience is more fully developed. This progressive method is recognized as desirable in matters of purity and sex-instruction, but it is by no means valuable in these alone. It is a vexed question as to whether writing should be used in preparation. It seems most practical to do so, at least for the young, both to ensure reasonable conciseness and also adequate care. Three points should, however, be made clear: (i) that the writer should use his own language and words, and (ii) that special emphasis should be laid on the frequency of commission and on the worst instances of sin. (iii) That all written matter should be carefully guarded and eventually destroyed. Those who are taught in some such way as this will make their confessions the natural outpourings of the soul's desire for relief from the burden of sin and for the joy of pardon.

II. Ways of Prayer

Supplementary to the use of the Sacraments as essential in the " after-care " of young people must be their development in ways of prayer. This may be done corporately in the class or Catechism, by example as well as precept, where the form used should include the five essentials for their private prayers : Praise, Thanksgiving, Penitence, Petition, and Intercession. From time to time the opportunity may arise for applying the same lessons individually. Probably it will be found necessary to stress the two points included in the description of prayer as " speaking with a real Person about real things." (1) *The reality of God's presence* must be dwelt on in the opening moments of prayer, for the obvious reason of attaining a right *direction* of prayer, but also because this is the strongest remedy for the so-called forgetfulness of prayer, more especially in the hurried mornings of those who have just started out in the business world. For indeed the forgetfulness is only the omission of something which seems very unreal, compared with the pressing realities of the day's work. (2) *Real things* must be the objects for prayer. The outworn forms of one age must be changed with growing years. It is a good rule to insist that no day's prayers should be exactly the same as those of any other day. Another that evening prayers should often be almost entirely examination for subjects for thanksgiving, petition, and intercession as well as penitence, suggested by the past day, all summed up in an " Our Father " at the end.

The use of the Bible also is extremely important, yet often omitted. Instruction is indeed needed. The boy or girl is not unknown who has set out to read the whole Book, but has lost heart on arriving at Deuteronomy. Some priests draw up lists of short passages from the Bible for their young people, which if used conscientiously provide an idea of the whole contents and aim of the Book. Very often school teaching has left an impression of disjointed facts and stories which have no relation to each other. It is important, however, not to attach the passages selected to days of the month. The reader is otherwise thrown into confusion if he omits one day, whereas in many cases a weekly rule is best to begin with. Some members of a class of boys from fifteen to eighteen years old were helped by the following easy scheme, which may be called *meditation* in embryo : (*a*) Having found some saying of our Lord, set aside five minutes for the task of thinking about it. (*b*) In the first minute dwell on the Presence of God. (*c*) In the second minute make some short acts of worship, etc. (*d*) In each of the remaining minutes ask a question :

(i) What did our Lord say or mean *then* ?
(ii) What does He say to me now ?
(iii) What do I say to Him in reply ?

This plan may, of course, be expanded or elaborated for use with other parts of the Bible as well.

It is impossible to do more than indicate one or two elementary ways which young people have found useful. The same kind of step-by-step method is the best with regard to *alms-giving* and *rules of life* in other directions. They should be so small and light as to seem almost foolish at first to the more advanced Christian, but they are meant to grow side by side with the other capacities and interests of the growing man or woman. The preparation of Lent rules may, of course, be an exceptionally useful opportunity for helping individuals to take a forward step. Special hours for interviews for this purpose should always be announced before the season begins.

III. Instruction in the Faith

Hitherto we have regarded our young people as so many individual souls, to be trained in the ways of God. We pass on now to consider the best method of grouping them for their training: hitherto the subject has been that which is to be taught, now it is to be the organization for teaching.

The writer is one of those who are convinced that the best and most practicable method is that known generally as the Method of the Catechism, not of necessity in all the fulness of detail described in the many admirable books on the subject, but with its general principles obeyed and its outline followed. Granted so much, the priest must have in mind a family life for his boys and girls—a family in which he himself is the father, taking cognizance of, though not managing, all its details—a family in which there are brothers and sisters of all ages and in which the seniors are willing and ready to take up the privileges and duties which are theirs by right. In this family provision will be made for all their needs: spiritual first, as being the chief aim of their religion; intellectual next, as its chief support; but bodily also, as its outward expression. In the happiest cases their Church will become a second Christian home for the members. In very many sad cases which exist, it will be the only one worthy of the name of Christian which they know, and will often be the place where Christian homes are formed for the future. When this happens, and the young people of one generation in the Catechism have married and become fathers and mothers of the next, then a stage has been well completed in the long, slow life-training which is to be the goal of after-care work. The family ideal will also be a true guide in dealing with questions concerning the relations between the sexes, between seniors and juniors, and between the spiritual and temporal sides of life.

There are, then, at least three essentials to be observed for the Catechism (this name will be used here for the purpose of convenience, though any other [1] may be used in practice if so desired). In the present instance it means the senior branch only, disregarding the carefully graded junior branches which will exist.

(1) *It must meet in the church*, where alone the right devotional atmosphere is possible. One of the greatest difficulties connected with a Bible-class, however well conducted, is in avoiding the impression that it is merely a glorified school or a friendly talk, while at the same time many of its members will tend to regard it as their chief Sunday duty—a duty of getting instruction, not of giving worship.

(2) *It must consist of boys and girls together.* For certain kinds of teaching they must be separated, but for the natural spirit of the family they must be together, both in church and in their social events. In the former they will usually sit on different sides of the church. Specialized services every week for separate groups, men and women, boys and girls, teachers and servers, etc., are a mistake. As a general rule, all need the same one Christian faith and religion taught in the same way. They may usually be trusted to make their own particular application of it for special needs of age, sex, or class. It will, however, be generally admitted that occasional sectional services are of value.

(3) *It must be systematized in method*, and nothing must be left to chance. The system must include—

(*a*) *the whole subject*, the Catholic faith and practice, dealt with in a carefully planned course covering three or four years :

(*b*) *the whole man*, i.e. each Sunday the subject in hand must be presented to the various faculties of the members, intellectual, emotional, and devotional ;

(*c*) *the whole activities*—thought, word, and action must all have their part.

---

[1] The name Children's or Young People's Church is to be avoided. It carries with it an implication that this particular meeting or service is to them the only, or at least the main part, of their duty to God. The same kind of danger exists to a less degree in calling one particular service a Children's Eucharist or Children's Mass, implying that juniors have a duty distinct from that of adults.

In a carefully planned meeting of the Catechism, hymns and prayers, instruction and catechizing, Bible reading and sermon, will all be in proper relation to one another, and will all emphasize the special subject in the complete course which has its place on that particular day.

Now, there are clearly *difficulties* which will appear to anyone whose care and anxiety it is to do his best for his young people in some such way as this.

(1) While he will recognize that by Divine commission and his Ordination vow the work is a priest's primary duty, yet the magnitude and difficulty of the task seem to make it an impossibility, especially if he is single-handed. There is so much to learn, and there are so many diverse things to do in this one branch of his work alone, if it is to be at all adequately performed. Certainly theories of education and some elements of psychology should form part of his study, but equally certainly the average man must rely largely on the guidance of experts, which will enable him to use the knowledge which he has of theology and other subjects for the best advantage of his young people.

(2) There are a few exceptional men who have the gift of quickly knowing and remembering individually any number of separate people. Most of us are less fortunate. It takes some time to acquire separate knowledge of the members of a large class, longer still to put them at their ease and to win their confidence. How, then, will the priest manage who has charge of a Catechism, containing perhaps several hundred members? He may remember, for his comfort, that great intimacy has its dangers, not the least being that of encouraging excessive dependence on the teacher, and that it is often true that young people will not seek guidance on the deepest problems from one they know too well. They must learn to respect and honour, it may be perhaps at a distance, their guide in matters spiritual. They will, moreover, always give him the credit of knowing them more intimately than he does in fact. But the priest must also enlist the help of others, both men and women, who will have charge of smaller groups of children. Perhaps a troop of scouts, a company of guides, or a class of some kind will provide the

opportunity for their more intimate intercourse with some responsible senior. In any case, it is of great assistance to have in a Catechism certain older people, who will have small numbers allotted to them whom they are to know and help in indirect ways whenever the opportunity arises. This difficult and tact-needing work is of special importance with those recently promoted to a senior Catechism, and with new-comers from outside—which touches one of the biggest problems of all. Certainly it should be expected that those boys and girls who have been brought up in the Church for five, six, or more years should have attained to a comparatively high standard of prayer and instruction. Certainly, therefore, the new-comer will feel rather out of it, and will need special help. There ought to be a probationers' class in the charge of some reliable person, who will take special care of the new-comers until they begin to understand the work that is expected of them and to feel at home. It is not exactly a matter of after-care, but it is none the less sad to notice how few of those who join up between the ages of thirteen and sixteen continue to persevere. The remedy must not lie in lowering the standard, but in trying hard to get the children to begin their instruction at an early age.

(3) A third objection which is often made to a method such as has been suggested is that with such large numbers it is impossible to get at the minds of the pupils and to answer their problems of faith. At first sight this is very serious. It is, however, true to say that in the main we are not yet dealing with an age which has religious difficulties in the sense which is implied. There are a few stock problems, perhaps not more than half a dozen, which are perpetually arising. These can be dealt with from time to time in the normal course of instruction. Others more serious may come forward as the young people near the twenties, by which time ten years of friendship should have broken down a good many barriers of reserve between them and their priest and provide in one way and another the opportunities for the help that may be needed ; moreover, there are very few untrained teachers who would have sufficient skill either to get at the real difficulties which

may be deep down in the minds of the members of a class, or to answer them adequately if they have appeared. Herein in most parishes will lie the weakness of a system of classes.

So much for the difficulties. On the positive side there is a great deal to be said in favour of a well-managed senior Catechism. A visit on some Sunday afternoon when it is at work will first give an impression of prayerfulness. There is no doubting the fact that these youngsters are trying to learn to pray. It is only on rare occasions that there is any question at all of discipline or behaviour ; certainly less frequently than in an average congregation of adults. Next to prayer comes work. Of course some arc lazy, but it is true to say that most of the members come to work in their degree, and often enough new-comers leave because they do not find the Sunday afternoon doze which they had anticipated, and parents have declared themselves shocked that work should be done on Sundays.

Further advantages appear as the work of the Catechism is investigated more thoroughly. There are almost count-less chances of holding offices or being chosen for some special work, many necessary, some ornamental only, such as delight the hearts of boys and girls—monitors of various grades, secretaries, clerks, sidesmen, visitors, servers, treasurers, bellringers, and so on. The highest office should be for those who will take the trouble to learn something of teaching, that they may help those who are in charge of the infants or junior Catechism. All of these, however, should be most carefully allotted only to those who are communicants ; while the age of fourteen, so often declared to be the signal for leaving the Church, should come to be recognized as that at which it is first possible to become an officer. It is an excellent plan to have an elected council of senior members, who will be responsible under the priest in charge for the conduct of activities both within the church and outside. The whole of this scheme has in view the training of future Church-men and women who will be ready later to take up offices in their parish church as servers and choristers, district visitors and parish councillors, and in the end the parochial officers and churchwardens will have been Catechism members.

As time goes on, that which may be called the " curriculum " will grow of itself. There will be a *missionary band*, with its study circles or groups with their own special interests at home and abroad. Periodically they will unite in a festival or exhibition. It has been found of exceptional value if mothers (or even fathers) of members can be induced to adopt a mission of their own, and with it their share in the annual festival. The rivalry between children and parents is the greatest help. There will be a systematic scheme of *Almsgiving*—perhaps a branch of a Duplex or Freewill Fund—in any case, it should be managed by the young people themselves, though, especially where money is concerned, under most careful supervision. There will be *days or times for corporate intercessions* ; there will be special festivals and special arrangements for times such as *Lent* ; there will be *social evenings and clubs* : all, in fact, which can make for the delightful family life which will develop the boys and girls on their spiritual side amid the happiest surroundings.

IV. Sundry Notes

In conclusion, some notes may be of value on various and somewhat disconnected topics.

(*a*) Of *retreats* for young people the present writer has little experience. Clearly they should be valuable, but expert advice should be sought. It is easy when a movement is in its infancy to pack into it those who are fitted and unfitted alike. Often the way may be prepared by two or three successive " quiet evenings " with the ensuing early mornings, but anything like a " quiet afternoon " should not be attempted. It tends to crowd far too much spiritual effort into a short space of time.

(*b*) In a *parochial mission* there may well be a special section and missioner for those between fourteen and twenty. This is really better than singling them out for a mission of their own. Perhaps best of all is to divide a mission into two parts. The children and young people would have their own days first, and the mission for the general congregation would follow after a brief interval. The difficulty is then avoided of the church being needed for several purposes at the same time. With a mission for boys and girls, instruction must play a large part, and the danger of excitement and over-emotion must be perpetually borne in mind. Conversions are indeed possible and frequent, usually of a very quiet and gradual nature ; but so too are dangerous half-resolutions and false beginnings. As with adults, so here also, the preparation time is all-important ; the arrangements should be to a large extent in the hands of the Catechism officers and council. Courses of mission or Lent services for those of this age are very useful, especially in following up a mission.

(c) *Social evenings and clubs* of any and every kind according to opportunity should certainly have their place in the work, but several principles must clearly be borne in mind.

(i) They should be essentially *self-supporting*, though it may be necessary to begin with some outside help and occasionally to seek it for special needs.

(ii) They should be *self-managing*, though always under the strict guidance of some priest or responsible adult.

(iii) The central club should be *for both boys and girls*, while it may have its separate branches for each sex. There are those who have serious doubts about this, and especially about social evenings and dances. If, however, the idea of the family is kept to the fore, it will be recognized that the family must naturally unite for its pleasures outside the church as well as for worship within it. Just as wise parents invite to their homes the boy-friends of their daughters and the girl-friends of their sons, so will such friendships be frankly and naturally recognized in the family of the Church. The very openness of their intercourse removes more than half of its perils.

(iv) The club must be *for those who are already members of the Catechism*, and not vice versa. It is quite useless to hope to attract outsiders to the Church by offering social privileges to all and sundry. Such a course always ends by lowering the standard of those who are already members. It is recommended by some in opening up a new mission district, but even then it is difficult to believe that it is not a bad mistake to begin with the impression that amusements come first, and religion afterwards. It is always possible to have special evenings in a closed club, to which non-members are invited. Sometimes this will result in new members for the Catechism, but it is very rarely indeed that they persevere for more than a few weeks. The club may have many branches— dancing, theatrical, drill, games, indoor and out, according to opportunity. It is most inadvisable to join leagues or associations of any kind. Competition with others which are run on less strict lines, and perhaps exist primarily for the sake of the club, and not of the Church, always leads to difficulties of membership. Clearly the football club which exists solely for the sake of the game and can enrol the best talent in the neighbourhood, starts with an unfair advantage over the " closed " club. Before long the members of our club will produce friends who are excellent half-backs, and are willing to come to the church. It is hard to refuse them and to go on losing matches, especially as they are most attractive fellows. But once admit them and it is the beginning of the end. Let them be told once and for all that they are more than welcome at the church, but the question of club membership must be shelved for the present.

(d) *Employment.*—The difficulties in the world of labour have fatal results for the younger generation. They leave school soon after attaining the magic age of fourteen. They can find no suitable job, and either hang about the streets with nothing to do until their characters are ruined, or get into worthless " blind-alley " occupations, merely postponing the evil day. If more fortunate, they get a post in some business firm to become a little cog in a soul- less machine. It is possible to get the men of a con- gregation to manage a labour bureau. They will keep lists of the boys who are leaving school or are in need of work, and to them the employers, whether on a small or large scale, will apply if they have a post vacant. Not only will work thus be found, but the boys will not be friendless in their situations. The master will have an interest in his man. It is most just and excellent that the men of a Church should realize in this way their responsibilities towards their younger brothers. It will foster in a unique way the Christian spirit in the industrial world. Such a plan has been found useful for the men and boys. There seems no reason why it should not work equally well, with certain limitations, for the women and girls of a parish.

It has proved a disquieting task to write this article, and probably it will prove disquieting to read it. The after-care of the Confirmation candidate is indeed a difficult matter. Everyone to whom it has been entrusted will, like the present writer, have made his own experiments, forged his own weapons, been encouraged by some successes and disheartened by many failures. Sometimes he will have been reminded that many failures are only temporary, and will gratefully acknowledge at some death-bed or in the crisis of a life that the lessons once learnt have not been forgotten, even if long disregarded. So he will go on trying to find the best methods, but will remember most humbly that after all it is not the method that in the last resort will matter most, but the prayerfulness and spiritual influence of the man. Above all, let him keep the standard of his own life high, so that he may dare to demand a high standard from those who are entrusted to his care.

*Made and Printed in Great Britain
by Hazell, Watson & Viney Ld.
London and Aylesbury*